Race and
Reconciliation

PUBLIC WORLDS

Series Editors: Dilip Gaonkar and Benjamin Lee

D ANIEL   H ERWITZ

Race and

Reconciliation

Essays from the

New South Africa

PUBLIC WORLDS, VOLUME 11

UNIVERSITY OF MINNESOTA PRESS

MINNEAPOLIS   LONDON

The University of Minnesota Press acknowledges the work of Edward Dimendberg, editorial consultant, on this project.

An earlier version of chapter 2 originally appeared as "Comedies of Mastery and Reconciliation: South Africa's *Taxi* and America's *Rib*," *Common Knowledge* 8, no. 1 (Winter 2002): 80–101; copyright 2002 Duke University Press.

Published by the University of Minnesota Press
111 Third Avenue South, Suite 290
Minneapolis, MN 55401-2520
http://www.upress.umn.edu

Library of Congress Cataloging-in-Publication Data

Herwitz, Daniel.
　　Race and reconciliation : essays from the new South Africa / Daniel Herwitz.
　　　p.　　cm. — (Public worlds ; v. 11)
　　Includes bibliographical references and index.
　　ISBN 0-8166-4107-2 (HC : alk. paper) — ISBN 0-8166-4108-0 (PB : alk. paper)
　　1. South Africa—Race relations. 2. South Africa. Truth and Reconciliation
Commission. 3. Reconciliation—Political aspects—South Africa. 4. South Africa—
Politics and government—1994- I. Title. II. Series.
　　DT1756 .H477 2003
　　305.8'00968—dc21

　　　　　　　　　　　　　　　　　　　　　　　　　　　　　　　　2003010934

Printed in the United States of America on acid-free paper

The University of Minnesota is an equal-opportunity educator and employer.

12　11　10　09　08　07　06　05　04　03　　　　　　　10　9　8　7　6　5　4　3　2　1

≈

This book is dedicated to Sophia Saks-Herwitz,

born in Los Angeles,

raised in Durban.

And to her mother, Lucia.

Contents

Acknowledgments

Earlier versions of parts of this book have appeared in the journals *Common Knowledge*, *Theoria*, *The South African Journal of Philosophy*, and *Current Writing*, and in the edited volume *blank: architecture, apartheid, and after*. Sections of the book have been presented to the Cornell University Humanities Center; the Philosophical Society of Southern Africa; the philosophy department of the City College of New York/CUNY; history, English, and philosophy seminars at the University of Natal; the Rhodes University Philosophy Colloquium; and the University of Witwatersrand School of Art and Drama. My inaugural address to the University of Natal has also found its way into parts of the manuscript. Each and every one of these occasions offered something significant for an American in South Africa to learn as he felt his way into the momentous instant of transition. The philosophy I brought to this experience I owe to Stephen Toulmin more than to anyone else because he impressed on me the unique capacity of the philosophical essay to probe philosophical ideas through the encounter with new times. Without his *Cosmopolis: The Hidden Agenda of Modernity*, this book could not have been written.

Other individuals also deserve special mention. These include Raphael de Kadt, Lucia Saks, Ahmed Bawa, Patrick Lenta, Deepak Mistrey, Julia Clare, Andries Gouws, Lynn Matisonn, Michael Steinberg, David Bunn, Ivan Vladislavic, Hilton Judin, Jeffrey Perl, Douw Van Zyl, Michael Chapman, and Ronnie Miller. Ed Dimendberg, editor-at-large for the University of Minnesota Press and a member of the faculty of the University of

Michigan, was crucial in the matchmaking process that goes under the name of publishing, as was the calm and stalwart Carrie Mullen, executive editor at Minnesota. Yolanda Hordyk of the University of Natal provided invaluable editorial assistance.

Support for this research was supplied by the University of Natal Research Fund and the National Research Foundation of South Africa.

Introduction

Historical Background

The inauguration of a new nation.

1985. P. W. Botha, expected to make a speech announcing massive re-form of the crumbling apartheid state, instead refuses to "cross the Rubicon." Overnight the rand devalues by more than 100 percent in a country already embroiled in war, chaos, township violence, and spiraling state terror.

1985 and 1987. The business and academic communities secretly meet the African National Congress, first in Lusaka and then in Dakar. The African National Congress begins to consider the idea of a negotiated settlement rather than an outright victory. All parties to the South African conflict fear the massive social upheaval that would come with a civil war in the country. No side can expect easy "victory" or even victory at all.

1989. Communism collapses, eroding the African National Congress's most important financial and military support bases. The National Party begins to realize that the likelihood of a Soviet-style state in South Africa is evaporating. This catalyzes the party into preparations for a negotiated settlement.

1990. Nelson Mandela is released from prison.

1991. The apartheid state is formally ended and the CODESA talks (Coalition for a Democratic South Africa) take place at Kempton Park, outside of Johannesburg. The African National Congress has decided to forgo the continuation of the armed struggle, which it now believes will lead to nothing beyond a destructive stalemate. Mandela immediately attacks the African National Congress for having formally disbanded "MK," the arm of the revolution. The talks promise to be stormy. They are boycotted by the Pan Africanist Congress (the PAC), which declares that the only serious way to achieve power-sharing is through direct election of representatives, thus achieving popular democracy. The CODESA talks are tumultuous, breaking down at least once. However, they eventually lead to a power-sharing arrangement (the interim government) and set out time lines and power lines for the transition to a broad-based South African electoral democracy. The African National Congress relinquishes the brunt of its leftist position during these talks in exchange for what it sees as peace and stability in the wake of an ongoing fear of revolt from the far right in South Africa. It has agreed to respect the rule of property, even though its official position has been that property acquired in a context of racist capitalism could not be deemed morally, legally, or politically valid in the new, more just society. Moreover, it has relinquished what was a personal credo of Mandela's, namely the nationalization of the gold and diamond mines. The National Party has agreed to retrench itself from control over the state apparatus, but has managed to give its employees huge pensions. What the National Party gives up is essentially its claim on governance, since it knows that in the first election it will lose power.

The CODESA talks and the formation of the interim government take place in the context of massive social insecurity. Forty-nine percent of white people vote against the ending of apartheid. The spiral of violence between Inkatha (the "pro-Zulu" party) and the ANC that will grip the KwaZulu-Natal province in the first half of the 1990s will just possibly claim more lives by the gun, the knife, and the "necklace" (tire-burning) than apartheid ever did. It is a well-known historical fact that two major threats to any incipient democracy are the dictatorship of the majority and the breakaway of the minorities into separate states. Inkatha fears the dictatorship of the Xhosa-based African National Congress and is in favor of, at minimum, a Federated South Africa in which it has the autonomy of a Zulu kingdom. (Zulu nationalism remains dominant in the province. Even in the year 2001 the Zulu king receives more funding from the provincial budget than that dispensed in the fight against HIV/AIDS—this, although 39 percent of all persons in the province are HIV positive.) And so the leopard and the lion draw knives and fight it out, with the help of the secret Third Force, always vigilant to stamp out potential communist threats in these insecure and less than salad days of the new nation.

The interim government, meanwhile, protects the interests of business, which will remain the most powerful and richest sector of the South

African state in the new dispensation. And so what Marxist theorist Antonio Gramsci calls a "weak revolution" is instituted, in which the state becomes constitutionally secure but weak in relation to business, and weaker still in the delivery of economic justice.

In 1994 the interim constitution is negotiated into creation. Its preamble stresses reconciliation ("ubuntu"), the values of humanity, and a form of decolonizing redress maximally sensitive to all South Africans but not harsh and punitive. It is a masterpiece of nation-building, radiant with the glow of harmony. The interim constitution mandates the creation, moreover, of the three committees that will form the basis of the Truth and Reconciliation Commission: the Truth and Reconciliation Committee, the Amnesty Committee, and the Reparations and Rehabilitations Committee. The issue of qualified amnesty (which I discuss in a later essay) is so controversial that it is resolved only in time to be included in a postscript to the constitution.

1994 is also the date of the first free and fair elections in the history of South Africa, leading to the government of Madiba (Mandela). The elections almost do not come off. In the wake of intense violence in the KwaZulu-Natal province, Inkatha has vowed to boycott the elections and turn election day into a day of blood. Inkatha is brought back into the fold only days before the electoral process, but most middle-class people in the province have already stocked up on long-life milk and canned soups in preparation for massive disruptions. Their gates are locked and they are staying put out of fear. And yet they show up: everyone votes. Everyone except those in the PAC and on the far right, who remain adamantly opposed.

1995 and 1996 are the years of glory. With a leader admired the world over, enough moral capital earned through him, through the struggle, and through the dignity of the transition to finance a generation's worth of European Union projects; with the commencement of the proceedings of the Truth and Reconciliation Commission under the sublime pastoral eye of Archbishop Desmond Tutu; with a new state-sponsored television network thrilled to commute the new nation into joyous spectacle; with universities inaugurating transformation; with a blessedly excited (if underfunded) civil society; with everybody claiming they have shaken hands or are about to shake hands with everyone else—it is a moment in which the so-called Rainbow Nation appears after the storm, and it seems, in the words of Thabo Mbeki, that truly the African renaissance is upon us.

I include myself in this "us" because it was in 1996 that I arrived in South Africa with my family. My wife, a South African by birth and nationality, had wanted to return to South Africa after many years in the

United States, and in 1992 we had spent a short time at the University of Natal while she began a research project on South Africa and the media for the University of Southern California School of Film and Television, where I briefly taught. It was during that stay that I became fascinated with the idea of being in South Africa during the moment at which constitutional democracy was being inaugurated.

The Constitution and Liberalism

Yes, the African renaissance was upon us. 1996 was above all the moment when the most advanced constitution in the world was negotiated to completion under the able leadership of Cyril Ramaphosa and Roelf Meyer—the former, a trade-union activist and, in the mind of many, the best person to follow Mandela as president of the country; the latter, a member of the National Party but liberal, independent-minded, and soon to bail out. That constitution, a marvel of liberal philosophy, mandated instruction and news in all eleven official languages; protected community rights in a number of fascinating, if inconsistent, ways; enshrined powerful labor laws along with civil and political rights; and provided, in Article 39, for a new regime of interpretation that required constant deference to "the spirit of the constitution as a whole." While ubuntu was dropped from its preamble, the preamble continued to stress the "healing of divisions" and opened to the kind of ongoing humanistic questioning that Article 39 prescribed. No judgment could take place without reflection on the spirit of the constitution as a whole, on its core values and their relationship to particular statutes, and on how these statutes might be revised in the light of a world in transition. Article 39 understood that a country characterized by diversity and change, a country (like any other) in which the fabric of reality is multiplex and tenebrous, would need flexibility built into its interpretive questioning of statutes. The core values of the constitution would have to admit of incessant reevaluation and also disagreement. What was being mandated was a regime of philosophical reflection internal to constitutional judgment, in which the inner meaning and truth of the constitution would always remain at issue for any particular judgment. Moreover, the expectation was that while constitutional judgments would require a certain degree of consistency, they would also admit of disagreement, and that this was, within bounds, a good thing, for it invited the conversation of democracy into the substance of law. No doubt this conversation has always been there, as, for example, the history of American constitutional debates has shown. However, now it was prescribed that the judge approach the constitution as philosopher, rediscovering and re-inventing its power every day as he or she sat in the courtroom.

This constitution, conceived at the moment of nation-building, was meant to be exemplary. The conversation of justice built into constitutional interpretation would be a model for the conversation of democracy within broad areas of civil society and the public sphere: a conversation philosophical in its reflective questioning and impelled by the double virtues of consensus and dissensus—that is, the virtues of an entire citizenry actively engaged in the casting and recasting of democracy through its conversation.

Since it is a sign of liberalism that such conversations are central to public life, and since those conversations are by nature reflections on meaning, truth, and justice, philosophy is fundamental to democracy, for such conversations are nothing if not philosophical. It was in the context of the fledgling democracy of Athens that Socrates preached the need for an education of the young that would train them in exactly this kind of conversation, a conversation in which one stood before the values of law, decency, truth, and justice and cross-examined claims to their interpretation, always remaining open to one's interpretive failures and the difficulty of achieving hard and fast answers to such weighty matters of public and private concern. Socrates is perhaps the original model of a public intellectual, and following him there is a history of the type, a history inclusive of Voltaire, Rousseau, Jefferson, Marx, Nietzsche, Russell, Sartre, Said, Govan Mbeki, Chief Luthuli, Chomsky, Fukuyama, and the brutally assassinated Rick Turner (pupil of Sartre and Aron, trade-union activist in the 1970s, anti-apartheid Marxist, gunned down by the security forces in his home and in front of his young children in 1978). Reflection on the core values of a social order and, on a related note, on the revision of those values, is itself a paradigmatically core value. Since questions of knowledge are inevitably occasioned by this reflection, it cannot help but become truly philosophical. Moreover, in a society as dramatically in transition as postapartheid South Africa's—that is, in the process of moving from one system of estates to another—the scope of reflection is particularly vast, the need particularly urgent, for here is a society in which everything is in transformation, or in resistance to such. Here is a society in which the values and institutions of citizenship, and the scope of political, civil, social, economic, traditional, and linguistic rights, are in flux and under renegotiation by people who hardly agree and have been, historically, at strife. Rights are sometimes negotiated not through words but through actions, as the recent occupations of land in this country, following suit on the problematic—indeed, socially devastating—nature of land reform in Zimbabwe, have shown. But without words, such actions remain, finally, inchoate invitations to chaos (a historical fault of what has been called "popular democracy").

The University and Public Intellectuals

It is a sign of a robust civil society that universities ought to be central to such discussions, since they are places where knowledge is meant to be generated, places with a density of research communities, and places where the legacy of the liberal arts is meant to be housed. It is the sign of a society with a disturbed, repressed, or atrophied public sphere when universities remain silent during such tumult. (One general marker for the robustness of a society's public sphere is whether and how universities are part of it. Authoritarian societies occlude the contribution of universities through censorship, political correctness, and intimidation. In America, where you are free to say almost whatever you like, the problem is that you can't get a hearing on the *Larry King Live* show, where, increasingly, presidential elections are debated and decided.)

South African universities have been all too silent during the tumult of change, and for complex reasons. Certain universities took powerful public stances during the old regime. The University of Witwatersrand, formed by mining money and Scottish missionaries, and a fine university in an urban center, had been fiercely dedicated to liberalism during the regime and a hotbed of activist research, Marxist dialogue, and protest. Some of the "black universities" (now referred to as "historically disadvantaged") developed profound activist cultures and received significant European funds to build their campuses and continue to speak their voices. The University of Natal, ambivalent in its position, accepted black students but prevented them from using the libraries or mixing with any other students, teaching them in warehouses downtown, while the venerable university sat perched on the hill above the docks, its statue of King George V proudly ushering students to Howard College, which is now the law faculty. And yet when Richard Turner was banned and placed under house arrest, the university paid his salary for three years. On the other hand, they replaced him after he was assassinated by the security forces in 1978 (one year after the Soweto uprising, when protest took a new and violent turn in the country and became dominated by youths rather than the old regime of comrades) with a man so conservative he could pose little threat to anything or anyone other than the struggle itself. Stellenbosch, Pretoria, and Potchefstroom universities were institutionally connected to the regime of power, and received extra government funding because of this.

The brave stances taken by South African universities in the days of the former regime were also, often epistemically, too facile to be sustainable today. It took no genius to speak in the name of equality when there was clearly none, to study economic injustice when it was so obvious, or to detail the trajectories of state terror, enshrined in law, when they were on the books and were scars on the land. Universities developed activist research paradigms, often along Marxist lines. These were brave and (then) to the point; they are now out of date. And universities have found it hard to invent new paradigms of activist research and social critique that would ensure new public stances at the moment of transition. To an extent this is because they are afraid to criticize the government, which has in the past few years enjoyed such high moral status (this has quickly evaporated with corruption, inefficiency, and failure of delivery). To an extent it is because they have been busy remaking their own houses. To an extent it is because, at a moment of financial limitation and downsizing, they are just trying to survive. To an extent it is because, when universities have engaged the public sphere, the response has been less than salutary. I want to dwell on two of these points.

The first point is getting one's own house in order: by 1996 everything from the composition of students (Natal is now more or less one-third Indian, one-third Zulu, and one-third white, reflecting the population of the Durban metropolitan area) to the nature of the curriculum was in flux. It was, again, a philosophical moment, calling for reflection on everything from the universal character of education in the humanities, the social sciences, and the hard sciences to the nature of training in citizenship and civility for diverse students from multilingual backgrounds who had been formerly dissociated from each other. Questions of who was, and what it was, to be an African, of the place of South Africa in Africa and in global affairs, of the nature of the new democracy and the kind of education relevant to it, of how to negotiate a country where diversity is reflected in racial categories (past and present), language, religion, class, education, culture, knowledge: these questions have informed curricular and research agendas and been the topic of public conversations within universities. Were universities to engage the public sphere with the care and intensity they have applied to themselves, it would be a fine thing.

This remaking of the university in the light of social exigency has led to a certain schizophrenia. The requirements of building up a middle class in a country where the majority of people are poor, the requirements of building human capital in a country of depleted skills, and the desire to cut cost in an irrational and overburdened educational sector—these have pushed educational management in the direction of outcomes, skills, and professional training at the expense of the social sciences and humanities. And there is a need to build a new class of professionals in a country with a skills deficit and vast inequality in the composition of the middle classes along racial lines. One understands the pushing of resources in the direction of the professions. On the other hand, skills for a new society include the capacity to digest complex knowledge flows and respond critically to social life, and this pushes professionalization back to the humanities. Moreover, the need for new forms of activist research in a society with dire needs pushes universities back in the direction of the social sciences. The schizophrenia is not resolvable, given the social exigencies of the country and the scarcity of resources. This partial inconsistency of forces guiding the university at a time of transitional justice (reconciliation, reparation, redress, democratization, globalization, development) is part, I will later argue, of a deeper inconsistency built into the very forces guiding transitional justice per se.

The second point is engaging in the public sphere: When new public voices or new forms of socially driven activist research have entered the new public sphere, the response from the state has been competitive and sometimes highly destructive. My own university (the University of Natal) has developed important new forms of socially driven research, including HIV/AIDS projects in rural areas, projects on urban violence and education, and projects on leadership. The research is especially creative, but not unique. The government values decentralization of research and social activism, but at the same time values control and state authority. Within this ambivalent power position things can work well, but they always operate under threat.

There are four main ways that research is funded in South Africa (as of the year 2001): (1) Through the National Research Foundation, which is a standard funding body to which researchers may apply in various categories for money. Evaluation is based on the quality of the project, its relevance to a research funding category, the researcher's record, and so forth. (2) Through the Innovation Fund, which develops what is often called "mode 2 research," following the work of Michael Gibbons—that is, partnerships between universities and other social actors like business, nongovernmental organizations, or the state. Should urban planners, architects, economists, and businesspeople wish to develop a project to restructure the Durban Port Authority in conjunction with city stakeholders, they might find money available from this government agency. Such research might or might not lead to the traditional fare of conference papers, books, articles, and the like, but it will, it is hoped, generate new knowledge of a socially relevant kind, and it is through virtue of that that a project will receive funding. (3) Through the Medical Research Council, which funds all medically related research (the lines of demarcation between its domain and that of the National Research Foundation are highly contested, but that is not my concern here). (4) Through independent funding, whether from the private sector or from abroad.

The Medical Research Council has existed in a tacit agreement with government. Government does not like the council's HIV/AIDS research and has said so publicly, and yet in private it funds the very research it castigates. At the moment when President Thabo Mbeki was busy lambasting the MRC, his government was funding vaccine research through the MRC—research obviously rooted in the established hypothesis that HIV causes AIDS. This unholy alliance was, until recently, working. The government could claim Africanist control over the understanding of the disease, while in a decentralized way allow science to progress. However, at a certain point, decentralized research, given its degree of outside funding, its international prestige, and its leading role in the activist agenda of Health, Prevention, and Disease Management, has threatened the state, given the state's obsession with images of legitimacy and its desire for increasingly authoritarian control over national procedures. This is a general character of weak states: that they demand public legitimacy through spectacles, rituals, demonstrations, ideologies, conferences, proclamations, etcetera, since their power is otherwise compromised. Similarly, weak states demand control over the events of the nation since they cannot facilitate social delivery and control populations through implementation of the rule of law (either because law is itself inadequate or because, in the case of South Africa, there is too much crime, not enough police, and a poor system of judges). So they desire decentralized production from the institutions of civil society and then, at a certain point, are scandalized by it. HIV/AIDS research at Natal has been under ongoing threat on account of this internal, bureaucratic warfare between state, the MRC, and its projects. And this is a general condition of knowledge production in the kind of political state that South Africa is today.

The state is weak with respect to business, the rule of law, and delivery, and so strives to proclaim itself by asserting its presence in civil society. It goes after newspapers, accusing them of racism, but seldom attacks business, where racism is probably far worse. Moreover, among the institutions of civil society, universities are funded by the state and dependent upon it. This allows the state to vacillate between respecting universities and treating them as vassals. Last, the African National Congress has never entirely gotten over its Stalinist past, and therefore has, from time to time, the liability of reverting to tactics of state control.

Hence the drama of the public intellectual, caught in the net of this conflict. It is productive, exhilarating, and daunting.

The Philosophical Essay

These essays are meant to be those of a public intellectual meditating on aspects of public life in the new South Africa, including the forces that occasion and constrain intellectual voices themselves. That I want these essays to pertain to public life is related to their form. They are *essays*. What Émile Zola said about painting may be adopted as a remark about the philosophical essay: that it pictures a "corner of nature seen through a [philosophical] temperament." The essay allows philosophy, journalism, political analysis, sociology, cultural criticism, and art history to become intermingled. It is a testament to the temporality of things; it does not seek universal truths but the establishment of new lines of relevance for philosophical ideas in the light of what is required of the understanding of a place and time. It seeks new places and times to widen the scope of relevance for philosophical ideas (about justice, truth, personhood, identity, society, knowledge), while also beginning from the thought that it is a concrete, historical reality that one wants to understand without sacrificing its richness and complexity for the sake of generality and abstraction. It seeks to probe, test, critically scrutinize received notions in the light of the social reality it addresses.

My project is to give a philosophical reading of society. My work does not centrally involve analytical reconstruction of any philosopher's system, but instead works through certain philosophical concepts, prying them apart from others to prove (or limit) their relevance for that reading of society. It is a central theme of these essays that one reason a philosophical reading of a society such as South Africa *is* possible is that the society is already relying on implicitly philosophical concepts—or giving its concepts implicitly philosophical constructions—in its social and political agendas. I believe this to be true of the way South Africa has constructed key concepts of race, reconciliation, and renaissance, all of which have been central to the South African transition. My essays seek to understand and criticize how race, reconciliation, and renaissance have been constructed. Since these concepts are not simply philosophical but also political, and indeed aesthetic, their analysis must be more than just philosophical. Moreover, since I am writing as a public intellectual, intending to enter the fray of discussions about what, for example, reconciliation ought best to mean, as well as about the meanings attached to it in current social usages, I cannot claim the detachment of the metaphysician, but instead take myself to be part of the politics of definition and description in the new South Africa.

The essay as a philosophical form is about probing philosophical ideas in the light of new realities. But the essay is also about the conviction that there is no set of master concepts capable of characterizing those new realities. I do not believe race, reconciliation, and renaissance are the definitive concepts pertinent to the South African transition, since the list would also contain concepts of economy, civil society, the rule of law, identity, and many other things (which indeed make their appearance in this book). Were the reader to read only one of these essays, it might appear that I am prescribing a specific concept paramount to the understanding of transition: reconciliation, for example, or diversity, nation-building, or race. It is only when the whole lot of them are read that this pretense disappears. A number of concepts are important in the understanding of the South African transition, and to social transition in general.

The way South Africa has constructed its concepts of reconciliation (in the work and writing of the Truth and Reconciliation Commission, in discussions about human identity and nation-building, in its postapartheid art and culture), the way it has constructed its concepts of return (in the African renaissance), and the way race is being rethought, reimagined, reexperienced, relabeled, repoliticized, all are wide-ranging features of South Africa's historical emergence. Since these features crisscross in distinctive ways, the essays do the same: looping back on each other in ways the reader will discover only in the course of reading. In *Philosophical Investigations* Ludwig Wittgenstein prefaces his text by speaking of the need imposed by his terrain of study (language and concepts) for the philosopher "to travel over a wide field of thoughts [that] criss-cross in every direction."[1] He began, he claims, by trying to write a more straightforward book, but failed. For his thoughts were

> crippled if I tried to force them on in any single direction against their natural inclination.—And this was, of course, connected with the very nature of the investigation. . . . The same or almost the same points were always being

approached afresh from different directions, and new sketches made . . . so that if you looked at them you could get a picture of the landscape.[2]

Wittgenstein is, in this part of his preface, directing the reader to expect certain things to happen in his book and *not* to expect other things—associated with traditional philosophy—to happen. And he is saying that his book is as it is because of the way his field of investigations continually loops back upon itself. Not only that, the way the reader is brought to understand this field must involve a similar looping mechanism, an ongoing act of return through which development in understanding takes place.

Another central feature of the philosophical essay is that, often as not, it aims to be controversial rather than to resolve an issue to the satisfaction of human understanding in general. This is related to my desire to write as a public intellectual. I do not think there is a single story, or single answer, to the questions of what race, reconciliation, and renaissance are and ought to be in the new South Africa, or how they are relevant to philosophy. What is clear is that to reflect on any of these is to enter the debate about South African democracy, and not just to stand above and speak as a "theorist." The line between philosophical thinking at a plane of abstraction above the fray of social debate within a society and the act of contributing to that debate is a line I could, given my topics, never hope to sort out. Neither institutionally nor philosophically. Neither philosophically nor politically. Therefore, my essays do not solicit agreement but conversation. I hope for interest, not consensus.

All of these essays are about justice in one form or another. The kind of justice pertinent to a society in transition from an authoritarian regime with a record of gross human-rights violations to a liberal democracy is distinctive in a number of ways—with respect to questions of constitutional construction, the nature of truth commissions, the remaking of civil as well as political society, the way identity politics and cultural production are recast. I often reach for comparisons between South Africa and other places (transitional or not), but, in keeping with the spirit of what I previously stated, I do not subscribe to the idea that a general theory of "transitional justice" can be produced that would be adequate to the complexity of transition. In the next chapter I discuss the concept of transitional justice, an important concept originally developed to explain the importance of Truth Commissions for transitional nations like South Africa, along with the way constitutional law must be evaluated for such societies. The concept is indeed such a good one, and from one perspective it would be reasonable to generalize it to all aspects of social transformation (civil, political, cultural, economic). However, it is the implicit point of these essays that if one were to do this, the concept would exfoliate into a number of crisscrossing concepts, or "language games," in Wittgenstein's sense, thus losing its theoretical integrity in the course of retaining its subject. There are various kinds of justice, there are various types of human rights, there are various kinds of concepts that are in play in articulating and explaining them.

Genealogy

One way of encapsulating contemporary events is to write their genealogy, and in these essays I produce a number of genealogies. What is a genealogy? In its paradigmatic form, that provided by the Bible, a genealogy is a definition of a person's identity by placing it in a lineage, by showing how it came about, as when to say who Jacob was is to say who begat him and who in turn begat him, back to the forefather Abraham. This biblical genealogy is a paradigmatically patriarchal form of the placement of persons, since it states that it was Abraham who begat Isaac rather than Sarah, even though Sarah's tremendous energy of pregnancy and birthing overwhelmed Abraham's miniscule contribution to the gestation of Isaac.

A Nietzschean genealogy of power is a history of progressive empowerment; really, of progressive *disempowerment*. What it shows is how, by a series of stages, a set of concepts becomes internalized in a culture in tandem with a set of cultural practices, and how together these concepts and practices produce the mortification of human thought, desire, and imagination. What made Nietzsche untimely to the nineteenth-century Europe of his time (or, we might say, early to the future) was his claim that certain templates of thought formed a vast and monstrous system by which European identities were mortified. The object of his attack was the entire history of Judeo-Christian morality, which he believed played this role in conjunction with the regimes of truth found in European philosophy and culture. To speak of an error in thinking as massive (for Nietzsche) as the histories of Judeo-Christianity and philosophy combined was to diagnose the ascendancy of weakness over strength, disempowerment over empowerment, the gradual construction by stages of a system of thought and practice that asserted moral hegemony over the individual, causing him or her to freeze sensation and replace it with frozen forms of intellection; to mortify taste and replace it with propriety, desire with duty, spontaneity with contemplation or excessive politeness, individual subjectivity with common group identity, debt with guilt, redress with the sense of an ineradicable stain of sin, imagination with definition, excitement with envy, and flexibility with the aggressive stance of the philosopher ready to belittle everyone else through pedantry and small-minded argument. Painting an enormous picture of a culture increasingly regulated by attitudes of resentment, envy, cruelty, and masochism, Nietzsche introduced a style of philosophico-historical interrogation into the repertoire of Western thinking, a style that is meant to gradually free the human from enchainment by a force so great and overriding as to be practically unnoticed.

Genealogies need to be written about civil society, legal interpretation, politics, the history of thinking, culture, monuments and their legacies, public space, the public sphere and its lack—and about every detail of these new times—which will bring to light the extent, the enormous extent, to which thought and reaction are here and now styled in deforming rather than empowering ways, for so many South Africans are not free of the templates of thought and response that a legacy of belief, attitude, and practice have imbued in them. Therefore, the reader of this book will see that genealogy is a unifying theme of the essays. There are genealogies (complete or partial) that run through chapters on the Truth and Reconciliation Committee, the African renaissance, President Thabo Mbeki's controversial view on HIV/AIDS, and the history of public space and architecture.

Embryonic Postapartheid South Africa

Collectively, these genealogies might be thought of as the genealogy of an embryo. For what has been exciting about the South Africa of the 1990s for a foreigner like myself has been its embryonic state. To arrive from the frantically imaginative and totally self-sentimentalizing identity politics of various Californian universities, from a condition of endless business-as-usual in American life, to a university and a nation in the process of dramatic crystallization is to be privileged with the prospect of nothing less than a return to the nascent. As a rule, one can assimilate any experience to philosophy by pressing it into critique and reflection. My teacher Ted Cohen used to quip that one can read the newspaper philosophically, more or less in the way that Marx claimed to read the history of the world in his morning newspaper (he must have been very good at reading between the lines, especially reading what is left out on purpose). It is a general fact of life that experience is underread rather than overread, nowhere more so than in a transitional South Africa.

When everything is new, everything becomes philosophical in an instant, for no template of thought or practice can remain immune from the potential of destabilization. Everything must be placed under the scrutiny of Socratic cross-examination. No value is free from this critique, nor is any article of language immune from the traces of a colonial map whose borders demand interrogation, nor is any practice free from the sociological pressure of others who may now also be privileged to engage it. South Africa is among the special places in the world for a philosopher to be at the present time since so much is in transformation, and so much in need of it. This nascent state is a natural habitat of philosophy, the place where it lives. The moment of my arrival in South Africa was neonatal, a moment in which citizens were thrust into the condition of the prenatal infant, born before its lungs are developed and its powers of ingestion are complete. In this push into an inchoate world in transition, university, place, and nation find themselves appearing too early on the scene of a history-in-the-making to think and project the world except in liminal form. Here they are, these new times, and in South Africa everything must be digested, explained, and rebuilt, yet everything is too early in the process of gestation to admit of explanation, and too fragmented to admit of clear construction. Citizens of the new South Africa are too early for "the test of time to decide very much." Our constitution is a largely untried document; we have little precedent to rely on. We exist, here and now, in a state of absence of knowledge about which models, if any, to follow or which specific outcomes are most likely and/or most desirable. Everything must therefore be put forward with the sense of what the philosopher Richard Rorty calls its "contingency" and what we may call its transitional nature. Everything must be referred to the process of immediate critique or even withdrawal.

Traditional concepts are increasingly unhinged at such a moment, occasioning the free and experimental work of their recasting. Ubuntu is a perfect example of this. From one perspective, ubuntu continues to mean what it has always meant: a traditional form of life in which persons are formed and take on identities only in terms of whole villages. Hardly a concept at all, but rather a placeholder for a form of life with its attachments, self-definitions, and values—values that can be seen in our students today insofar as they use, as the South African historian Charles Van Onselen has suggested, their scholarship money to support a family back home, as if being a student were the latest form of migrant labor in which checks from the city were sent back to rural areas, thus turning the university into a purveyor of social welfare. But as soon as ubuntu is removed from that particular form of life and is rethought as a *philosophical concept* of modern relevance—relevant, say, to the nation where group allegiances are subject to the constraint of the national interest, or to the world of diasporic individualities of South African exiles now returned from abroad to face the future—the meaning and force of the concept are no longer evident. After all, the "village" is now national and global. To state that ubuntu remains a specifically African concept is to admit that we no longer know what African thought is, granted its own entry into the whirl of a modernity not its own and now its own, granted its own neonatal condition. This is especially true in that ubuntu is a practical ethics, which is community-preserving and communitarian in form. It is a way of life, a set of moral instincts manifesting themselves in tacit choices: a moral capital, not a "philosophy" in any obvious sense of this word. When a gardener refuses a job he really wants to have and instead offers it to his brother because his brother is the one who is supporting their parents, this is ubuntu. When a female KwaZulu-Natal worker allows six unemployed members of her extended family to live in her one-room apartment because they have no work, this is ubuntu. On the other hand, when that same woman is expected to go and cohabit with her dead husband's brother to "keep the women in the family," that is also ubuntu. Community values and duties may be inhibiting of individual liberty. To return to ubuntu is to do so critically. My point is the further one: that to render ubuntu into a philosophical signifier and (in the national push) to recast this concept in as many ways as possible is already to have subjected it to an operation of modernity, one that converts moral practice into moral theory and thinks ubuntu comparatively, vis-à-vis various philosophical doctrines about community, justice, decency, and humanity. This may be—let me say, this *is*—a creative and rewarding endeavor for a liberal/African society in the midst of decolonization, since hybridizing traditions is one way people may be brought together. It is a way of creating new ideas about Africa and Africans by returning to old practices.

I date the inaugural moment of South African society, its neonatal moment, its moment of birth, from 1994 to the year 2000. No doubt South Africa will remain young for a long time, perhaps forever. However, from 1994 to the millennium the whole society existed in a utopian state. I date the end of the moment to the Durban HIV/AIDS conference. It is a terrible irony of history that 1992 was the date at which HIV infection rates began to soar in South Africa, especially among the black African poor (who carry the disease in the highest numbers). It is an irony because the end of apartheid brought with it the possibility of freedom of migration internally and, more important, across national borders, which dramatically spread the disease. Should there be no more infections at all in this country, fully a quarter of the population will die in the next fifteen to twenty years. And the rate remains at 12 to 20 percent, depending on whom you consult in this year of 2001. By 2000 all of this had come to light, along with the government's intransigence in addressing the problem and its ideological response.

The increasing authoritarianism of the state, its failure of delivery, its mounting corruption, its wasting of European Union money; the failure of policy to have produced foreign investment; the spiral of crime, the corruption of the judiciary, the incapacity to help the poorest of the poor—all are problems that are overwhelming the optimism. Globalization has not happened, and this is a global failure. South Africa is a new nation on paper where materially things are in so many ways worse than before. The scenario is bleak since, with a quarter of the population scheduled to die even if there is not a single new HIV infection in the country, all areas of society and economy will be affected, from medical systems to primary education (where teachers are dying at the rate of a thousand a year). Who can celebrate a new nation in such dire circumstances? Who can presume to take the stance of a prophet and speak of what will be?

On the other hand, important processes are at work, such as current challenges in the courts to state policy on anti-retroviral delivery by the Treatment Action Campaign, which may end up empowering the courts as countertendencies to the centralization of state power. The results could be important for the fledgling democracy and its need to establish templates of genuine conflict of interest between state, judiciary, and civil society—perhaps as important as *Marbury v. Madison* or, later, *Brown v. the Board of Education, Topeka, Kansas*, were for the United States. When one writes as a public intellectual about the present, one's book stops in a way that history does not. This book stops at the end of 2001. Perhaps by the time it hits the bookshelves in 2003, things will already be different. I can live with that if the reader can, given that the point of this book is to map the initial moment of the South African transition (1994–2000) and to do so by reflecting philosophically upon it in a way that is also a reflection upon philosophy. The future of the neonatal infant is, finally, beyond this book's purview, even if it is the reader's own present tense.

1

The Coat of Many Colors: Truth and Reconciliation

The Bible

Joseph, seventeen years old, was a shepherd, along with his brothers. Israel, their father, loved Joseph more than his other sons, for he was his father's late lamb, the son of his old age. One day, Israel had a special coat, sewn of long sleeves and dazzling colors, made for him. Joseph's brothers, knowing that their father loved Joseph best, hated him so much that they could not utter a civil word to him. One day Joseph's brothers went to pasture their father's flock at Shechem. Israel told Joseph to go and see how his brothers and the flock were doing, and to bring him word of it. Later a man found Joseph wandering the countryside and asked him, "What are you looking for?" "I am looking for my brothers," was his reply.

The rest of the story is well known. Joseph's brothers conspired to kill him, only to have Ruben, the best of the lot, intercede, saying that Joseph should be spared but put into a well. It was done. Spying a group of Ishmaelites laden with goods, the brothers thought to themselves, "Why kill him? He is, after all, our brother. Instead, let us sell him into slavery and make profit from it." While the discussions went on, another group of traders, the Midianites, saw Joseph, drew him up from the well, and sold him to the Ishmaelites. Horrified to find Joseph gone from the well, the brothers feared their father's wrath. To deceive him, they drenched Joseph's coat of many colors in the blood of a goat and brought the stained coat to their father, asking him to identify it. The father, seeing it, immediately knew that it was Joseph's and, lamenting that wild beasts must have devoured him, put on sackcloth and went into mourning over the loss of his son.

Israel, the father of Joseph, lived a long time without knowing that his son was alive, a slave to Potiphar, a stranger in a strange land. Joseph found himself thrown in prison because of his refusal to submit to the overtures of Potiphar's wife. In prison, Joseph became the interpreter of dreams, master of prophecy. Called on to decipher a dream of the pharaoh himself, Joseph responded that it told of seven good years, followed by seven lean years, advising the pharaoh to make provision for the lean years to come by stocking up his granaries so that his people would have bread, and so that Egypt might make profit from those who had not secured their stocks for the times ahead.

Seven good years followed by seven lean years came as Joseph foretold, and among those who came to Egypt in search of grain were his brothers, sent by their father in desperation. Withholding recognition until the last moment, Joseph finally revealed himself to his brothers, who were shocked and expected immediate retribution. Instead, Joseph embraced them, saying that they were still his blood kin and his loves. Inviting the whole family to leave its lands and come to Egypt, where they might live prosperously on the rich land of Goshen, he and his act of forgiveness led to the reuniting of Joseph with his family.

Joseph forgives; Moses returns. South Africa becomes a rainbow nation, a coat of many colors. Moses returns with a people who are now a *people*, no longer a mere family defined by lines of shared belief and shared blood, or by a history of quarrels and inseminations. This family returns as a *people* because, formed by shared oppression, solidified by forty years in the desert, ready to learn freedom slowly, led by a Mosaic figure, severely and from the mountaintop, they are now a people with a Torah—the Five Books of Moses, the holy tablets—a people with a document, a revelation, a prescription, a historical archive before which no idols may stand. They are formed by betrayal and slavery, but also by forgiveness and law.

The Bible is a story, the greatest story on earth, the biggest seller of all time, a telling of what was (supposedly or in fact) and is (supposedly or in fact) a gift from God. Literal and allegorical, simple and opaque, it is a moral guide that narrates a people and provides law, so that by this providence they might become and remain a people by reciting its script and fulfilling its commandments. From generation to generation many have done this: many peoples, not one, some of whom have wreaked a violence on the others worthy of inclusion in the Bible itself. Even, especially, in South Africa, where the history of religion and the history of blood are, in many respects, the same, from the pulpits of the Afrikaans preacher—who charged those people, "the Afrikaans *volk*" (or so they said and believed), to honor the day of the vow, December 16, Dingaan's Day, on which the *volk* took a sacred vow to beat the Zulu—to the hands of Father Michael Lapsley, blown off, along with one of his eyes, by a letter bomb sent by the security police, a "postcard" that reached its destination. The blood of religion has reached the lion and the lamb, who now sit down, each with the other, and sometimes forgive. Father Lapsley asked for the names of those who perpetrated the act against him, because without their names he would not know who to "endeavor to forgive."[1] Almost a century earlier, in 1913, the Anglican Ministry in South Africa sat easy while the Land Act, instituted in that year, deprived black Africans of 90 percent of their land, thus sending them onto the roads and into the mines, a people dispossessed. On the other side, Father Huddleston, who worked in Sophiatown, outside of Johannesburg, in the 1950s until being deported by the apartheid regime, is remembered today for his many acts of generosity, as are many others. Dr. Andries Treurnicht is also remembered, by the man who held before me the chair in philosophy at the University of Natal, Professor Koos Stofberg. Treurnicht was instrumental in barring Koos from teaching in Afrikaans universities because Stofberg, while a young student in Holland in the 1970s, wrote Treurnicht a letter that burned his temples, rather than blow off his hands, with its detailed and unassailable argument against biblical justification for the apartheid regime—upon which the National Party had relied for its mythologies of self.

Religion is, in South Africa, soaked in blood. Because of this, it is perhaps uniquely suited (if suited at all) to allegorize the moment of breakaway from the past, to turn memory into prophecy through the events of the Truth and Reconciliation Commission, to archive the past in the form of a moral code for the future. It is not for nothing that Archbishop Desmond Tutu has served as the moral beacon and acting chair of this august assembly for his impeccable antiapartheid credentials, his international reputation, his position in a patriarchal society as a moral father, a man of the cloth who resides close to God, a man of impeccable integrity, a man who also comes from humble origins and is black. Religion, once poison, is now cure. Perhaps signal among the vocabularies of the present in its capability of freeing the South African past from religion, of turning religion into moral infrastructure, of commuting the appeal of Christ into a capacity for forgiveness in civil and political society, is religion itself. This cure of religion by religion can also produce a failure of cure, a reopiation of the people, a mode of avoiding the hard facts of poverty, illiteracy, disease, unemployment, lack of housing—what Thabo Mbeki calls the problem of "two nations," in the name of a good biblical story about truth and reconciliation, a story seductive in its moral impressiveness. That the Truth and Reconciliation Commission is a national drug is a thought held by certain people, some of whom have impossibly huge expectations about history—a thought that shall haunt the biblical when it reappears on the scene of history.

Certain moments in history appear to call forth biblical allegory because those who inhabit such moments are trained in the ways of the Bible and are liable to its recitations, and because their time is one in which fact and story, archive and revelation, memory and moral code, reality and allegory, past and present conspire into blending as a people gestates into a *people*. Or so we are told, or so the events of the nation, some of them but not others, bespeak and intend. To what effect it is unknown. At such moments, foundational in their biblicality, the lines between historiography and homily, archive and revelation, recitation and invention, converge in a fit of border-crossing and voices take on an aura beyond their words. So it is with Archbishop Tutu; so it is with the South African Truth and Reconciliation Commission, one of the greatest shows on earth during the 1990s. What is the power of the biblical today, at a moment of what is called nation-building, and what is called reconciliation? What is the power of truth when harnessed to religion and when not harnessed? When, given the way in which moral infrastructure developed out of religion in the history of Europe—a history that recurs in the language of the Truth and Reconciliation Commission, hybridized as it is to the philosophy of ubuntu—is truth *not* harnessed to religion? Needless to say, an analysis of power would be at stake in these questions, as would an analysis of certain relations between science, liberalism, and the Enlightenment. Given the fragmentary and complex systems through which power circulates in these interrelated forms, this would be an enormous, perhaps impossible, task. And yet it would be a task that would have everything to do with the Truth and Reconciliation Commission, which has been the greatest show on earth because it has been the only show around in which the secular moral codes of conduct (which are its historical offspring) appear within the larger biblical framework of homily, allegory, nationalism, and the history of religion without being fundamentalist in character, but instead the opposite. A rare historical experience is required today for this to happen, and perhaps at any time for it to happen well (insofar as it happens well); a history that has everything to do with the project of reconciliation, an equally rare event today. The world watches because there are so few places today where a formative moment in the history of moral infrastructure is taking place in this seminal way: from the seminary to the commission of inquiry.

The moral integrity of the Truth and Reconciliation Commission, both in its conduct during the heady occasions of its interviewing and in its findings published in its report, is astonishing to the point where it places the philosopher in a position of considerable trepidation. For philosophers are accustomed to writing about people who are smarter than they (e.g., Plato, Aristotle, Kant, Hegel, Nietzsche) as if they are full of holes (then what does that make the ones who write about them?), but unaccustomed to having anything to say about events that are morally superior to them and, quite possibly, morally sublime. What words are adequate to such events?

To ruminate on the relevance or irrelevance of philosophy to these weighty matters is not to come to the conclusion that philosophy is irrelevant. It is to suggest that *not* to so ruminate, that not to take such doubts seriously, is not to engage the event in a way crucial to what philosophy is about. If philosophy were proved irrelevant, that would in itself be a philosophical conclusion of interest. The report of the commission already ruminates extensively on its own limitations—moral, conceptual, historical, national, epistemic. In so doing, one might think it has short-circuited philosophical critique already. Whether this is the case or not depends on what one takes to be enough rumination, or rumination of the right kind. Moreover, there are portentous reasons to doubt that philosophy has anything to say about the goings-on of the Truth and Reconciliation Commission, reasons that have to do with the issue of keeping silent. It is a question of what words by the philosopher should follow testimonies like these, spoken about children of violence by their loved ones:

"That morning I did something I had never done before. My husband was still at his desk busy with the accounts of our business. I went up to him and stood behind his chair. I put my hands under his arms and tickled him . . . he looked surprised and unexpectedly happy."

"'And now?' he asked.

"'I am going to make tea,' I said.

"While I poured water on the tea bags, I heard this devastating noise.

Six men stormed into our study and blew his head off. My five-year-old daughter was present. . . . That Christmas I found a letter on his desk: 'Dear Father Christmas, please bring me a soft teddy bear with friendly eyes. . . . My daddy is dead. If he was here I would not have bothered you.' I put her in a boarding school. The morning we drove there we had a flat tyre. 'You see,' she said, 'Daddy does not want me to go there. . . . He wants me to stay with you. . . . I have watched him die, I must be there when you die. . . . ' She is now a teenager and has tried twice to commit suicide.[2]

"When I came home, I saw there were many white men, they kicked my door . . . and they went in. I am sure I nearly died that day. They missed when they shot—they missed me on my forehead. Another soldier approached—the soldier was sitting on top of the car and he was pointed at me. He started shooting at me while I was trying to open the door. Now these bullets looked like pellets and they were black. Then I went in next door and I tried to wonder how did my children survive.

"My fifteen-year-old son Bonisile ran away with his sisters. When they arrived they found out that their father was already dead. They cried. Some of the men who survived that day came to my house, now these men picked up my husband. He was—he was put on top of his own son. . . . This child, who was also full of blood, kept on asking—'Daddy, can you see me, can you see me?' Now I heard when they got there at Condradie Hospital, when they were in this passage on their way to Condradie, he died. . . . My son Bonisile, who was smeared with his father's blood on him, was never well again after that, he was psychologically disturbed." (Krog: 79–80)

Silence would seem to be the appropriate response for me, although not for the commission, to whom they were originally spoken. When the commissioners spoke, their words were spoken in a particular place at a particular time to a set of individuals, and also to a room filled with translators and journalists. Antjie Krog, poet and journalist, witnessed the words and recorded them in her powerful book, Country of My Skull, from which I reproduce them. To these words the commissioners and especially their chair, Archbishop Tutu, might have responded with thanks and with encouragement—about the capacity for these words, perhaps, to help in the process of healing for the people who spoke them, and perhaps also about the general importance of the Truth Commission for healing in South Africa. Such responses were typical to the commission, which also, occasionally, would be asked, again by its chair, to stand in silence or to engage in prayer. A commissioner might also have asked for more information or pursued a "subjective" angle ("How did you feel when . . . ," "What do you think today about . . . ").

To the first of these two pieces of testimony Krog chooses not to "speak" directly in her book, for it occurs in a string of testimonies of a similar kind and then in the book followed by a line space and a new paragraph, as if to suggest that the reader pause and let these words ring in his or her ears before reading those supplied by Krog. Her words, therefore, become indirectly connected to what has been read. This moment of silence represents a brief acknowledgment of the enormity of what is heard, of its proximity to that which cannot be understood at all and to what is understood all too well, of its sublimity. Such a moment is also that of respect for what the other has gone through, a moment in which the difference between the other's experience and one's own is acknowledged. It is the kind of moment one must allow to happen upon hearing that someone has suffered a terrible loss (father, child). It is also the moment of the psychoanalyst, who must often say nothing at all, so that the one on the couch does not feel "crowded in" by the psychoanalyst's words, so that the one who speaks is assured that her experience is given validation rather than rendered supplementary to the language of the one sitting behind her and "quietly taking notes." There are many times in life when such silence is called for as a part of the process of reception—by everybody, not simply the philosopher, whatever or whomever he or she is. Here the silence is double: first, an act of respect, of acknowledgment of the gap between self and other, and second, an acknowledgment that the story told has proximity to that which, in the words of Theodor Adorno, "breaks the clocks of measurement" and is morally unfathomable. This is also a silence specifically directed to the philosopher.

With the Holocaust, Adorno famously remarked, "All the clocks of measurement were broken." Perhaps they have been reset by now, given that this terrible event was followed by the murderous events of Cambodia, Rwanda, and Serbia, and preceded by the attempted extermination of the Armenians by the Turks, and now appears as the most signal in a series that must be understood as part of modernity and its systems of violence. And yet, although this series, each by itself and each in relation to the others, requires the project of explanation, in all cases the attitude of silence is an obligation, one aspect of "understanding" or acknowledgment, given that the enormity of the horror is, from the human point of view, incomprehensible—the modern fact of extermination being the point at which the human becomes permanently unrecognizable to itself.

The gross violations of human rights that have been the focus of the commission in South Africa are not events of extermination, and the series of examples (of racism, of state terror) in which they line up as similar and different provides one with less reason to feel that all measurement is broken in their explanation. A field of psychology, historical studies, sociology, political science, economics, and much more may be activated in responding to the following excerpt from the commission's inquiries:

> Amongst those who questioned Captain [Jeffrey T.] Benzien at his amnesty hearing was Mr. Tony Yengeni, one of his victims, who asked him to demonstrate his torture methods:
>
> CAPTAIN BENZIEN: It was a cloth bag that would be submerged in water to get it completely wet. And then the way I applied it was: I get the person to lie down on the ground, on his stomach, normally on a mat or something similar, with that person's hands handcuffed behind his back.
>
> Then I would take up a position in the small of the person's back, put my feet through between his arms to maintain my balance and then pull the bag over the person's head and twist it closed around the neck in that way, cutting off the air supply to the person . . .
> MR. TONY YENGENI: Would the person groan, moan, cry, scream? What would the person do?
> CAPTAIN BENZIEN: Yes, the person would moan, cry, although muffled; yes, it does happen.
> MR. TONY YENGENI: And you did this to each and every one of us?
> CAPTAIN BENZIEN: To the majority of you, yes . . .
> MR. TONY YENGENI: What kind of man uses a method like this— one of the wet bag, to people, to other human beings, repeatedly, and listening to those moans and cries and groans and taking each of those people very near to their deaths—what kind of man are you? What kind of man is that, that can do that kind of—what kind of human being is that, Mr. Benzien?
>
> I want to understand really why, what happened? I am not talking now about the politics or your family. I am talking about the man behind the wet bag. When you do those things, what happens to you as a human being? What goes through your head, your mind? You know, what effect does that torture activity do to you as a human being?
> CAPTAIN BENZIEN: Mr. Yengeni, not only you have asked me that question. I—I, Jeff Benzien, have asked myself that question to such

an extent that I voluntarily—and it is not easy for me to say this in a full court with a lot of people who do not know me . . . approached psychiatrists to have myself evaluated, to find out what type of person I am. . . . If you ask me what type of person is it that can do that, I ask myself the same question. (5: 368–70)

It is notable that Yengeni's need to know his torturer is profound. It is also notable that when each man speaks, he slides between descriptions of the torture in the past tense and in the present tense, as if each is, in his own mind, especially within the intensity of their face-to-face exchange, still there at the moment of torture, a moment that is a specter of nonresolution, a ghost that lives between the past and present, blurring the gap. Last, it is notable that Benzien is both hiding and revealing himself, his hiding paradoxically being in his somewhat smug description of visiting a psychiatrist, as if he should score some points in the direction of amnesty on account of it ("I voluntarily—and it is not easy for me to say this in a full court with a lot of people who do not know me . . . approached psychiatrists to have myself evaluated, to find out what type of person I am"). This gesture was not one of therapy but of merely "finding something out," as if about another. So that this other, never touched or disturbed, can be presented to the Truth and Reconciliation Commission as an other, a ghost from the past. Benzien's true self is instead betrayed by his use of the present tense when speaking of what he did. He is still that person. (Yengeni has recently been under investigation for considerable corruption in his office of parliamentary whip for the African National Congress. In the townships, a "Yengeni" is the new word for a fancy four-wheel-drive automobile.)

Now, philosophy is hardly the best discipline for speaking to the question of who Jeffrey Benzien is, given the extensive writings on torture by psychoanalysis, critical theory, political science, and history, not to mention a host of nongovernmental organizations, victims, perpetrators, families related to the events, journalists, and the like. It would be presumptuous for philosophy to assume any special vocabulary for the answering of this question. It must be admitted that insofar as the commission takes itself to be in the business of explaining such matters, which in one voice it does, its explanations are of a most incomplete, superficial nature. Which the commission also, in another voice, more or less concedes, depending on how you read the report. My point is that, although the question remains open of who Jeffrey Benzien is—and what that says about the human becoming unrecognizable to itself, or recognizable in another form, through the production of new and terrible knowledge—even in relation to Adorno's remarks about the resetting of clocks, philosophy does not immediately enter the scene in addressing it, at least not until enough is said by other disciplines so as to allow philosophy to take up the thread of that question in a better way. What philosophy can say at the start is the obvious: that Benzien's character, evidenced in what he did and in the cool detachment of his describing and "demonstrating" it before the commission, is sufficiently disturbing to force a moment of silence, of contemplation, of anxiety.

After that brief pause in testimony in Krog's book, the words with which she follows the pause are those of a poet:

> In the beginning it was seeing. Seeing for ages, filling the head with ash. No air. No tendril. Now to seeing, speaking is added and the eye plunges into the mouth. Present at the birth of this country's language itself. (Krog: 29)

Journalism becomes poetry at the moment when witnessing is that of the "eye [plunging] into the mouth," which is the eye of the one who gives this description or report: the victim, the one whose seeing is now that of speaking. The eye is also Krog's eye, the mouth her mouth, as she reports her having witnessed the victim saying these words, that vision again now in her mouth, that ashen suffering and memory now hers and hers to share. What this poetry does is to place writer and victim in the same space of seeing, of speaking, of transmission. The moment is haunted by the spreading of ashes of the dead, of dying again through speaking of the dead. It calls for words that hang in the air, that sear without the analytical detachments of thought. It calls for reception.

One might recall these words of Dori Laub on the double structure of witnessing:

> The listener . . . is also a separate human being and will experience hazards and struggles of his own, while carrying out his function of a witness to the trauma witness [the one who is giving testimony]. While overlapping, to a degree, with the experience of the victim, he nonetheless does not become the victim—he preserves his own separate place, position and perspective; a battleground for forces raging in himself, to which he has to pay attention and respect if he is to properly carry out his task.
>
> The listener, therefore, has to be at the same time a witness to the trauma witness and a witness to himself. It is only in this way, through his simultaneous awareness of the continuous flow of those inner hazards both in the trauma witness and in himself, that he can become the enabler of the testimony—the one who triggers its initiation, as well as the guardian of its process and of its momentum.[3]

Some may find Krog's incantation of birth out of place, but it is in keeping with Laub's double structure of witnessing. For while Krog is witnessing the language of others, their first chance at speaking the truth as they know it in a public, national forum, it is *her own language* that is being born in the country of her skull: her skull with the ash in it. This is her own praise poetry about what is happening, her sleepless nights, and her fury. Some, especially some South Africans fed up with "Afrikaner browbeating," may think of her language as the final gasp of a tiny intellectual elite for whom the country remains imagined as "theirs." For it is no country of her skull that South Africa is, but rather one of fifty million other people, some of whom are doing the real talking in this Truth and Reconciliation Commission event. Some may further find her book a retreat into the kind of poetic aestheticization of violence that drains it of its windowless edge by commuting it into modernist Afrikaans poetry: the latest in a history of precious and biblicalized mythologizations. For what it is worth, I do not find it thus. It is saved by being a new genre, one of journalism as well as poetry. Jean-François Lyotard speaks of the liminal experiences of our time as demanding new genres adequate to, or attempting to be adequate to, their unspeakability: one must speak, one cannot speak. It seems to me that the mixture of poetry and journalism, which cuts from reporting to witnessing to imagining to remembering and continually loops between these in an *opera furiosa*, breaks through the mould of mere subjectivity and the illusion of poetic ownership to address one deep reaction to among the most intense events of our time. If there can be no poetry after Auschwitz, then this is more than poetry for precisely that reason: that to respect the event of Auschwitz, of its enormity, is to always bear in mind that one's need to imagine it is also always a need to acknowledge one's failure to imagine it. In Krog's work, imagination gives way to fact: she is a reporter and witness, and this book is also a book of reportage. It is in the movement from poetry to reportage that, paradoxically, the enormity of the event is there, as is its dialectic of achieving the position of a witness, who must at once report and *imagine*. She does not seek to master the event, to present it as a seamless, aesthetic whole, but rather to describe the whirl of being part of it, the way no one can quite take being in the rooms of the commission day after day, or take the intensity, the wear and tear on family and soul, the *journalese* of it. For this reason, hers is not an aestheticization of politics.

Krog's language performs a movement from ash to birth, death to regeneration, which is curative without *curing*. (Freud says the end of psychoanalysis is not cure but the capacity for working through. Krog's language works through, which would be, for the victims and their families and also for all other witnesses such as she, an endless task.) Her language speaks of witnessing, but also gives her a certain distance from the burden of witnessing close up and so being drowned by the thing. "Present at the birth of this country's language," she says. She was present then, when it happened, when the victim gave birth to language. She is present to the birth of language now, her language, the language she is making happen herself. "Present at the birth of this country's language" is incomplete, a sentence fragment that lacks a subject and a verb. The subject alluded to is, in the first instance, herself ("I am present at this birth," "I was present at this birth"), and, by extension, everyone who was there in the room where these words were spoken by a victim, and everyone who is reading her book now, as the victim's language and hers are happening again. By "language" is meant a transaction in which voice gives itself the power of speech but through an institution (that of the commission, that of literature), which occasions the reception of this speech by others. What is meant is communication, which in South Africa has not happened very often about real things, between persons of different colors in the many-colored coat of South African peoples. There is a kind of birth of communication here; she is not lying, although she is precisely making it up, turning it into poetry, which is also its birth. Call it the birth of the varieties of language, of the capacity for a victim to report a set of events straightforwardly and the capacity of a journalist to then take this language and sear it into the reader's brain by letting it speak, giving pause, and then performing certain poetic twists in relation to what has been reported.

The more important aspect of the deletion of a verb in the incomplete sentence ("Present at the birth of this country's language") is that the tense of the sentence remains ambiguous. We do not know if the subject (call it "Antjie Krog") *was* present at this birth or if she is present at it now in the writing, through the writing. More likely, this birth itself is a doubling process that begins with the speech of the victim (witnessed by her) and continues into her own prose. The birth of a language is a complex event in which words recur to be given multiple births, multiple identities. The ambiguity is also one pertinent to trauma, to the birth of a language of trauma, of the birth of language through trauma. The haunting of the past in the present is also found in the time travels of Yengeni and Benzien between present and past tense, and allows her to imply the haunting presence of the victim's words in her own brain, haunting being a way in which the past recurs in the present. It is an ambiguity that allows Krog to gain a certain curative distance from this haunting by implying that she was there in the past and is not now, or not in the same way. She was present at the birth of this language, receptive to its power, passive in its transmission of ash, made anxious by its hint of death. But by saying she was present, she is also putting it in the past. Not completely, but partly so. Last, she is present at the birth of her language, her commutation of witnessing into a poetry of communication, just as are we "present at" this invention through the receptivity of reading. We are also, naturally, not present; she is. Hence the evocative nature of the sentence fragment that bespeaks a literature of overcoming.

It remains to be said that in Krog's testimony there is also a hint that birth is not free of memorialization, for where there is ash that remains in the head, there is the presence of the dead who live on. It is through the ash in the head that the birth of this country's language, of its capacity for speaking and writing, will take place. One might think of the Truth and Reconciliation Commission as a memorializing exercise, which is a chief reason why religious men and women were right to lead it, and also why its report contains a long list of all the victims, as if a litany of the dead.

The Relevance of Philosophy to the TRC

What, then, does make the Truth and Reconciliation Commission pertinent to *philosophy*? This philosophical essay has already stated that to doubt the relevance of philosophy to the TRC is crucial to philosophical reflection on the TRC. Sublime events carry great ideas; they are moral beacons. This does not ensure that philosophy follows from them. Quite the contrary: it might ensure that no philosophy follows, depending, of course, on what one means by philosophy. However, if the great ideas carried in sublime events were already philosophical in gel, then philosophy *would* follow from the events themselves. In the following parts, I discuss how the TRC is already philosophical in gel, how this gives rise to further philosophical reflection, and what that says about transitional justice.

Consider Tutu's language. I want to call it the language of *religious homily*. The language typically used by Tutu to respond to the testimony he hears is as peculiar, as idiomatic, as Krog's. He gravitates towards the preacher's platitude, truism, reminder. (I remind you that this is an essay about the Truth Commission and the Bible.) The sweet, singsong character of his voice augments these ways of talking. For the philosopher Ludwig Wittgenstein, philosophy consists of "the assembling of reminders for a particular purpose." The kind of reminders one assembles depends on the purpose. Wittgenstein tells us that were anyone to assert the propositions of philosophy, they would be so trivial that everyone would agree to them and nothing would be accomplished. It is all a matter of timing, context, interpretation—of bringing home what everyone already knows, but in a way that cuts through something, some veil of obfuscation, some illusion, some unclarity, and accomplishes a freeing of the mind from what Wittgenstein calls a fixation, or haunting. Tutu's language (the homiletic, the truistic, the becalming, the platitudinous) is a way of drawing on remarks of such startling obviousness that only Tutu—on this particular occasion, speaking in his calm, singsonging way, in an orchestrated visual spectacle, on a stage where the commissioners sit, facing victims and perpetrators, above the crowd, before the television audience, as in a service of the heart or a public confessional—only Tutu, dressed in the glorious robes of the archbishop, can say these remarks, can *mean* these remarks, can *bring them home*, for they are one inch from preposterousness or kitsch. Tutu is a man of the cloth, and not only is he, the chair, a man of the cloth, but so are the vice chair, Reverend Alex Boraine, and the commissioner, Reverend Bongani Finca. A typical kind of response by the commission to the terrible words of a victim's testimony is this offered by Tutu to Puleng Moloko and family after testimony given about a relative called Maki:

> Puleng Moloko and the family, we would like you to note that the death of Maki was a national shame. South Africa was looked upon internationally, more especially those who were fighting against apartheid, as beasts, as carnivores and that the family managed to stand by Maki even at a time when everybody was saying, away with that family. We salute you . . . Maki and the family have emerged, after all these disclosures, as heroes. I would say this hearing and this hall have witnessed . . . how noble Maki was, and I will, without shame, request this house to stand and observe a moment of silence. (5: 365)

Here Tutu is responding to the testimony of Maki, a comrade from the struggle who was falsely accused of being a spy for the authorities but who refused to run away and hide, knowing she was innocent. Her injuries forced her to undergo open-heart surgery, left shrapnel in her body, and caused extensive, indelible scarring.

Tutu listens to the testimony of Mrs. Beth Savage, severely hurt during a bomb blast by the Pan African Congress in 1992, and six months later suffered a "nervous breakdown." She states to the committee, "There but for the grace of God go I," when asked how she feels about the perpetrators. To her response, Tutu says,

Thank you. I just want to say, we are, I think, a fantastic country. We have some quite extraordinary people. Yesterday, I had spoken about how proud I was to be black in seeing the kind of spirit that people showed in adversity, and now we're seeing another example, and I think it just augers so wonderfully well for our country. We thank you for the spirit that you are showing and pray that those who hear you, who see you, will say, "Hey, we do have an incredible country with quite extraordinary people of all races." (5: 374)

If Tutu's language has the character of a series of reminders, it is not obvious that it is meant for a philosophical purpose, nor is it even obvious what a "philosophical purpose" would be. Tutu's language is, in the first instance, biblical in resonance, the language of a sacred man of the cloth. I suggest that his reminders are philosophical because of the deep inheritance of biblico-philosophical language they draw upon, and that they are philosophical because they are connected to a truth construction that is precisely a connecting truth to reconciliation, a truth construction explicitly contained in the report. These themes, along with the theme of transitional justice, occupy most of the rest of the essay, although not in this order.

It seems to me that to consider the appropriateness, the power of Tutu's remarks, you must consider what you yourself might have said (if anything) in response to Beth Savage's testimony, were you in his position. I do not say, "Consider what words you would use if you were he," for if you were he, you would, it follows, use the same words as he, and the thought experiment becomes trivial. Rather, if you were you, but somehow found yourself in his position, what would you say that would be worthy of the occasion? Would you use any words at all? Should you? Other than "Thank you for your testimony, Mrs. Savage"? What words generate the right response, *a* right response? I take this question to be internal to the evaluation of *Tutu's* words, to the evaluation of their purpose and effectiveness, given the circumstance of their utterance. And, by extension, I take this question to be about the appropriateness of the homily per se in certain kinds of circumstances, or the role of religion today (a role for religion in secular society today). For although the Truth and Reconciliation Commission is mandated by law, what is unique about it concerns its religious character. There have been many Truth Commissions in the past decade, some more successful than others in various ways, each unique to circumstances. Some (the Chilean example) have offered blanket amnesty. Others have addressed interrogation and prosecution. Milosevic is "on trial" for crimes against humanity. The South African Truth Commission is the only one that has been driven by a religious principle and rhetoric, and, in a related way, the only one that has occurred as a nation-building exercise at a moment of transition. It is this, a fact internally related to its position of qualified amnesty (see below), that makes it unique. In another *kind* of inquiry, one of the Nuremberg type, where punishment was the object in the name of justice-as-retribution, words like Tutu's would be absurd, as would his style of visual gesture. Instead, another set of words would be in place, such as, "We shall now proceed to further investigate the case so as to bring those to justice who committed this heinous crime," or something of that nature—words of retribution, judgment, decisions taken. Tutu, Boraine, and Finca would surely have been the wrong people to drive such a commission of inquiry. It would have been given over to lawyers, human-rights activists, constitutional court judge Richard Goldstone (also head of numerous national and international human-rights commissions) perhaps. Tutu's homilies can accomplish what they accomplish only because qualified amnesty is in place. These homilies are part of what allows the language of the TRC to be the kind of restorative/nation-building exercise it has been.

What Tutu's language shares with philosophy is not only its character as a kind of reminder, but its heritage of utopian imaginings of liberal democracy, nation, and the oneness of a people, existing in a state of reconciliation before God. It is as "trivial" as Wittgenstein believes the propositions of philosophy to be, and for a similar reason: it recites what everyone knows for purposes of a specific kind of acknowledgment (of the victims) and a specific kind of nation-building exercise. It brings home the obvious for these particular purposes. I shall point out below that the report of the TRC constructs, out of a grab bag of homilies and theory bits, its theory of truth for a particular purpose. Indeed, the commission's theory of truth operated as a homily throughout the proceedings literally under the banner of truth, for hanging above the seated commissioners was always a cloth banner, stating, "Truth—the Road to Reconciliation." Tutu's remarks are idealizations about human dignity, human community, human suffering, human forgiveness, human society, human justice. They shepherd the words of the victims into an idealized space in which those words are no longer merely those of individuals, but words reverberating with the sound of a nation-building exercise before an invisible God. Tutu commutes individual stories into biblical narratives, precisely by dignifying the individuals who speak as individuals before God, before community, before the future. The homiletic brings home the biblical character of the event. It makes the event biblical.

Since biblical images of community are also philosophical images taken from the Christian Enlightenment of ideal justice, ideal society, ideal nation, Tutu's language carries what I want to call "our philosophical heritage" in crystallized form. Put another way, it is because Tutu's language is so homiletic, so simple, so drained of anything but the most common and deeply felt morality that it can command the attention of a community, which feels it as theirs. It is because his is philosophy reduced to homily (crystallized as homily) that each of us feels that we are brought together under its wing, that we are shepherded by it.

Last, Tutu's language calls upon South African heritages of ubuntu because it is about people becoming people (becoming human) only through the care of the community as a whole. What Tutu's language shows is that to speak in the name of an entire nation as diverse and filled with strife as South Africa, one must speak homiletically, in language so simple and deep that everyone believes it because they already know it.

This is, in itself, philosophy enough. Or is it? After all, many have had grave doubts about the TRC and about the role of forgiveness, amnesty, etcetera, in it. Perhaps, then, to all this Christianity, a Nietzschean response is required? A Marxist response? A Freudian response? Each of which is—as a critique of certain belief systems, as a critique of the human capacity to believe, and believe *fervently*—a critique both philosophical and contemptuous of the mere abstraction of (certain kinds of) philosophy.

This brings us to the topic of amnesty, and of the justice associated with amnesty.

The Rules of the TRC

Everything in the appropriateness of the language used by Tutu depends on the issue of qualified amnesty and its connection to the larger project of reconciliation through truth. The South African Truth and Reconciliation Commission invented the concept of qualified amnesty. In the past, either Truth Commissions had been of the Nuremberg type (delivering retribution) or of the Chilean type, where unqualified amnesty was given to all in exchange for truthful participation. In a Nuremberg situation, I have already said, Tutu's language would be out of place; this is also perhaps true for a situation of unqualified amnesty, where his language of forgiveness and being close to God would be harder to take, given that all the perpetrators had been "forgiven" already by being let off scot-free.

The facts are these: The Truth and Reconciliation Commission was mandated by the interim constitution, worked out by the power-sharing government and a negotiating team, including other factions of South African political society. Its mandate was more formally stated in the Promotion of National Unity and Reconciliation Act, No. 34, of 1995, which set forth its terms. The issue of qualified amnesty was so problematic that it was resolved only at the last minute and included in a postamble to the interim constitution. Amnesty was the result of a stalemate in the war of the late 1980s. Neither side found itself capable of winning, which led to the power-sharing interim government. The African National Congress had had the idea of a Truth Commission for some time, but found that, given the stalemate, it could not expect the National Party, with whom it was sharing power, to agree to a Truth Commission without the carrot of amnesty. In turn, the National Party's desire for unqualified amnesty was rejected by most of the other parties, including the ANC. Out of this stalemate came the idea for qualified amnesty, which in turn would produce the incentive on the part of perpetrators to tell "the whole truth" for the record and in the interests of justice.

Three committees were set up. The Truth and Reconciliation Committee (what is popularly called "the Commission" or the "Truth and Reconciliation Commission," a form of words I am using here) was charged with

> establishing as complete a picture as possible of the causes, nature and extent of the gross violations of human rights which were committed during the period from 1 March 1960 until the cut off day in 1994, including the antecedents, circumstances, factors and contexts of such violations, as well as the perspectives of the victims and the motives and perspectives of the persons responsible for the commission of the violations, by conducting investigations and holding hearings. (1: 55)

The Amnesty Committee was charged with the review of applications for amnesty. Since full disclosure was among the criteria for the granting of amnesty, two persons from the Truth Commission were allowed onto this one, which is otherwise independent. Last, a committee was established to consider the issue of reparations to victims, the Reparation and Rehabilitations Committee. It has, as of 1999, produced a set of recommendations that the government has done nothing to implement, with the exception of a special President's Fund to aid those in immediate, dire need. An investigations unit was also set up.

To be granted amnesty, the perpetrator must have provided full disclosure of the truth, in addition to satisfying further criteria. These criteria were (1) their acts must have been politically motivated, and (2) their acts must have been "in proportion" to the political motivation (more on that below). As of the date of publication of the report, namely its presentation to then President Nelson Mandela on October 29, 1998, amnesty had been granted to 150 persons out of between seven thousand and eight thousand applications, with two thousand still left to evaluate. So the numbers are *relatively small*, although the stakes are enormous, given the magnitude of the crimes committed.

The story that led to the amnesty provision is well known. Given the political stalemate between warring parties, which led to the establishment of both the interim government and the Truth Commission, qualified amnesty became the only negotiable possibility. All were afraid of massive instability from the left and the right, and this lent the negotiations a profound urgency. There are circumstances other than the South African ones in which any kind of amnesty would have been unthinkable, Nuremberg being one of them. There, the stakes had been genocide and millions were still warm in their ashen graves. Moreover, since every Jew who had not left the burning fires of Europe in time had been exterminated, there was little role for "national reconciliation and unity" between Jews and other Europeans. Things were different in South Africa on all counts, and it is because of this that Tutu had the role that he did.

These facts explain the setting up of qualified amnesty. It is another thing to explain why so many victims and families of victims embraced the process. Some—for example, the family of Steve Biko—refused to participate, arguing that an amnesty process for brutal killers was not acceptable to them, to the memory of Biko, or to the new nation predicated on justice. Some former prisoners from Robbin Island I have talked with feel the same way. Members of the Pan Africanist Congress have strongly voiced this view in public. Others in South Africa welcomed the commission's proceedings and tried to embrace the ideal of reconciliation. Forgiveness runs astonishingly deep in South African cultures, and it is hard to explain why. To call them Christianized is true enough but not enough, and the African roots (most victims and families were black) demand study. No doubt the force of the commission, with its biblical emphasis on reconciliation and national unity, figured centrally in predisposing families and victims toward these ideals. Tutu himself was maybe more important than anything else. And it also should not be forgotten that many of the families and victims had never had the opportunity to speak before any social institution and have their concerns taken utterly seriously. Their expectations of civil and political participation were low, and they enthusiastically grasped what was offered, which was indeed significant. Finally, it should not be forgotten that some kind of reparations have been promised to compensate for suffering and to offset the amnesty that may be offered to perpetrators. To date, the little that has been organized is nothing short of a scandal.

The question of how to evaluate the qualified-amnesty provision is philosophical, because it quickly leads to larger issues of justice. What needs to be kept in mind is this human-rights background. Ours is an age of the exfoliation of rights—in the form of international agreements and international courts of law, of political and civil rights, of human and substantive rights, economic rights, cultural and linguistic rights, the rights of poor countries, the rights of future generations, of the unborn, even of animals. There is force in the extrapolation to new domains, which are then codified (at least in rhetoric and on paper) as nonnegotiable domains in which things are given and things must be respected, be they citizenship or housing, instruction in one's native language, or even the right for a tree to thrive in the ecosystem. Needless to say, as rights are multiplied and codified in moral laws or actual legal systems, they have the tendency to become both more controversial and more inconsistent. It is a fact of life that, often as not, what one does in the name of a single right can end up violating another. The world of rights is the world of trade-offs—between liberty and equality, housing and the environment, the demands of free trade and those of human flourishing. How one negotiates the gaps, difficulties, inconsistencies between rights, how one interprets one vis-à-vis another, depends on whether one is a libertarian or a social democrat, a member of the World Bank or a demonstrator in Seattle or Geneva, a pro-life activist or a believer in the right to "free choice."

This liability of rights to come into conflict in the name of justice is not merely a defect in the practice of justice; it is internal to the very idea of what justice is, for justice is nothing apart from rights, and conflicts in the understanding and application of rights are not guided by a superhuman ideal or theory of justice. On the contrary: theories of justice themselves come into conflict as issues of the understanding of rights, and their application in practice, continually crop up. They may be theories of justice stressing distribution as opposed to stressing recognition, or theories of justice stressing impartial observers as opposed to stressing situated historical subjects in a diverse, liberal colloquy, or theories of justice stressing constitutional rights as opposed to stressing communitarian moral sources. There is no more a way of resolving these disputes between theories than there is of resolving actual conflicts in the understanding and application of rights. Both are of the same sort. Justice is therefore always a negotiation in a particular circumstance that can change, and is open to disagreement. As Jean-François Lyotard says in *Just Gaming*, there are many kinds of justice and many language games involving justice.[4] Between these there is only structure, system, negotiation, conflict, resolution, agreement, disagreement.

Since it is a general condition (I want to say *norm*) of justice that rights are liable to come into conflict, and since it is a general condition *(norm)* of justice that different persons may negotiate these rights in different ways, it should hardly be expected that the Truth and Reconciliation Commission be measured in terms of a coherent, consistent, ideal of justice, against which it will surely fall short in this or that way.

One way that this point has been made is in terms of transitional justice. Recent work on transitional justice argued that the kind of justice pertinent to a country's transition from dispensation of terror to democratic rule of law is distinctive (not the same as the kind of justice pertinent to stable democracies). Countries in transition have special needs, including (1) the need to punish perpetrators from the past regime and in this manner to thereby strengthen the rule of law against forces of terror remaining in the society; (2) the need for the kind of social healing that comes from public punishment; (3) the need for the kind of social healing that comes not from punishment but instead from public images of reconciliation, which allow citizens to reimagine themselves as at one with each other, this as a nation-building exercise; (4) the need for specific spectacles of transition, often in an international forum, which will build the moral capital of the new regime and garner support; and (5) the need to delicately appease those from the old regime, so that transition will not be derailed by a coup or other means. These needs are not exactly consistent, hence the *dilemma* of transition.[5]

Geoffrey Robertson has stated:

> The starkness of the dilemma—whether to pardon or to punish gross violations of human rights by former government and military officials—has been temporarily resolved in many South African and African countries by the intermediate device of the truth commission. . . . That is because truth commissions have reported enough of the truth to discomfort the perpetrators of crimes against humanity who still hold rank in the military and the police: their continued influence frightens politicians, who in consequence invoke the "interests of national reconciliation" as an excuse for granting them amnesties and pardons, despite emerging evidence of their guilt.[6]

Robertson is skeptical of the kind of justice that resides in amnesty, as many are—and especially judges such as himself. The South African Truth and Reconciliation Commission came at a moment of transition and must be understood in that light: its goal was reconciliation as a nation-building exercise, which, for a country like the United States today, would smack of absurdity. The TRC was mandated by the *interim* constitution, and at a moment when something had to happen to push the future forward. This is internal to the evaluation of the TRC. The TRC was a negotiation motivated by the five special needs previously outlined, all pertinent to transitional justice. Since such demands are not prima facie compatible, the TRC was not simply a "second best" trade-off between warring parties, each committed to those claims that suit their interests. It was a trade-off between *kinds of claims.* Its innovation was qualified amnesty.

Whether the TRC found the best solution in qualified amnesty—which reserves the right to punishment but also provides an incentive for perpetrators to tell the truth (namely, that qualified amnesty requires "full disclosure"), which punishes but also allows the religious nation-building exercise around reconciliation to be proclaimed at the early moment of the new South African nation—this is a question about which persons may reasonably disagree. The larger philosophical point is that there is no alternative within justice other than some trade-off or other, each alternative formulation of the TRC being also something that would have to preserve some arrangement between the right to punish, the right to truth, and the right to reconciliation. These rights, both in their interpretation and their application, form no ultimately stable relationship and will never be free of some potential inconsistency, once you look into the situation closely enough.

Some of the potential goods that have come from the qualified-amnesty provision have included (1) the fomenting political stability in the context of a new nation with a weak state and, in the mid-1990s, the threat of violence from the left and right; (2) the gathering, through testimony, of a massive record of violence that otherwise would have been impossible to construct, that is, the buildup of the archive that perpetrators had the incentive to disclose, since full disclosure (judged by the relevant committee) was a criterion for amnesty; (3) the further goal of a nation-building exercise from which flowed at a crucial juncture in the nation's transitional history the beautiful and sublime, that is, aesthetic rhetoric of reconciliation, directed by Tutu and other men of the cloth. All of these goods are by now well known. Unqualified amnesty would not have been a reasonable option, since it would have given perpetrators no incentive to tell the truth and would have felt to many people to be a degradation of the enormity of the apartheid crime. As for the option of offering no amnesty (thinking theoretically, since this was not a viable historical option, given the power held by the National Party and fears about instability fomented by the right), it would have erased the Tutu voice and all associated with it, and, to my mind, produced a far less comprehensive archive.

Whether one remains skeptical of the role of amnesty in the TRC or not, it cannot be measured against business-as-usual law; that is but one language game, deep in the texture of our idea of justice, which has force in human life; and in societies in transition like the South Africa of 1994 there was no socially binding rule of law remotely capable of application to an entire domain of such criminals from the past. Not only that, the goods that flowed from the qualified-amnesty provision would not have so flowed. Which would have been better, more just? The rule of law (punishment) or qualified amnesty? The choice is not a real one, since it is an imaginative choice between what did happen and what did not The what-might-have-been is, at best, provisionally imaginable. History is always like this; there is no way to compare the what-was with the what-might-have-been that is not highly speculative and tentative.

Whatever immediate *conceptual* problems there are with the criteria for amnesty come, above all, from the issue of defining what proportionality consists in. Proportionality is a mathematical measure transposed into a metaphorical realm where any attempt to regulate the concept is bound to be artificial. The Amnesty Committee cobbled together a series of protocols from the past that, for example, permanently exclude rape of women or children, the killing of children, and the like as ever "in proportion to any political motive." However, given that one is dealing with heinous crimes in every case, any attempt to decide which of these gross violations of human rights should be awarded amnesty (given full disclosure of the truth) and which should not must be ad hoc. Jeffrey Benzien's torturing was in 1999 ruled in proportion to his political motivation, for he was granted amnesty. There is, moreover, no way to argue, based on the criteria, that this was a misjudgment. This is enough, I think, to show that the criteria are incoherent. No doubt Benzien gave a convincingly honest and self-flagellating performance, which helped in the "Judeo-Christian" atmosphere of forgiveness, and no doubt his psychopathic personality made that self-representation easy for him. Dirk Coetzee, among the most powerful and vicious members of the Third Force, was granted amnesty in 1997.

Father Michael Lapsley, who is deeply committed to the process of forgiving, nevertheless also gave testimony before the commission—stated on

South African television during a talk show on the Day of Reconciliation, December 16, 1999, formerly the Day of the Vow, and now a national holiday with a different religious character—to the effect that the commission has become too "perpetrator friendly," with amnesty being generously, if also stringently, offered for perpetrators, but without, to date, reparation offered for victims. This is so, and it points to the deepest flaw in the commission, namely, the way the religiosity of the language carries a tenor of redemption, when in fact little has happened other than the importance of these words and their vague effects in a population of very different people, many of whom refused to follow the proceedings at all or were unable to (no access to television, or to the report, etc.). One might then retreat to the position that the real work of the commission consists in establishing the archive, which is always for the future, and in setting a tone for reconciliation to come by providing a beacon in the night. To which others, deeply exasperated with ongoing conditions of suffering in South Africa, respond with the thought that, once again, religion has reopiated the people, being drunk on its own powers of forgiveness and its rosy complexion on life, when nothing concrete has happened other than letting some perpetrators go free. Moreover, those at the top were never brought into the ambit of the commission in a proper way. When P. W. Botha, under whose reign the security forces were vastly and openly expanded, is let free after a ridiculous stalemate, then it is the frogs and foot soldiers rather than the sharks with pretty teeth (or in Botha's case, the big crocodile, as he was often called) who are hooked—again, unlike Nuremberg.

The mandate of the three committees, taken together, was superhuman, which is part of what makes it biblical. In the words of Antjie Krog:

> It [the whole process] was supposed to finish its work in eighteen months. Broadly stated, the aims of the commission were to return to victims their civil rights; to restore the moral order of the society; to seek the truth, record it, and make it known to the public; to create a culture of human rights and respect for the rule of law; and to prevent the shameful events of the past from happening again.
>
> The first hearings were held in April 1996. Over the following two years, South Africans were exposed almost daily to revelations about their traumatic past. In the cities and in many smaller towns, in improvised courtrooms fashioned out of town halls and community centres and churches, the drama of Apartheid and the struggle against it was played out. The Commission received 20000 statements from victims, 2000 in

public hearings and [it has been stated earlier that] it received nearly 8000 applications for Amnesty. (Krog: vii)

The concept of a gross violation of human rights was given definition in the light of protocols set forth by the four Geneva conventions of 1949. These protocols include:

(a) violence to the life and person, in particular murder of all kinds, mutilation, cruel treatment and torture;
(b) taking of hostages;
(c) outrages upon personal dignity, in particular humiliating and degrading treatment;
(d) the passing of sentences and the carrying out of executions without previous judgement pronounced by a regularly constituted court, affording all the juridical guarantees which are recognized as indispensable by civilised peoples. (1: 75)

Certain forms of violence between warring armies, in accord with the protocols of war, were excluded (e.g., killing a soldier on the opposing side while in the midst of a battle).

Amazingly few serious conceptual disputes between parties arose over whether this or that counted as a gross violation of human rights, and this was no doubt due to the victim-centered sympathies of the commission, which applied less stringent criteria for whether a victim had suffered an abuse than it did in judging *who* had committed it, insofar as a distinction could be made between this pair of judgments. It is also because of the amnesty carrot that was offered as a condition of full disclosure, which predisposed perpetrators not to fight about the details of whether their crimes were "gross violations" but instead to argue for appropriate political motivation for them.

While the commission investigated gross human-rights violations in all quarters of the South African past, concluding that the African National Congress, Winnie Mandela, the Pan Africanist Congress, and others had unequivocally committed such violations, it also found it crucial to draw a moral distinction between violations that happened in resistance to apartheid and those that were committed in defense of that racist regime, given global consensus that apartheid represented a crime against humanity. The commission might have chosen to address at least in a single session what Mahmood Mamdani has called the "routine degradations of apartheid," given its concurrence with the view that apartheid represented a crime against humanity, for there would have been good reason to take the view that such degradations were gross violations of *political* rights—political rights being among what are called human rights. I consider this a missed opportunity, given the broad and grandiose formulation of the mandate, which included investigation into the background causes of gross violations of human rights, and which surely included a climate of such "routine degradations." Such a session or group of sessions would have made a strong and needed statement about that past.

As Krog implies by her terse and ironic tone, the mandate of the commission was clearly impossible to fulfill. Indeed, its goals were utopian and impossible to fulfill by *any* group of commissions or researchers in the neonatal beginning of a new regime out of the shards of the old. I have described the impossibility of the commission's goals as internal to the strength of its nation-building exercise. This fault, I think, was (also) a virtue. Deborah Posel, in a trenchant article on the commission, speaks more strongly and more negatively than Krog, however:

> The TRC's mandate was simultaneously deeply moral: access to truth was to lay the foundation for a more humane, just, social order, passing resolute moral judgement on the past but in ways which reconciled a previously divided society to a common future rooted in a "respect for human rights." The "reconciliation" dimension was itself variegated, inspired by a cluster of meanings of the idea. The TRC was to initiate processes of individual, interpersonal and collective "healing," through the catharsis of finally expunging the truth about gross human rights violations previously hidden. Here, reconciliation was to be an affirmation of "ubuntu," a "recognition of the humanity of the other." The idea of reconciliation was also explicitly tied to the project of nation-building, "imagining" a new form of national community based on a "collective memory," a "shared history." Exposure to truth was to lay the basis for a national consensus about the past and how to overcome its legacy in the future—"some essential lessons for the future of the people of this country." Lastly, reconciliation was also understood as an act of compromise, borne of the country's negotiated transition. As itself the product of a political compromise, the TRC was seen as a crucial vehicle in attempts to stabilize and reproduce the politics of transitional justice. Finally, all of this was to be undertaken "as expeditiously as possible," within a period of two years.[7]

A coat of many colors, an impossible mandate, a this-and-that about all things, a utopian plan, a report then saturated in the ecstatic rhetoric of the Christian service—the commission and its report have been the object of sophisticated historiographic and epistemological critique within

South African academic circles, and usually by persons who fail to address the commission's often considerable remarks about its own inadequacy and other self-criticisms. These remarks do not invalidate such criticisms from the academy, but they cast them in a different light.

The Historiographic Critique of the TRC

The historiographic critique is developed by Deborah Posel and then taken further by Colin Bundy.[8] Posel asserts that the report exhibits

> [an] inability to grapple with the complexities of social causation [which] is compounded by the TRC's having to tie its account of apartheid to the story of gross human rights violations. Having to focus a narration of the past around the clash between "victims" and "perpetrators" provides very blunt tools for the craft of history writing.[9]

"The TRC's 'truth' about the past," she states, "is neither 'complex' nor particularly 'extensive'":

> With little explanatory and analytical power, the report reads less as a history, more as a moral narrative about the fact of moral wrongdoing across the political spectrum, spawned by the overriding evil of the apartheid system. In so doing, the TRC report achieves some notable successes that go a long way towards fulfilling some parts of the Commission's mandate—but to the exclusion of others.[10]

Bundy concurs, arguing that the report represses historical complexity by deleting competing positions and by focusing on apartheid as a narrative of individual deaths rather than a *political system with a historical genealogy of a specific kind*, thus reducing apartheid to a "series of myths," or what we may call a biblical narrative (of betrayal, going too far, death, rupture, individual conscience, the warring of tribes). This emphasis on individual volition and victimization is compounded by the time line chosen by the commission, which restricts its investigation of crimes to the period from 1960 to 1994, thus foreclosing on the larger political genealogy.

Last, Bundy argues that the report is hopelessly ambiguous in its conceptualization of apartheid. On the one hand, it takes the unconditional Kantian stance (also that of Amnesty International) that any gross violation is equally unacceptable to the moral imagination, and that, for a culture of reconciliation, all must be investigated equally. It doesn't matter on whose side the violation happened, the pro-apartheid side or the anti-apartheid side. On the other hand, the commission's report (five volumes,

1998) wants to find a way of stating that crimes committed against the racist regime of apartheid cannot be viewed in the same light as those committed in its name. Apartheid was itself a crime against humanity, and this, one wants to say, doubles the stakes of gross human-rights violations committed on its side. It is my own view, in Bundy's spirit, that were the report to have carried the logic of calling apartheid a crime against humanity to its conclusions, then it would have had to rethink the amnesty apportioned to each side, since one side would have been "doubly guilty," to speak in a metaphor of measurement. (The measure of proportionality would have been affected.) The downside is that such a rethinking of the conditions of "measurement" would have affected the larger prospects for "the culture of reconciliation"—perhaps. Hence, the commission had to have it both ways—perhaps. Had to take a morally inconsistent theoretical position—perhaps. On moral grounds—perhaps.

There are two things to say about Posel and Bundy: first, that they are not fair to the report, and second, that they are right. To grasp why will be to advance understanding of the work of the commission, and the report, considerably.

The report says this about its own mandate:

> One of the reasons for this [the Commission's own] failure of emphasis is the fact that the greater part of the Commission's focus has been on what could be regarded as the "exceptional"—on gross violations of human rights rather than the more mundane but nonetheless traumatizing dimensions of apartheid life that affected every single black South African. (1: 132–33)

So the commission is hardly unaware of the limitations in its mode of procedure. Moreover, it does not stop at merely stating this self-critical truth; it elsewhere tries to bring home that a culture of routine degradations was part of the violence of the past. (See, for example, the long discussion by Judge Pius Langa about the daily degradation of waiting in interminable queues at the mercy of "bad tempered clerks and officials [who] might reward one with some endorsement or other in the 'dompas'" (or "pass book") (1: 62–63). Langa there describes the bureaucratic degradations of daily life for people of color under apartheid. No doubt it is all a matter of emphasis: were the commission to have focused on routine degradations, its picture of reconciliation would have looked materially different, for it would have been about redress—moral, social, psychological, material, human. Mamdani is right: it did not do that, and its picture of reconciliation, being overly idealized, could be taken to avoid such an equally compelling picture of rights. One answer is: no commission can do everything. The other is that intellectuals are always required, since the assertion of one kind of right always, inevitably, subdues the assertion of another. Here, it is the right to recognition of daily degradation and the picture of redress associated. A society in transformation must bootstrap itself through multiple commissions of inquiry, as the Human Rights Commission under the tutelage of Lindiwe Mokate is doing, or meant to be doing, now.

Posel argues that the "large chunks of the apartheid system" are left out of the report, and that this is an epistemic flaw in the way the report chooses to construct its terms for digging out and setting forth *the truth*. She is right that its rhetoric of truth is formulated from the perspective of its picture of reconciliation, and that any such formulation of a truth-predicate relevant to the work of a commission is liable to be incomplete and partisan. That the report does so construct a truth-predicate is a sign of its philosophical character, and, as such, it calls for philosophical critique along Posel's lines as well as for respect for what it did in fact accomplish.

The report states that it is concerned with four aspects of truth: factual truth, social truth, dialogue truth, and restorative truth.

> (1) *Factual truth* is described in two ways:
> (a) truth about individual events (what happened, who was killed, by whom, etcetera), more specifically "accurate information through reliable (impartial, objective) procedures";
> (b) findings on the contexts, causes, and patterns of violations. (1: 111)

In describing the second part of factual truth, the report takes a most interesting position on itself:

> In this respect, the commission was required to report on the broader patterns underlying gross human violations of human rights and to explore the causes of such violations. To do this, it had to analyse, interpret and draw inferences from the information it received. In this regard, it became necessary for the Commission to adopt a social scientist's approach—making use of the information contained in its database and form a range of secondary sources. (1: 111)

Posel believes this kind of language, including this parsing of truth into categories or kinds, allows the report to indulge in an illusion of positivism: thinking its findings are empirically established, built from simple building blocks according to transparent forms of construction, clear as to where one kind of truth meets the next, clear as to where fact and explanation meet, ready for the archive as an epistemically indubitable body of truth.

She may have a point. However, I find her reading vastly oversimplified as a view of how the report regards its results, and, more important, why it has organized "categories of truth" in the way that it has.

If one reads the next few sentences, which continue the remarks just quoted about "adopting a social scientist's attitude," one finds Michael Ignatieff quoted, approvingly, as saying this: "All that a truth commission can achieve is to reduce the number of lies that can be circulated unchallenged in public discourse" (1: 111). A few lines later, the report then says:

> Applying Ignatieff's notion of reducing the number of lies, one can say that the information in the hands of the Commission made it impossible to claim, for example, that: the practice of torture by state security forces was not systematic and widespread; the state was not directly and indirectly involved in "black-on-black" violence . . . [etcetera]. (1: 111–12)

This is hardly the stuff of positivism, if by positivism one means a conception of scientific practice that believes that fact, appropriately established by verifiable procedures, can be arranged in a transparent form of organization, from simple to complex, such that larger conclusions follow transparently from each and every simple fact, and do so independently of all but logical inference. It is not even the positivist twist of Karl Popper, who substituted the criterion of falsifiability for that of verifiability as the criterion of propositional meaning, for Popper's falsifiability criterion requires a clear formulation of what would count as the falsification of (1) a statement of fact and (2) more generally, a theory, and there can be no such criterion offered here. What the commission is saying is that the best it can do by way of reliable truth is to collect enough evidence, with enough overall reliability, so that, put together as a whole, it can be convincing *enough* as to overrule, once and for all, the big lie so crucial in the twentieth century. This does not ring of positivism, but rather of skeptical modesty combined with moral urgency. Think of Jean-Marie Le Pen in France, who still refuses to believe that the Holocaust happened, because "he has not made a study of it and was not there." What Truth Commissions do is to raise the stakes of the lie, so that those who refuse to believe will have to try harder to be convincing to the public. And it is public truth, the truth of the archive and the mode of circulation in civil society, that matters. For there is no limit to what people can do to one another apart from the restraints of truth, and these restraints are in turn a matter of what they can be brought to *believe*. Voltaire said it: Get someone to believe an absurdity and you can get them to commit an atrocity. There is always the possibility of willful skepticism, given the failure of evidence to mount up in a way that is more reliable than it is—given, that is, the fallibility attaching to each and every procedure. The question is how far must one now go in making the skeptical position believable, convincing, anything other than the product of willful fabrication. Think of the Europe of Serbian justice and Austrian deserts.

Jean-Marie Le Pen's claim that whether six million died and how they died is not his concern, since he has not made a study of it, is really the claim that the Holocaust remains an open question. Le Pen, whose party has most recently celebrated the election of Jorge Haider's party to the Austrian government in the millennial year, is intimating that in all probability the study would leave him just as uncertain as he is now. This degradation of the archive by its avoidance is again a classic strategy for denying the facts, for speaking against them by not "making a study of them."

The apartheid state was not Nazi Germany, nor is the role of the big lie in South Africa today the same as its role in Europe. There are many reasons for this, the most obvious being that the big lie can continue in Europe because there are so very few Jews left, while the victims of the apartheid past have become the majority of new South African citizens and, more important, the state. It is unclear how much people knew in the old days about things like the security police and the Third Force. On the one hand, many South Africans had children in the army (conscription was required), and they brought back all kinds of stories of atrocity; on the other, many South Africans have told me that they had no idea of the extent of human-rights violations that had occurred in their country. Whether they should have known must remain an issue of conscience; the point is that, given the archive of atrocity, no longer can they remain in states of partial self-deception or misinformation. Finally, while the current power structures do not allow for revisionist views of the South African past along the lines of the big lie (which was the old apartheid line), who knows what it will be possible to say in one hundred years' time?

The report, rather than engaging in the illusion of positivism, is about the moral conviction in the buildup of the archive, in the massification of fact—even if all kinds of reasonable uncertainties remain concerning that body of fact. Were there not a distinction between little uncertainties and big ones, between uncertainties of detail and of overall shape and scope, between fact and explanation at the broad level, the capacity for humanity to look itself in the mirror and know what it has done would evaporate— hence the importance of the archive in raising the stakes for those who would deny these distinctions. And by the archive is also meant here a series of stories that relate the facts to a picture of things. Such stories may be inadequate in many ways, as pictures invariably also conceal, exaggerate, and distort. And yet, without an archive that also tells and shows, there could be no argument against the far right and no intellectual way of preventing its radiation of vile fantasy.

Let us pursue this question of the reasonableness of the report's evidence more specifically. Posel argues that

> [i]n line with the genre of an official state commission, the TRC report presents itself as the work of a team of "observers" on the past, who collated and assembled a series of facts about gross human rights violations, to produce the objective, authorized, version of the country's recent past. But a closer reading reveals a different process of knowledge production. The report contains a version of the past which has been actively crafted according to particular strategies of inclusion and exclusion.[11]

I will suggest that she is right, but at a more abstract level than she imagines. I will suggest that the strategies of exclusion and inclusion do not fundamentally pertain to the assembling of "the facts," but to a larger narrative that relates the facts to the project of reconciliation. It is there that the Foucauldian epistemic regime kicks in, if you will, the construction of a system of truth-predicates and operations that empowers the commission and those associated with its proceedings with "the route to reconciliation," and that, as a form of empowerment, is a construction of an epistemic regime, that of truth that deals power.

We must first consider the assembling of versions of the truth, and what is or is not there regulated by strategies of inclusion and exclusion. Consider an example, that of three versions of the killing of Sergeant Mothasi[12] and his wife in 1987, reported by Antjie Krog and then the commission's version. We first hear from three members of the security forces about what happened. Krog says:[13]

I transcribe Captain Jacques Hechter's version:

"We got out a distance from the house. We were wearing dark clothes and balaclavas. Mamasela's wasn't over his face, just rolled down low. He knocked on the Mothasi's door and asked if he [Richard] was in. We were standing around the corner and listening. When Mamasela told us that Richard's wife was expecting him, we decided to wait for him inside. Mamasela knocked on the door again. When the woman opened the door, Mamasela pushed her with a gun to a back room, where he had to keep her from seeing us. We switched off the lights, but left the television on so that it seemed that someone was there. We then hid behind the couch. Then a vehicle arrived: His Mazda. He came to the door and found it locked. He was struggling with the lock when we jerked him inside. He immediately realized there was trouble. He struggled violently—he fought like a tiger and he shouted wildly. To bring him under control I started to strangle him . . . and Van Vuuren smothered him with a pillow over his face. He then fired four shots with his AK-47—the pillow was a silencer. Loots was also present and he accidentally hit me with the stock of his AK-47 against the arm. Then we called Mamasela: 'Come on! We're finished.' Just as we were walking out we heard a shot from inside the house. When Mamasela joined us we asked what the shooting was about. He told us that he killed the woman because she saw his face. It was also only afterwards that we learned that there was a child in the house." (Krog: 82)

This is Paul Van Vuuren's version:

"There was a big noise, he was screaming terribly. And . . . me and Captain Hechter . . . (sighs) worked together without talking. Each knew what he had to do . . .

"I can just explain to you that at this stage in the operation . . . time is a factor and one only acts without thinking. . . . On that specific night we were not discussing whether the woman would see Mamasela. We did not take it into consideration, which was a mistake on our part, we should have considered it. But I knew that Captain Hechter's wife was divorcing him at the time and we did not put pressure on each other.

"After we fought with Richard Mothasi and Captain Hechter put the pillow over his head, and I fired four shots with an AK-47, Captain Loots and Captain Hechter put the pillow over his head, and I fired four shots with an AK-47, Captain Loots and Captain Hechter went out the door . . . and I can't remember correctly, the woman's head was under the blanket, or the sheet, but her head was covered. I told Mamasela: 'You must come, we are finished'—and then I turned around and ran out. Heard shots. When I got outside, Mamasela was next to me. I said, 'What did you do?' He told me that he shot the woman also because she saw his face. I just want to mention that at the time it was not strange that people would recognize Mamasela. Because Mamasela and I were reasonably big friends and he told me that he was going to get plastic surgery at the state's expense. He often spoke to me about his personal stuff. So as far as I'm concerned Mamasela's face was to be changed later." (Krog, 85–86)

. . . Joe Mamasela gave his version of the Mothasi murders in an unbroken stream of words:

The Coat of Many Colors

"I was talking to her [Irene Mothasi—in the back room of her home] to lie to her that her husband was involved in robberies and stuff like that and I asked, didn't he bring in any money, and generally she was quite concerned that no, the man did not bring any money, at the back of my mind you know I felt pity . . . I did not know what I can do to help her . . . and then all of a sudden Hechter came in, and when they were fighting with her husband she got concerned, she was calm all the time because I tried as much as possible to keep her calm, but during the struggle, myself I was disturbed, I was perturbed, and she was uncontrollably agitated, and Hechter came in and said: . . . 'you're standing there gaping, why don't you kill the woman' [spoken by Mamasela to the Commission in Afrikaans]. Then he took my revolver and HE ordered her to get into the bed and he shot her about four times in the direction of her head, I could see the body, the blood . . . the child was in the other room. He was sleeping. THEN he gave me the gun and said: [Again reported in Afrikaans] 'Now go and kill . . . go and shoot that child.' So I took the gun and I opened the door where he was sleeping and I saw this innocent little thing, and his face mirrored the face of my own child. I just couldn't do it. . . . I then fired two shots in the direction of the bedroom, where the wife lay, then I closed the door. Then Hechter said to me, 'You did not shoot, I did not hear any shots.' I said, 'No I shot.' He said, 'Bring the weapon here.' And he took the gun and opened it and I was glad that I managed to shoot at random, otherwise I would be killed for defying an order. So in a way I believe I'm happy that I didn't kill the child whilst that thing was going to haunt me for the rest of my life. I don't think I would have retained my sanity the way I've retained it." (Krog: 87)

Now the differences are obvious. As Krog says: "It's worth noting where these stories differ—on the question of accountability. No one will admit to killing Irene Mothasi, because no political reason could possibly exist why an ordinary nurse had to be killed" (Krog: 88). The question of amnesty received, as opposed to a life behind bars, can hang on whose version is correct. But there is also the issue of the perpetrator's need to preserve his own integrity, as he sees it, by highlighting what he refused to do. Hence Mamasela: "I saw this innocent little thing, and his face mirrored the face of my own child . . . I just couldn't do it." It is the oldest strategy in the book to stress, as a perpetrator, the danger one put oneself in, on account of disobeying an order, so as to identify with the victims and remove the stain of one's guilt. Hence Mamasela: "I was glad that I managed to shoot at random, otherwise I would be killed for defying an order." Mamasela achieves, so he feels, a double gain through these words:

to preserve his sense of his own moral high ground by stressing what he would *not* do as opposed to what he routinely did, and he betters his case before the commission by denying responsibility for the killing of the wife. On psychological grounds alone, Mamasela's rhetoric is in effect a confession of guilt. No one else of the three feels the need to indulge in the gesture of stressing his own moral bottom line—which to me suggests that he is the one who is hiding something.

Now, consider how the event is reported in the Truth Commission's report:

> Sergeant Mothasi was based at the Police College at Hammanskraal. He had laid a charge against a Colonel Van Zyl who had assaulted him, leaving him with a burst eardrum. Unsuccessful efforts were made to put pressure on him to withdraw charges.
>
> On 30 November 1987, Hechter, Mamasela and Van Vuuren went to the Mothasi house. After ascertaining that Mothasi was not at home, Mamasela reported back to Hechter and Van Vuuren, who instructed him to return and to take Ms. Irene Busi Mothasi into one of the back rooms. Hechter and Van Vuuren then entered the house and sat in darkness until Mothasi had returned, when they tackled him. Van Vuuren put a pillow over his head to act as a silencer and then shot him. Mamasela claims that he was also instructed to kill Ms. Mothasi, but left the child. This is disputed by Hechter and Van Vuuren who claim that they were unaware of the child and that Mamasela killed Ms. Mothasi of his own accord. Neighbors subsequently reported hearing the child crying through the night.
>
> . . . Captain Jacques Hechter . . . and Paul van Vuuren have applied for amnesty for the killing, but claim that they were told that Mothasi was passing information on to the ANC. (2: 271)

Other than a spelling difference in the name (which Krog has gotten wrong), and a certain deletion of personal voice, there is no fundamental loss in the conflictual character of the testimony here, since the dispute over responsibility for the killing of the wife remains in the report. Again, it is wrong to generalize from a single example, but in the interests of space and time I am doing this, suggesting that such disputes over factual truth are not atypical to the report, which cannot rightly be accused of the systematic deletion of contesting views.

The commission acknowledges uncertainty in this case. This is important, but it is not the only thing that is important. What also matters is the powerful level of *agreement* that exists among the three versions and that is acknowledged in the report. Each version admits to the fact of the killing of Mothasi, each admits that the wife was killed by someone, each admits that the child was spared. None of *this* is in doubt, which is to say the doubt concerns the issue of perpetrator guilt rather than whether a gross violation of human rights occurred. I want to hazard the remark, and hazard it in the absence of further presentation of cases here, that such levels of disagreement and agreement about "factual truth" and related issues of guilt and innocence are typical to the body of evidence that the commission received and processed.

At the next level, as it were, of "factual truth" (the commission's term), things are far less certain. That level concerns issues of perpetrator responsibility, and each fabricates in various respects; we are unsure who fabricates the most. These men saw themselves as foot soldiers in a "dirty war." Their self-descriptions, no doubt half-believed and half-produced for the purposes of truth-telling and amnesty-getting, are highly debatable and uncertain with respect to believability. (Is this how they really saw themselves? To what degree were they also motivated by raw, undiluted racist rage, even Mamasela?) In terms of explaining the background that produced the likes of them, the broader explanatory models that must be relied on to describe their formation are also powerfully debatable. Even the *range* of explanation—involving reference to the importance of apartheid structures, of state technologies of power crucial to modernity in general, of racist formations that are also those of white tribalism (Afrikaner nationalism)—while up to a point evident, is hardly indubitable, as the many competing theories of modernity, colonialism, power, and state terror will attest.

At the first level of factual truth, there is no disagreement that the killings took place. There were gross violations, according to the terms of the definition of that, which are themselves the product of a partially debatable but also highly convincing framework of definition. At the first level, questions of perpetrator guilt are uncertain, and *precisely* uncertain where questions of retribution for the perpetrators arise in pointed form (who killed the nurse for what cannot be, to the commission, a "convincing" political reason). At the second level of truth, that of broader explanatory and causal frameworks, things are far less certain; indeed, it must be said, the line between fact and explanation is itself quite unclear. One might say that causal reference to the security forces is a fact, while to the political system a structural explanation. But the apartheid system is also, in certain contexts, an evident *fact*. Here Nietzsche's dictum that "there are no facts, only interpretations" takes on special aptness, since the line between fact and interpretation is itself a matter of debate (interpretation) rather than of fact. Where fact ends and reasoning about fact begins is, contra positivism, a matter of interpretation.

Posel is thus right in one respect: by assuming that factual truth is "the same," both at the first and the second levels, the commission indulges in an epistemic mistake, which points itself in the direction of an unthinking positivism, reducing explanation to the status of first-level fact—this even while retreating to the Ignatieff position.

We continue down the path of truth set forth in the report to the concepts of social and dialogue truth. Why, we shall see in a moment. Social truth is truth about social relations, as in a community's view of its prospects for cooperation. Added to social truth is "dialogue truth," a concept thought up by Albie Sachs, an important member of the ANC and currently a constitutional judge in South Africa. "Dialogue truth" is "the truth of experience that is established through interaction, discussion and debate" (1: 113), and for the philosophical reader it rather approximates Jurgen Habermas's notion of reflective truth, which is intersubjectively produced through the open dialogue of free, equal, and informed persons, and which leads to consensus. How such truth is represented, much less measured, in the report is totally unclear. There is something to Posel's view that by naming these kinds of truth, the report engenders for itself the illusion that it has covered all the bases of truth in its domain and range, although I think it more likely that if one reads the progression of kinds of "truth" that the commission articulates, beginning with factual truth, proceeding into social and dialogic truth and culminating in restorative truth, it is meant to read like a *Pilgrim's Progress*.

Indeed, the four truths are the product of a religious imagination more than anything else, as in the case of "the fourfold way" of Buddhism, or "the seven stages of enlightenment" that the young European hippie so admires when he reads his mystical literature on the airplane to an ashram in Poona. There are philosophical legacies of this in European history as well, from Aristotelianism to neo-Platonism. To sharpen the point, consider the idea of restorative truth, the "final and highest stage of truth," which is defined in this way: "There is also 'healing' truth, the kind of truth that places facts and what they mean within the context of [actual] human relationships—both among citizens and between the state and its citizens" (1: 114). This healing involves in the first instance:

> Acknowledgement . . . acknowledgement refers to placing information that is (or becomes) known on public, national record. It is not merely the factual information about past human rights violations that counts; often

the basic facts about what happened are already known, at least by those who were affected. What is critical is that these facts be fully and publicly acknowledged. Acknowledgement is an affirmation that a person's pain is real and worthy of attention. It is thus central to the restoration of dignity of victims. (1: 114)

Restorative truth is the *placing* of truth in the human context where it effects, or may point in the direction of, reconciliation. This involves placing "the facts" in the public archive, but goes beyond that to the dynamic power of truth *set to work*, as Heidegger might have put it, in human relations. It is the appropriate recognition of truth, the appropriate inscription of it, the appropriate interpolation of it, the appropriate communalization of it, that restores—in a way that is "truthful to" human nature and perfectibility, if you will. The concept is literally about "truth-telling," "truth-remembering," and "truth-instituting," both in the institution of the archive and in the fabric of human life. This leads to reconciliation between persons and with the state. Restorative truth, the "restoration of dignity," is already reconciliation in gel.

The inner logic of this bricolage of truth categories, articulated in the impromptu way it has been, is less about positivism and more about a logic of movement from truth to reconciliation. It is about the formulation and formalization of a mode of progression: about a nation-building exercise for postapartheid South Africa, a transition for an interim nation through the desert led by the Mosaic law, the Mosaic tablets; a way forward according to an allegorical formula that is literalized through these analytics of truth. This allegory of the stages of truth, this way forward from truth to reconciliation, which includes the concept of the archive, of the archive as place and as site of script at work, is a recasting of the great Protestant ethic of perfectibility under a different title but with the same metaphysico-religious basis. It is this idea of truth as constituting a *path*, of fact as hardly inert but instead energized by the larger movement of life in a godlike way. It is a picture of Christian progress. Tutu's homilies are the heir to an entire tradition of philosophico-religious conceptualization, which the report's theory of truth cobbles together in the manner of a momentary coup de grace, but which has the scope of centuries of intellectual preparation. Such concepts are the daily bread, the wine and wafer of those versed in the verses, of the cloth, of those who wear the coat of many colors, of those who know in their bones what Kant called "the Judeo-Christian tradition." The report, in articulating this arrangement of concepts, from truth to reconciliation, in literalizing allegory (*Pilgrim's*

Progress, as the progression of truths) makes the work of truth-giving a gift of the biblical (in Derrida's sense of the gift), as if from Mount Sinai, from the Sermon on the Mount, or from the pages of Protestant literature.

I pile up these images because I think that the pileup of images and purposes was internal to the nation-building exercise the commission represented. And this leads to one way in which the grand narrative of truth (from factual all the way to restorative truth) has, in fact, been a *regulative mechanism* for the proceedings themselves, rather than a mere quixotic narrative about nation-building of little cash value as a description of the proceedings. Tutu constantly framed his questions and answers so that they passed beyond victim acknowledgment into larger homilies of nation-building. Indeed, a central reason for his use of homily was to make that connection. Recall what Tutu says to Beth Savage: "Thank you, I just want to say, we are, I think, a fantastic country." If that is not a sentence that passes from victim acknowledgment (of her) to a larger paean to the nation, then nothing is. Indeed, it is almost as if Tutu is *discovering* through these dark proceedings an inner light and humanity in the nation, which is itself of restorative value. There is a certain truth in this. Everyone intimately involved in the work of the commission spoke of the astonishing humanity found within so many victims (a humanity the terms of the commission also constructed by making it near impossible for rage, violence, and retribution to enter into their language).

At the initial moment of nation-building, when a script of harmony was what was required for the very terms of a peaceful transition (where civil war threatened and group violence was daily reality), there was pragmatic, political force to these larger images of nation-building and restorative truth. In short, the grand narrative of truth was politically crucial at this moment of transition.

The report's construction of its idea or image of truth—its grand narrative relating evidence, testimony, interpretation, assignation, and archive to communalization, respect, working through, and finally, reconciliation— is illustrated by the banner that appeared above the commission every day it did its work: *"Truth—the Road to Reconciliation."* They meant it literally. Naturally, it was utopian, therefore also an illusion, but it was also a truth-predicate, invented for the occasion and crucial to it. And from the moral point of view, a template was being instituted for future generations that would inhabit a new nation and look back (one hopes) on these proceedings as exemplary (as people continue to derive moral lessons from the Bible). This too contributed to the moment of transition, where regimes of remembrance, commuting past atrocity into future harmony, are instituted for future generations as ways of stabilizing the chaos of transition and working through its ills.

J. L. Austin taught that the utterance of words, or their writing in a report, is a way of making something happen in the world and not simply a way of describing the world. The "Way of Truth" is a description of the dynamics of the proceedings (up to a point, anyway), but also a speech act that was, along with the larger domain of speech acts that constituted the work of the commission, a way of doing something in the world, of making something happen. Call it the invention of a truth regime, procedural as well as didactic. As such it must be understood as an articulation of a structure of power. It is, I want to say, the *attempt* to produce an archaeology: a set of rules for the production of true statements, for statements that will be taken to count as true within the system. As an attempt to institute an archaeology (which no one being or micro-event can succeed in doing on its own), the way of truth has been a regulative mechanism that, in Foucault's sense, both produced and constrained the domain of research, interviews, and victim and perpetrator statements. Like any archaeology, the rules relating fact to restoration or reconciliation would produce reconciliation, but also serve to place clear constraints on the set of possible statements that any of the players could successfully make. Here, Posel and Bundy are absolutely right: the terms of the commission constrained the possibility and appropriateness of victim (and perpetrator) testimony, so that were one unable to abide by them, one would have to bow out of the proceedings altogether, as the family of Steve Biko, the black-consciousness activist murdered by the security forces, chose to do. For those victims who did choose to play the "game" when asked what they would like to have happen, it was considered inappropriate to say, "I want the head of the perpetrator on a plate so that I can throw it in the river like they did to my little boy." Even if the victim felt this, and even if the commissioners solicited deep, authentic, *honest* responses, the "atmosphere" was such that it would have "violated" the truth regime set up by the commission had such a thing been said. It rarely was said, hence "the beautiful humanity of the victims." Indeed, given the rules, it was easy for a pathological figure like Benzien to lie his way through to a successful outcome (amnesty).

One further reason why a truth-predicate was introduced was that, while regulating the work of the commission, the truth-predicate aimed at greater generality. Hence my point of a regime of truth, an attempt at an archaeology. The truth-predicate announced in the report is not simply a statement about the mechanisms internal to this truth commission itself, placed at a given historical time, but a statement about how all persons at all times should behave: in short, it is a bible for the future about social interaction. Naturally, this is problematical, especially because there is and ought to be a moment, also crucial to the nation, when quite other terms are crucial: terms of dissensus, rage, trade-union strikes, fierce debates between parties, and, quite frankly, terms crucial to strengthening the retributive character of the rule of law. Thus, for example, it would prove contrary to the second and third levels of truth that at the end of the day social agents should disagree about matters of society, justice, and, indeed, reconciliation itself, for "agreement" is mandated by those levels of truth and as a condition for restoration.

Naturally, the commission knows that its truth-predicate is, since a generalization, problematical. Naturally, they forget it, and do this because it is crucial to the *utopian* moment of the commission's work that a general template of truth and human behavior be imagined: that the commission indulge in the illusion that it is exemplary, when it is a specific artifact of transitional justice (of the moment of transition). This is, one might say, its mandate. Nietzsche spoke of the exigency of lying at certain moments of history, including lying about history. This is one such moment. The Bible was another.

There are many ways to think about truth, some more abstract than others. Speech acts inventing pictures of truth, narratives of movement from one truth to another, are contextual, and must be understood as such. They are never free of power, which means both the power to constrain and the power to empower. This epistemic regime is *productive* of truth in Foucault's sense, or aims to be. It allows statements, sometimes profound statements, about fact, dialogue, reconciliation to be created, or aims to do so. It also imposes, I have said, constraint, refusing many other kinds of statements. I have analyzed it in terms of its political—and moral—pragmatics.

Reconciliation

The way of truth is not the only fictional construction regulating the procedures of the TRC. The very idea of *reconciliation* in South Africa, of reconciliation as process and as goal or ideal, is, strictly speaking, a fiction as well. Reconciliation implies that beings were once one, came apart, and are now back together again. This is hardly, from the historical point of view, the case. From the moment settler set foot in Algoa Bay, there has been constant conflict. Through the Xhosa wars, the Zulu empire, the great Trek, and the Boer war to the apartheid state, there has been little oneness between peoples. So the very image of reconciliation is already a way of picturing a deep unity that was not there. This is, of course, part of the nation-building exercise.

The metaphysical fiction in terms of which people are thought of as originally as one, and hence in need of re-conciliation (like re-naissance), is in Tutu's case the Christian ideal of a people (the South African one) that has fallen out of relationship with God. This Christian drama of a trinity, in which Christ is called on to reconcile man and God, is the textual unconscious of the fiction. It is in terms of this drama that the script of reconciliation can be written as a script of re-conciliation. We shall find that another kind of script is required to write the African renaissance, another example of the mysterious re: the mysterious thing, the *big other*, for those with a penchant for the work of Jacques Lacan. In the case of the African renaissance, it will be the history of pan-African racialism, itself related (in part) to a reading of the Bible by W. E. B. DuBois.

The concept of reconciliation entered into the stream of philosophical thinking from its Christian origins in the work of G. W. F. Hegel, who thought of history as a process of diremption (fragmentation) followed by return and restoration. It is tacitly being relied upon here. In the course of human history this act of reconciliation is identified by Hegel with the construction by humanity of modernity: with law to encode liberty, equality, communal values; with structures of the state to ensure good human flourishing; with forms of spirit to express the inner life and subjectivity of "the people." For Hegel, truth and reconciliation are the same: the way humans come to know themselves is the same as the way they come to realize themselves in social forms that achieve reconciliation. Hegel's idea of reconciliation, an inheritance from the Reformation, is one that—at least in *The Philosophy of Right*, where it is given its most comprehensive elaboration—presumes the end of history as its starting point. It is about coming to a more truthful and better relation to the world as it is, in a way that will both make the individual subject a more contented and better citizen, and will make the world itself better. Whereas in the South African case reconciliation is something the society in transition has to bring about, for Hegel it is something that has already happened in history, only people are not aware of this. As Michael Hardimon puts it, the project of reconciliation is for Hegel to show citizens that they are already reconciled to their social world, to show them what reconciliation rightly consists in (they have delusions of grandeur), and to show them that their society is indeed a happy (enough) home, a home that is as good as it could possibly get, given the metaphysical shape of history and the nature of the human mind:

People who attain reconciliation come to see that the fact that their unreasonable expectations were not fulfilled does not constitute a real loss at all. It should be pointed out, however, that this form of reconciliation is not simply the result of recognizing the irrationality of one's original expectations alone. It is not a form of adaptive preference formation, or adaptive preference change. Rather we are supposing that the situation one becomes reconciled to is genuinely good. The role that recognizing the irrationality of one's original expectations plays in this form of reconciliation is that of making it possible to grasp the goodness of one's situation, which in turn brings about a state of reconciliation.

Reconciliation is not a matter of thinking that everything is wonderful. Hegel's celebrated rich and suggestive claim that reconciliation consists in recognizing "reason as the rose in the cross of the present" . . . illustrates this point.[14]

Everything therefore hangs on what would or does count as a real loss, a loss one cannot abide, a loss one cannot rationalize in the best sense of this term, a loss that would and should prevent one, on rational grounds, from believing that the world one inhabits is a home:

> "Reconciliation" in Hegel's technical sense of the term refers to both a process . . . and a state. The process is that of overcoming alienation from the social world, and the state, that of being at home in the social world, which is its result.[15]

For the social world to be a home, it must, on the Hegelian view, be capable of fostering human autonomy and social connectedness, a complex condition of self in which the self is free to follow its own course while also understanding its essential interconnection in social life.

Naturally, reconciliation in a larger sense requires that a panoply of rights be satisfied. The Hegelian story takes reconciliation to be a process that can occur only at the end of history, when state, the rule of law, civil society, and common morality make society a "home" for all, whether they realize it or not. It is because society is a home that reconciliation to it is possible. *The Philosophy of Right* is meant to demonstrate that the social world is a *home* in a satisfactory sense of that term. Agents are therefore reconciled to the social world. However, reconciliation in South Africa is not simply between agents and the social world, which has been a world of depravation, indignation, and horror for so many. It is also between agents and other agents, between perpetrators and victims of human-rights abuses. The terms of transitional justice pertinent to reconciliation are therefore more complicated.

I have said that recent work on transitional justice has argued that the kind of justice pertinent to a country's transition from dispensation of terror to democratic rule of law involves trade-offs between partly inconsistent demands. These (to repeat earlier remarks of Geoffrey Robertson's) push transitional societies in the direction of truth commissions, which (it follows) represent choices made between competing parties and partly incompatible options. Some players will remain unsatisfied by the choices made (e.g., qualified amnesty); others will find themselves reconciled. Moreover, the larger scope of what constitutes genuine reconciliation may be a matter of fundamental disagreement between citizens. Thabo Mbeki had a sharply worded public debate in the newspapers with Bishop Tutu during the days of the TRC, Mbeki weighting the issue of social redistribution of goods as far more central to reconciliation than Tutu, who, while acknowledging the need for redistribution, argued that the basis of reconciliation resides in forgiveness, respect, and acknowledgment of past wrongs. While neither used the language of John Rawls or Charles Taylor, their debate echoed recent philosophical discussions about redistribution versus the politics of recognition.

It might be thought that the upshot of the debate between Mbeki and Tutu is that history is not yet over in South Africa, and that only at the end of history will true reconciliation be possible. Only, that is, when both redistribution of goods and the politics of just recognition are achieved. However, there is strong reason to doubt that there will ever be a time when all contradictions internal to the transitional process are fully resolvable. That process has been a trajectory of compromise between, for example, the demand for punishment and that of forgiveness. *Qualified amnesty* was the result of the attempt to bring these less than compatible demands together. Many South Africans were uneasy with it and some rejected it, including the family of Steve Biko. These trade-offs and their discontents, trade-offs built into the transitional process, will structure what will be called the end of history. There is no reason to surmise that that end of history will "resolve" them through a Hegelian process of "Aufhebung." Even at the reputed end of history, the justice obtained will depend on options excluded as well as roads taken. It will always be open to certain agents to argue either that because of options excluded earlier on, history is not over, or that it is over but the outcome is not satisfactory. For such agents, the reconciliation process will be compromised. And who is to say (in advance of the facts) that they will not be right, that their views will not be reasonable, given the fact that history is composed of inconsistent demands and best possible trade-offs? It is likely that at any moment in history, present or future, different concepts of justice held by different agents will result in different attitudes about the prospects of reconciliation. Reconciliation is, like all concepts of justice, debatable.

Brotherhood

Father Michael Lapsley, who lost both arms and an eye in a near fatal security-police parcel bomb attack in Harare in 1990, told the commission that he needs to know who to endeavor to forgive. He knows that his gesture of trying may fail, or at best meet with partial success. Meanwhile, one listens to the voices of the children:

> [A] facilitator at the special hearing on children and youth in Durban gave this feedback from children's testimonies and drawings: She quoted from the testimony of a thirteen-year-old girl about the killing of her father six years earlier on the South Coast of KwaZulu-Natal:

> "Another picture . . . I have here from an eight year old girl. She drew her father as a small or young man, and the mother being short, and when I asked the child why she is drawing the father short she said that [the] reason she drew her father short, it's because the father was helpless, and they surrounded her father and they poured petrol on him and burnt him. What is very sad about this is that these children, most of them they know the people who did this, and those people are still alive and they see them every day. And another child who is eight years old said, 'I am just waiting for my revenge.'" (5: 417–18)

We might say that Father Lapsley wishes, like Joseph, to go in search of his brothers so that he might make them again, for the first time, brothers. But so does this girl want to find her "brothers," although not to the same purpose. How far can one go in search of one's brothers or sisters, and with what attitude? Whom can you make your brother or sister, or sage, or friend, or partner, or king? Either in reality or in the imagination?

> Many victims justifiably insisted that they were not prepared to forgive if this meant that they must "close the book on the past, let bygones be bygones" . . . forgiveness is not about forgetting. It is about seeking to forgo bitterness, renouncing resentment, moving past old hurt, and becoming a survivor rather than a passive victim. (1: 116)

In 1992 my wife and I visited an artist's colony in a small village an hour inland from the Cape promontory, near the town of Paarl in the western

Cape province, where vineyards bathe in the sun beneath the rings of mountains that separate this fertile land from the drier, semidesert of the Little Karoo to the north and east. Paarl is historically one of the centers of Afrikaner nationalism, a place where the Afrikaans revival took place in the 1930s. There is a monument to the Afrikaans language there whose lunar, modernist shape is worthy of German kitsch. You do not, however, see it from Dal Josefat, where the colony was located: Dal Josefat, God's own country, the place of Joseph—the other Joseph, father of Jesus—perhaps the place of both Josephs. The village was designated a "colored town" during the apartheid days and many "colored" farm workers still lived there in feudal conditions. (In the old days the men were paid in alcohol, the women were paid nothing.)

The colony, set on soft rolling hills, consisted of a manor house in the Cape Dutch style, a barn, and a few small houses in which farm workers had lived and whose simple white walls, wooden doors, concrete floors, green sloping roofs, and clean, baroque porticos now opened to visitors like ourselves. In the distance, floating ethereally in a haze of effulgent October light, could be seen the dry cropped mountains of the Cape. Each morning sheep from a neighboring farm were brought to graze—gently, in the manner of a Bach cantata. The artists, lively and raucous, slept late, painted moderately, talked continuously, and consumed a large amount of robust red Cape wine, usually while sitting in their jeans, T-shirts, and sandals on the stone steps at the back of the old manor house, whose stately wooden floors and formerly elegant dining room led out to the sloping hill behind the house and beyond to the river.

It was by that river that one evening, a few years later, the young woman who, with her artist husband, ran the place was walking her baby in its carriage when she was brutally attacked by a local man. Beaten to a pulp, she suffered permanent facial disfigurement and numerous other injuries. When questioned about the assault, the man who did it said that he just wanted to lash out at someone. A "colored man," no doubt he had his own story. The baby, a silent and uncomprehending witness, could say nothing. Will that baby too want its revenge? The colony suffered other human tragedies and, in spite of assistance from the University of Stellenbosch, gradually fell into moral atrophy and financial ruin. I mention this story because the woman who was attacked is a daughter of one of the persons who sat on the Truth and Reconciliation Commission. I do not say the story is relevant.

2

Soweto's *Taxi*, America's *Rib*

Rainbow Nation, Communication, and Solidarity

Rainbow Nation: the guiding image of early postapartheid South Africa. Rainbow Nation: an image that had great currency during the mid- to late 1990s, the image of a society where, finally, each band of color would chromatically harmonize with all others while retaining its own distinctiveness. The South Africa of this nation-building slogan is one preaching difference alchemically harmonized by natural law. Such a law, according to which each group, each constituency, each colloquy is automatically rendered complementary to all others, is a law worthy of the utopian moment of nation-building. It is a law also of discovery, proclaiming that each may discover in an instant its hidden principle of complementarity with all others. This law can be understood as a replacement for the former system of laws—the apartheid racial estates—that predicated life on the necessary failure of complementarity, on the disjunction of color bands. This rainbow is preferable to the tornado that preceded it, even if it remains within the ambit of racialism, giving predominance within the new nation to differences based on color. And South Africa remains mired in huge differences that are still, in many ways, aligned with skin. Differences between black African and white settler, Indian and colored, English and

Afrikaans—and among Twana, Zulu, Xhosa, Pedi—remain profound, as do the racist and racialist concepts according to which people understand each other as belonging to such types. These genuinely profound differences between people, in combination with the categories people continue to rely on in interpreting each other, can ring fatal for communication: virtually prohibiting meaningful conversation about *difference*, much less agreement about such critical issues as heritage, democracy, family, education, and work. And the kind of harmony crucial to nation-building is certainly also compromised.

Harmonization and communication are hardly the same, and the image of the Rainbow Nation discounts the gap between them by proposing a nation in which complementarity, or likeness, replaces the hard work of communication, including and especially communication about difference. Within a rainbow, color difference is the object of immediate, natural correspondence, thus obviating the problem of desire and at the same time that of likeness. That is, the problem of desire is one of motivating the urge for meaningful communication between persons and groups in a nation where people have grown up often despising each other, and where they license the most virulent thoughts and remarks about each other, so long as these remain "in private." The problem of desire is that of motivating people to want to join and explore, understand, celebrate, accept, productively criticize, and, in some cases, resolve their differences. And the problem of likeness is that of getting people to become, or to recognize that they have become, similar enough to accomplish this work of communication.

There is a philosophical point to be made here about the bringing of human diversity to genuine communication. For two people to bring their differences to acknowledgment, they must not only want to communicate, they must also realize that they are (or have become) sufficiently alike to make their differences manifest, each one's to the other. They must achieve sufficient likeness. According to a well-known argument of Donald Davidson's, belief systems and languages must, at base, be similar enough to render differences coherent.[1] To speak coherently of differences in belief (or in linguistic meaning), one must have, in principle, a way of locating the differences within some scheme. For A and B to differ about the nature of objects, of time, space, identity, etcetera, they must share enough belief and meaning in common about objects, time, space, identity, etcetera, for their *differences* about such matters, however profound, to emerge. Remove the underlying pattern of commonalities and you remove any way of locating their differences, you remove the possibility of their *having* differences. Davidson's (which I have pared down to the minimum) is an argument against radical incommensurability of belief, an argument about radical relativism. However, his argument says nothing and is meant to say nothing about whether, in a particular circumstance, A and B will have enough in common to be able to communicate their differences, each to the other, with the right level of subtlety and perspicacity. Sufficient unto the day are the means, and all hangs on whether—in this context or that, for this purpose or that—enough is shared between humans to allow them to communicate "successfully" for whatever particular purposes, like building a just nation.

The concept of "successful communication" or "genuine communication" is context-bound. It is also a concept about which persons may, in this context or that, disagree—both with respect to its meaning and to its application in particular contexts. South Africa is a society beset, as I have said, by significant problems in communication. A goal of its social transformation is to enhance levels of communication, thus allowing human diversity to become an object of acknowledgment and reasonable dissensus to become part of the political process. But for those goals to be achieved, its people must become more *alike* through processes of democratization and globalization. A middle class must develop between former masters and former servants, and become ever more inclusive of the population. New values of respect and discovery must be inculcated. New styles of conversation must become normalized in a society whose forms of politeness can mask sullenness and silence. The society must develop political styles of multiparty communication, and so on and so forth, for one is speaking of a change in the map of things, in an overall topography.

In what follows, I discuss one particular aspect of postapartheid South Africa that is relevant to my training as a philosopher: the importance of "reversal" for this process of democratization and communication about diversity. What I mean by "reversal" should become clearer as I review the philosophical history of this concept, something I bother to do in order to approach the way reversal has been rendered thematic in South African cultural forms since the collapse of the apartheid state in 1991. I approach these matters, however, gradually, beginning with limitations in the work of Richard Rorty. I then turn to Montaigne and Hegel, before ending with the discussion of a postapartheid film.

Richard Rorty thinks of moral communication hinging on what he calls "solidarity." A leftist of the old Roosevelt/liberal variety, with deep instincts for human dignity and a skepticism about the appeal to "first principles" rooted in "reason," Rorty is communalist to the core. The bottom line for ethical justifications is, for him, nothing other than the "we," the community of believers in solidarity. "When I have reached bedrock," in Wittgenstein's famous phrase, "my spade is turned," and at that moment of appeal—when appeal to every reason has been given, appeal to every practice shown—if an alien community remains unconvinced, there is little else to which to appeal other than to stand one's ground. Solidarity becomes (instead of a universally binding ethical principle) the epistemological framework in terms of which ethics must be thought. And solidarity becomes as well the metaphor for the good ethical fight.

Solidarity is moreover the metaphor for the encounter with diversity, the bringing of others into community with oneself. As Rorty says:

> The right way to take the slogan "we have obligations to human beings simply as such" is as a means of reminding ourselves to keep trying to expand the sense of "us" as far as we can. That slogan urges us to extrapolate further in the direction set by certain events in the past—the inclusion among "us" of the . . . unbelievers beyond the seas (and perhaps, last of all, the menials who, all this time, have been doing our dirty work). This is a process we should try to keep going. . . . We should try to notice our similarities with them. The right way to construe the slogan is as urging us to *create* a more expansive sense of solidarity than we presently have. The wrong way is to think of it as urging us to *recognize* such a solidarity, as something that exists antecedently to our recognition of it.[2]

The inclusive stance of solidarity, which places the other inside the domain of one's community, is the substance of moral respect and identification, Rorty believes. We begin with "us" and expand it, learning to "notice" things about others that enhance lines of similarity. From these newly appreciated lines of similarity, we create more expansive terms of solidarity. We have, Rorty argues, no choice about this, since there is no appeal to reason or first principles that can establish the connection between these lines of similarity and our interest in respecting such people. We see them through our lens; the point is for us to try to expand that lens as much as possible to include them.

What Rorty never makes clear is what happens to that lens when we reach out to "unbelievers across the seas" and "menials" in our own basements. How might *we* change in the process? I ask this especially since the examples he uses are those achieving solidarity with persons who have formerly been the object of colonial or class-based castigation. It would be too easy (and quite possibly neocolonial) to assume that our reaching out to include them is simply a matter of our enlarging the scope of our terms of reference without further, more pervasive change within ourselves and our modes of ethical self-regard—as if what we are doing is simply granting them admittance into our country club without challenging the status of the club itself.

But note that a complementary picture, one less centrally reliant on solidarity and more on the toleration induced by skepticism, has long been available in thinking about what happens to "us" when we reach out to achieve solidarity with others. Montaigne's masterpiece "Of Cannibals" (1578–1580) conceives the evaluation of even cannibalism as inviting self-scrutiny by the "I" about his own "we"; the "I" cultivating an attitude of inclusion (or exclusion) toward the other is not the question raised.

Philosophical Pictures of Reversal

According to Montaigne, one does not say to the cannibal, "You are now an honorary bourgeois. Come and eat at my table." Nor does one begin by seeing him as a "human like us," if one wishes to take him seriously. The work of establishing likeness and humanity is more dialectical. It is a work through which the "I" changes its perspective on itself, and on the "we" of which it is part, in the course of evolving a perspective on the cannibal. This work in turn leads to skeptical results about both the "I" and the "other." Montaigne refuses both the posture of European superiority over the cannibal and that of moral relativism regarding her. He is famously ahead of his time in suggesting that a community that fails to rethink itself in the encounter with the other is a community aiming for domination rather than understanding. While he sticks to his own view that eating others cannot exactly be a good thing, just how bad it is remains deeply uncertain. "Bad with respect to what?" one must ask, realizing that there is no way of articulating a cultural criticism of the cannibal apart from a repertoire of comparisons. It is the received certainty of comparisons (between them and us) that becomes the subject of his attack, an attack performed in the form of a reversal. And by comparisons I mean cultural hierarchies, relegating the cannibal to an essentially lesser moral status than the westerner. Montaigne's reversal is articulated as follows: Cannibals are quite specific about whom they kill and devour. They only kill when they need to eat. By contrast, when Europeans wage war they engage in a rabid game of pillage, rape, and destruction against defenseless civilian populations, destroying in the process whole villages, towns, or communities. The cannibal is thereby placed on the same footing as the Europeans Montaigne lives among, while the Europeans are placed where they belong: in the jungle of cannibals. This reversal of values accorded to self and other allows him to raise an essentially skeptical question about which is finally the worse. The European is worse, he hints, but it is only a hint, for Montaigne is, as usual, uncertain.

Montaigne's goal is hardly that of articulating a sense of solidarity with the cannibal. It is instead to show that we do not have the means to evaluate him or her. Diversity, having arisen, cannot be brought to articulation except in the form of doubt. And diversity has arisen only by means of a reversal: "they" are shown to be more like how "we" conceive of ourselves than "we" could allow ourselves to admit, while "we" are shown to be far more like our vision of "them" than "we" could similarly ever say. After the reversal, the "we" is left as uncertain as the "they." Neither is in prospective solidarity. Instead, the two are merely placed on the same footing, with further terms of comparison remaining to be worked out. We do not assimilate them to us. Rather, having been recognized to be more like them than formerly thought, we exist in an opaque, somewhat borderless space, in which paths of similarity and difference between them and us remain unclear. The consequence of this process is that we can recognize the strange inexplicability of the other's difference from us *for the first time.* Whatever they are, they are not of our community, and we do not know quite why they do what they do (habit? necessity?). We know only that our framework for interpreting them is not adequate. Is it even adequate for the interpretation of ourselves? Why, for example, do we wage such violent war? It will take tomes of Marx, Nietzsche, and Freud to confirm by their multiple and contradictory stories that we do not. Since we are now as uncertain of ourselves as we are of them, a new concept of humanity has arisen that links them with us in a shared state of uncertainty. If Rorty should decide to employ this new concept as a way of producing solidarity between his "them" and his "us," there is no reason to balk.

Hegel's picture of reversal concerns not the colonial encounter of self meeting an unknown other, but the struggle between persons caught up in interlocking shapes. In a famous passage in the *Phenomenology of Spirit,*[3] Hegel claims that the master and slave arrive as an ensemble out of a struggle for existence. That struggle is a struggle for recognition in which neither can tolerate the existence of the other and so seeks to subsume the other into the self. The master is the one who wins. His victory renders the other into an utterly dependent slave who exists only to labor for the master, and as yet has no capacity to even conceive of working for himself. The slave is an incomplete person because he lacks the capacity to formulate his own desires. The master is an incomplete person because while he generates his own desires, he has no skill and depends on the slave for their fulfillment. The slave has no capacity for self-recognition; the master, for labor. Within the system of Hegel's thought the master/slave is meant to be both a sketch of actual human history—which has so often arranged itself into shapes of master and servant—and part of an analysis of the genetic conditions for the possibility of human knowledge, of the formulations the mind has to go through to arrive at the correct one. Hegel's belief that the master/slave as a concept performs both these jobs leads to many problems, one of which is that the shape is abstracted from too much historical content to serve as an adequate picture of historical development (even though it contains many interesting hints). For example, Hegel's picture of the slave is of a person who has as yet no sense of self-recognition, but no historical actor is like this. Rather, enslavement is about robbing agents of their culture and devaluing them in the process, or denying them equitable access to cultural goods and stunting their sense of the legitimacy of their desire.

Nevertheless, a resident of South Africa may be forgiven for seeing the modern history of his country hinted in this picture. In 1913, the African was denied the right to own land, thus sending him reeling onto the roads and into the gold and diamond mines. Later, he was deprived of most of his remaining rights, including the right to live where he had already staked home and hearth. This experience, and state, of being reduced to material and work force for the master is the essence, Hegel believes, of the slave's "phenomenology." Its experience, Frantz Fanon will add, is that of abjection. The slave's own life has stopped, his culture has been disenfranchised and devalued. Robbed of self-consciousness, the slave exists as an existential void for the master. The eyes of the master and his commands to the slave are omnipotent, as are the institutions of his regard (the museum, the colonial administrative system). Similarly, the narcissism of the master is expanded to the point of no return, since the slave, thus devalued, ceases to exist and becomes a mere shadow, whose bent and wizened figure cuts no force and attracts no attention, while the world is the master's oyster. A luxurious position: the master orders the slave about while simultaneously denying his existence.

Since Hegel has abstracted the master/slave from its historical richness, he cannot explain the full motivations slaves have for wanting to be free. The colonial slave is a double consciousness who at once desires recognition within the current world, fair access to its goods, and return to a former (precolonial) world where his culture flourished. This triple desire is what produces the complex movements of decolonization.

Now, Hegel's explanation of the dissolution of the shape is this: It is prompted by history when the slave comes to attain sufficient self-recognition through his skill to realize he is master to the master because the master depends upon his skill. The master in turn comes to realize that he is "slave to the slave" since he does no work and is nothing more than a pampered house cat who feeds on the work of the slave. This is a reversal in the regard each has for self and other, which is due to growth of mind within the shape itself. Again, it is an inadequate picture of historical growth that leaves out, for example, the effects of economic growth on the way agents change their perceptions of their world, not to mention the full force of the desire for liberation.

More apt is Hegel's picture of the master's *anxiety* at the moment when the ensemble becomes unstable. In the master/slave configuration, all is dog-eat-dog, cannibal-devour-cannibal. Either I belong to you or you to me. The master assumes that the slave must want the same kind of power he himself has wielded, but that now *he* will be its victim. As yet there is no comprehension of a third option by the master, so one can understand the deep anxiety that the master experiences when reversal takes place. He will see himself as swallowed and losing power, even body image, and ego boundaries. He may well emigrate to New Zealand; he will certainly turn, if only for a moment, resentful. He will be scared as hell. Naturally, this terror will prevent recognition of what the slave really does want.

Not entirely. The phenomenology of the slave *is* deeply rooted in envy, bitterness, and aggression, and, moreover, in the fantasy that by crushing the master one can take over his negotiation of the world, as if by osmosis. Revolutionary democracy has more than once led to mere reversals of victimization, with past masters reduced to present slaves by popular will.

Hegel believes that history moves forward insofar as the slave does not become mired in this desire to replace the master in an ensemble of domination. At the moment of reversal, the slave recognizes that while he has power over the master, he needs the master around because he needs to learn the master's art of self-recognition through work and culture. The slave needs the master as a model to appropriate.

Similarly, the master comes to realize the slave is not going to enslave him, and is ready to learn the secret of the slave's skill.

Reversal and Reconciliation

This Hegelian story of modernity has a happy ending in reconciliation because each party, having recognized that the other has what it lacks, becomes *like* the other, appropriates crucial aspects of the other's makeup. As each becomes like the other, *communication* becomes enhanced and mutual respect possible. The concept of a shared society based in equality can now arise, and with it the processes by which constitutional law, nation, and citizenship are established. At the same time communication becomes possible because each is now more like the other and each, under the new regime of respect, listens to the other. At the end of history, they become co-citizens of a nation, an "I that is we," able fully to communicate because finally they are the same people.

Hegel's is an Enlightenment fantasy in which everyone ends up the same. It therefore obviates the problem of diversity altogether.

Still, its lesson about the importance of a dialectic in establishing the means of communication should be remembered, for what the Hegelian story of truth and reconciliation can offer the Truth and Reconciliation Commission is this caveat: reconciliation requires more than the giving of testimony or the construction of a supportable self-image and an accurate memory. Reconciliation requires more than redress, the redistribution of wealth, or even the apportioning of blame and punishment. It also requires more than cultural reconstitution (at least of the kind urged on us in South Africa by President Thabo Mbeki's pan-Africanist "renaissance"). Reconciliation demands *reversal,* with all of the epistemological and historical complexity that that process involves. The master must undergo the rigors of reversal, rigors that tend to produce (in Montaigne's sense) skeptical conclusions. And the slave must learn the master's art of self-recognition, though in the former slave's own way and according to his or her own history and social style.

Much was said during the 1990s in South Africa about producing a culture of reconciliation, especially in the first few years of the postapartheid state, which is my immediate concern. Nelson Mandela, the first president of the new nation, tossed a rugby ball as a gesture of national unity and was cheered. The rains came to the parched landscape of the Karoo and ended with a luminescent rainbow that, by some act of national prestidigitation, spread mysteriously east and west, north and south, to both seas, and led to our reigning image of a Rainbow Nation. The Truth and Reconciliation Commission made great strides toward revising the past, documenting it for the archive and instituting an agenda of reconciliation through testimony, memory, and moral work. But such events hardly defined the complexity of South African social life, much of which had, and still has, little to do with reconciliation. J. M. Coetzee's 1998 novel *Disgrace* pictures postapartheid South Africa as a society where the proud events of the new nation are far removed from the lives of ordinary people, who have the liability to simply switch roles or absurdly cling to them. In both cases master and victim remain the dominant forms of life. When reversal does not always lead to reconciliation, it is liable to lead to a new dispensation of disgrace.

To say that master and slave must change places if reconciliation is to eventuate (and disgrace to be avoided) is to speak the language of dialectical necessity—a precipitous language inviting counterexamples. Is it not imaginable that a master/slave couple or something very like it could achieve reconciliation without reversal ever happening? What kind of necessity is this exactly, the one connecting reconciliation to reversal? Especially if reconciliation is and will probably—*should probably*—remain a matter of debate?

What the pages of history and the meditations of philosophy have shown is that reversal is empirically necessary insofar as one's concept of reconciliation is about the capacity for agents to communicate about diversity and to respect it. Slightly more strongly put, it is virtually unimaginable that such reconciliation could take place—given the starting point of the master/slave—without reversal. For we have no way, I submit, of imagining how agents could break out of their stultifying, deep-seated, historical roles and related perceptions apart from the process. The very image of the Rainbow Nation gives voice to a desire for this process to magically happen. There is no more necessity to the causal, or the conceptual, connection between reversal and reconciliation than this. And no less.

America's Rib

Given the anxiety internal to the moment of reversal, it is natural that its manifestation in art and culture tends to happen in the form of comedy. Comedy eases us into the terror of role reversals, leads us to suspect that something good can come out of it, and projects that good in a way that mostly avoids the hard issues of how social transformation is restricted by the existence of recalcitrant templates of power. Reversals have been required wherever relations of power have been those of domination and constraint, and where reconciliation has been a live option. Hence South Africa does not have a franchise on the genre of comedy that crops up at the moment when the master/slave relationship is ready to snap like a broken rib. South African comedies of reversal have American comedy—specifically, the "Hollywood comedy of remarriage," as Stanley Cavell calls it—as their screwball prototypes.[4] Among these, the most germane may be *Adam's Rib,* directed by George Cukor in 1949 and written by Ruth Gordon and Garson Kanin. *Adam's Rib* is one of the great films about human reversal, in particular about the reversibility of men and women. The film concerns the lives of one married couple, Adam and Amanda, two New York lawyers from the upper crust. They are known to each other as Pinky and Pinkie. They end up redefining the terms of their marriage by subjecting it to the dynamics of a courtroom case, in which they find themselves on opposite sides of an attempted-murder trial. In the course of the trial, she stands both procedure and her husband on their heads, wins the case, proves her point—that men and women are entitled to the same treatment under the law—and nearly loses her husband, who enters into a sulk of biblical proportions. Toward the end of the film this exemplary pair stand on the brink of divorce.

The two differ, it seems, only by the little extras attached to the ends of their pet names—Pinky has a *y* at the end of his, while his wife, Pinkie, sports an *ie* at the end of hers. Their names are so alike that when, in a spillover of private life into public drama, the discombobulated Adam calls her by her pet name instead of addressing her as the defense, the court reporter has to ask twice for its correct spelling. "Is that Pinky with a *y* or an *ie?*" the reporter drawls in his bored New York accent. Evidently it is easy to get these endings confused, even if men and women are supposed to be—and especially in the socially distant past of the 1940s were taken to be—as indelibly different as East from West, black from white, the rock of Gibraltar from the island of Santo Domingo, elite from subaltern. Adam is a definite rock, and no film audience could possibly have confused Spencer Tracy, the solid he-man who plays this paragon, with a representative of the fairer, slinkier sex—and especially not with the svelte and suave Katharine Hepburn, who plays Amanda, even if she beats Adam at his own game and announces halfway through the film its resolution: "Let us all be manly."

Cavell's *Pursuits of Happiness: The Hollywood Comedy of Remarriage,* the font of all writing on this film and on film comedies of this sort, makes it clear that the Shakespearean ambience of *Adam's Rib* depends on its movement between the real world and what, in a term borrowed from Northrop Frye, Cavell calls the "green world."[5] It is in the negotiation of these worlds, the one of quotidian reality, the other of dreamlike romance, that marriage is subject to the threat of divorce and/or brought to the land of happiness. In a marvelous turn of phrase, Cavell says that the green world of these films tends to be a place within a half day's drive (at that time) from New York City, namely Connecticut. *Adam's Rib* poses this negotiation between real and green worlds as one between, on the one hand, the courtroom in New York (where Adam and Amanda literally hit it off) and their duplex (where life between them becomes increasingly unbearable), and, on the other hand, the dream farm in Connecticut. In that green world their romantic absorption finds its apogee and their interminglings overrule categorical analysis in terms of "the law of gender," even while requiring that both be "equal under the law."

Both Adam and Amanda believe in the principle of equality before the law, yet each reserves the right to twist that principle to suit his or her purpose. Adam believes the principle to happily coexist with those categorical rules that distinguish one sex from the other: "I like there to be two sexes," he says. Amanda is less happy about this matter, since to her, these rules serve to mask a series of "unwritten laws" that operate in society to prevent women from having equal access to justice, thus keeping them downtrodden. What she objects to *personally* is his practice of buying her off with a new hat when women's rights are at issue. "You look cute when you're causey," he says to her over the phone, after telling her he's prosecuting the wife of Warren Attinger, the philandering husband caught, shot, and wounded by his wife, defended by Amanda. To her this is extortion, the extortion of the reserve of personal intimacy they have built up in a marriage of equality in privacy—the kind of equality that comes from being crazy about each other and playing together, like sexual children. Such capital is not a commodity that men can use, Amanda reasons to herself without saying so, except under the illusion that they truly are masters. It is again one of those unwritten (unacknowledged) practices that produce public inequality, in justice and in the public sphere. Later, she will announce to him in a fury, after he has slapped her, "Let us all be manly," meaning, let us all use such unwritten laws to get what we want. Some would call this a deserved redress, others a problematic intervention in equality. It is the first example in film, perhaps, of the ethical and legal problems associated with special rights, formulated contextually on the basis of redress. Amanda has in effect introduced an equity bill into their relationship, into courtroom practice. What follows, I have said, is that a courtroom is stood on its head and therefore forced to think.

Amanda convinces the jury that her client, Doris Attinger, is not guilty of any crime, since (1) she shot only to warn her husband off of his philandering and reconstitute her family, and (2) no one was fatally hurt in the act. In the course of her argument, Amanda demonstrates to the jury that it is only an "unwritten principle" that allows a man the right to protect his family by force, and that once this principle is applied equally to women,

Doris Attinger will be found not guilty. Adam is disgusted both with the argument and with Amanda's legal shenanigans, believing that the law can admit of no special circumstance: when a person shoots, he or she breaks the law, end of story, straight conviction.

When unwritten laws go up against written ones, and both stand in the name of equality, a variety of positions (his and hers) are both plausible, and the system of constitutional values, if one can call it that, breaks down into a number of incompatible, yet plausible, alternatives. It is here that written law gives way to flexibility in *judgment*. Amanda asks the jury to reflect on the spirit of law and to make its determination in that light. It could have been a leaf from the South African constitution.

Adam gets *his* when, after losing the case and also, it appears, the marriage, and in the guise of a male Doris Attinger, he breaks in upon Amanda and her spineless friend Kip, gun in hand, ready to shoot, just as Doris had done. At this point Amanda cries out that he has no right, that no one has the right to break the law. "Music to my tin ears," Adam replies. What he has demonstrated to her is that "you believe what I believe." He then points the gun at himself, to their horror, and takes a bite out of it, to their amazement and pique: "Mmm, my favorite, licorice." His music and food are of bitterness and tin, since his assertion of his "rights," having been forced on her in the form of a slap in the face, hardly brings them together. It will take the remainder of the film for him to realize that he can respect what she has done, even if it will never sit easily with him, and that their relationship must be one of equals who have the right to differ. He will come to realize it because he desires her, because he likes her, because he wants to be with her. The dawning of recognition is precipitated by his desire and catalyzed by her response.

How then does this couple sort itself out? In the terms of the silent home movie that's screened within this film, how do Adam and Amanda manage to go from mortgage to merriment? The resolution begins to happen over the issue of mortgage. They are at the office of their accountant, reckoning their quarterly taxes. Already Amanda has won the case and Adam has attacked her with his licorice pistol. Already all hell has broken out in the courtroom and in their private lives. Spencer Tracy the rock has crumbled like a cookie and in effect has become womanly, which raises the question of what it is to be womanly and to whom this state, as defined and practiced, belongs. To him it is a state of humiliation, to everyone else in the courtroom one of comedy. He has been stood on his head by a female weightlifter and acrobatist (coded as lesbian to Kip's equally acrobatic gay): she has cut him down to size by being twice his girth. He has babbled, screamed, argued, and in general become disoriented to the point of behaving like a hysterical female who has lost her purse. He has lost his name, his appendage, his Y chromosome, not to mention the hat he gave his wife to buy her off. Now he is ready to find that the state of being in between manly and womanly is one to which he can belong, and that this readiness will free him to reentangle himself with her. It happens during a discussion of the paying of the mortgage. The check in question is the final payment on their dream farm and apparently, Adam says, they got careless as the prospect of owning it outright approached and did not jot down what percentage of the payment was deductible. Adam grimaces, stops, and cries. "We own it now, free and clear," he exclaims between tears. "It took us six years but we made it." Tears flow from Adam's eyes at the prospect of its loss. Astonished, melted, she moves behind him, puts her arm around him, and says, "Listen, Pinky, if we start now, we could get there in time for dinner." Pinky: "You mean and see the dogs?" Pinkie: "You don't want to go." Pinky: "Yes, I do." Pinkie: "You don't really want to go." Etcetera.

What we see as this scene transpires are two reactions that are held by the camera long enough so they can happen in silence. It is these reactions that occasion what is said by each of the pair, as if what they say simply follows from what they have already shown—to each other. Wittgenstein suggested that the phrase "I am in pain" can be understood as a replacement of such pain behavior as happens, originally, in silence; and indeed, almost all of the melodramatic moments of this film happen silently, including the opening sequence with Doris Attinger (Judy Holliday) following her hubby to his love nest and shooting it out with her newly purchased gun. Watching Amanda and Adam watching one another during their court summations, one can see each expressing a silent delight and amusement in the other, which already betokens the possibility of their reunion.

The accountant tells them that, if they leave now, "It'll cost ya." Amanda replies that "the more we pay, the more we like it"—a homily whose purpose is to signal her return to the world of delight but also to the title of their already screened silent home movie: *The Mortgage the Merrier* and "the more we like it" echo off each other, as if silent and sound film are suddenly in harmony. Later that night, together again, in their dream world a happy couple, we are treated to another silent demonstration, one that is about the former and casts it in a most peculiar light. Adam opens his mail and exclaims that he has been invited to run for a local seat of government on the Republican ticket. Amanda says that she is very proud of him, to which he responds that he would rather hear that than anything. She then puts on the hat that has become the symbol of her power and their recent history, sits down on the bed in a beguiling, Chinese kind of manner, which he does not yet see but we do, and wonders aloud: "Adam, have they picked the Democratic candidate yet?" "You wouldn't," he replies. "How do you know?" she responds. "I'd cry," he says, "and then you wouldn't." She quizzically asks, "But those were real tears?"—meaning back in the office. "Course they were," he says, "but I can turn them on any time I want." As he says this, the camera closes in on Spencer Tracy's wide and gleaming Irish eye, which gradually occasions from itself the eruption of a single golden tear, then another, then a small but veritable stream, which is then turned off more or less at will. It is no surprise that this consummate Tracy performance carries the effect of a consummation, since the slow, inexorable, and excited forcing of a single magnified drop, then another from his quivering eye, replicates the pleasure of the male orgasm. Nor will it, therefore, come as a surprise that both partners find Tracy's, that is, Adam's, that is, Pinky's, performance unnerving and exciting. One might think of it as a sophisticated kind of foreplay: "Oh, yes, there aren't any of us don't have our little tricks, you know," Amanda responds with her usual aplomb. "Men, women, the same." "The same, huh?" "Well, maybe a little difference." And, finally, it will come as no surprise that the penultimate line of the film, more or less, is given over to him. "Vive la différence!" he exclaims. She asks what that means; he says that it is French for "Hurrah for that little difference," at which point the curtain is drawn, they are removed from our sight, evidently to do the desired in the pursuit of happiness, and the film, the Punch-and-Judy show, ends. As it did in the silent home movie.

The thought that those tears, back then in the office, were not spontaneous but intended, a thought that remains unresolved, brings up the question of performance in those life moments that precisely call forth the conviction that comes from sheer spontaneity. Tracy's gesture, performed (mostly) in silence, is an acknowledgment that all the silence between the pair has been a kind of talk, a performance, a nonverbal communication in which each directs his or her sulk, eye solicitation, or hamming at the other for the purpose of intimacy or its denial. (Between this pair, silence blurs the line that separates out hamming, acting, naturalness, and expression.) The demonstration that Adam gives Amanda is meant to suggest that he had more of a hand in bringing about this happy ending than had appeared—that he had willed and engineered it. But the production of tears at will is also meant, after the fact, to reinterpret that earlier moment in which his silence demanded (and received) the attention it deserved, and to reinterpret it in a way that makes him feel more comfortable, and also powerful, now. As if to say: "As I am doing now, so I did, or could have done, then." Adam is trying on his silence as she tries on the hat he gave her, the hat that caused him grief when he found it on the head of the woman he was meant to prosecute. What both husband and wife are convinced of is his sincerity now, and his ability to be comfortable in using the female role, in acting the female part when demanded.

Adam's translation of his final remark, *"Vive la difference!"* ("It means, 'Hurrah for that little difference,'" he says, and it is the last thing said by anyone in the film), is more in the nature of an *addition* to the meaning of what it translates than a translation. These two lines—the one in French, the other, its "translation," in the dialect of High American Hollywoodese—are related by the same kind of little difference as Adam is to Amanda. Each complements the other and adds to it, as again the film within the film in *Adam's Rib* adds to the film and vice versa. Each is, once stated, part of the other, part of its "meaning."[6] Together, these recited lines become *his*. They are addressed to her in particular, but also to what women in his view simply are. He knows their difference by translating it—that is, by making it his, which also means by assimilating it, not through law or essence but through desire. The translation cannot be effected apart from desire and is an artifact of it. His exclamation is in French because French is, to Hollywood, not only the language of endless romance (the "ooh la la!" language), but also because it is the language of popular liberty—as in the statue in New York that the French built as a universal image of liberty, a symbol of immigration, including that of Hollywood writers and directors from Europe, which has come to mean *the more the merrier*. For America is a land in which a motley crew of immigrants produces vitality through, one hopes, variety, to delightfully rib the language into new being.

Happy ending? Evidently. But note that, in the film, the question of who is different from whom, and, above all, the significance of such differences, is left unaccounted. As it must be: no longer objects of essentialized laws, they are freed again to be objects of *desire*, and of uncertainty. The task of public life, and of private marriages, is to unravel such similarities and differences by conversing about them, working them out, discovering them, and by finding that, as over time categories of gender fall away, men and women both do and do not actually become different in ways we may not expect. Such is the space of citizenship in a nation whose liberty requires the acknowledgment of diversity.

Reconciliation is a matter of placing the pair again on an equal footing, through court tactics of redress in public and the courting of similarity in private. In private, before the gaze of a million film viewers, meaning in public representation.

Soweto's Taxi

Adam's Rib is about married people who are already crazy about each other coming to appreciate their differences. It is this achievement that makes their attraction within marriage sustainable (that makes their *marriage* sustainable). What South African screwball comedy takes from such American cousins as *Adam's Rib* is a picture of sustainability, but within new terms of sociability and thus citizenship—this in the insecurities of a society with new and more decent prescriptions about liberty. South African comedy is not about remarriage but about *resocialization*—renationalization, if you will. This process is in many respects different from those of discovery and rediscovery, since it is about people who initially do not communicate and do not like each other. And so the screwball element enters when people accustomed to particular terms of inclusion and exclusion in the domain of citizenship—when people accustomed to terms of communication having basically to do with who gives and who follows orders—become embroiled in each other's lives. What happens is that, in a chaotic, borderless space, where the figure of Adam, the master, has to learn from, trust, depend on his thorn in the side (his rib), all hell breaks loose—and through all hell breaking loose, the possibility of human felicity and sociability emerges. I refer to the figure of Adam as the giver of law and order, but I should rather speak in the old palindrome: it's the madam who is Adam. In *Taxi to Soweto*, Jessica Du Toit is the master.

Taxi was made by Manie van Rensburg in the heyday of postapartheid South Africa, when reconciliation could appear as a quick and sustainable option, a signal of total national transformation in a utopian instant. A film about borders and their crossing, it takes place largely in a taxi and is about an urban Afrikaans couple, Horace Du Toit and his wife, Jessica, and what happens to them after Jessica's car has broken down somewhere on one of the Johannesburg freeways. With no help in sight, she hails a taxi. As she gets in, not without trepidation, she is greeted by Richard, the taxi driver and general trickster/factotum, to whom she introduces herself as "Miss Jessica" (as in: "Miss Jessica to the likes of you"). He smiles his ironic smile and proceeds to deliver her to her home—by way of the various downtown taxi stops he is making for his other passengers. In the course of this downtown route (Jessica would seldom find herself in such a chaotic and newly multiracial part of the city, since she remains holed up in her formerly white and still white suburb, a place called Parktown), the taxi is kidnapped to Soweto, where the fun (hell) begins. Expecting that her matronly voice still carries immediate authority, she tells the kidnapper in no uncertain terms to behave properly, and the instruction receives a most unexpected reply, which, fortunately for her, she cannot understand, since it is not in a language she understands. This will be the first of many unexpected responses, each of which will undercut the sense of comfortable command that she and her husband are accustomed to hold over all manner of natives, who were, after all, in the days of apartheid, not even South African citizens.

Meanwhile, Horace, in charge of negotiating a strike by his black African workers, remains unreachable by her: he greets her call for help from a fancy Soweto shebeen called Club 77 with the remark that she should not bother him when he is at work, and he follows that dismissal with a swift click of the phone. Unable to get home by calling for help, she is forced to rely on Richard, to rely on him so completely that, when he briefly loses sight of her, she collapses with anxiety. She is, after all, alone in a township where she does not want to be, and where she is the object of many a male eye, if not male proposition. This state of affairs disturbs her sense of self and authority (self as authority) to the point where, when Richard returns, she beats him with her fists and then collapses in tears into his arms, a lost child dependent on his wiles and his good nature. If this scene is not a representation of reversal, of becoming, to one's horror and distaste, the slave to the slave, then nothing is. Horace fares no better, if not worse, for, on returning home, he finds a message on his answering machine from Richard, inquiring after Jessica's safe return—but in a fatal idiom: "Jessica baby, this is Richard. I'm at Satchmo's." Assuming the worst, that his wife is off with a black African, Horace settles down into the night, drinks too much, and manages to get himself locked out of his house and nearly arrested by his own security company while trying to break back in. His appropriately violent dog, leftover and symbol of white security from the old days, manages to take a nice bite out of his hand in the process. Later, searching for Satchmo's (which he has no idea how to find and wrongly assumes is in a seedy part of downtown Johannesburg called Hillbrow), his car is stolen, he gets even more impossibly drunk, and ends up sleeping in a nearby flea-bitten hotel, where, since he relinquished his wallet to local beggars in a moment of dystopia, he cannot pay for the room the next morning. But it is the night before that interests us:

sitting in a seedy bar that he had thought might be Satchmo's, watching one of those corny Afrikaans-language melodramas with which apartheid overwhelmed South African television, our drunken hero confuses the actors he sees on the tele with himself and his wife. He sees (or thinks he sees) Jessica going off with Richard, and he hears (or thinks he hears) Richard speak directly to him off the TV screen and, with a grin, say, "Welcome to the new South Africa."

Taxi to Soweto is obviously a film about white fears. Played out as a collapse in spatial borders that under apartheid reflected and defined essentialized differences, the character of Horace Du Toit is swallowed whole by a city whose new betwixt-and-between spaces he has developed no skills to negotiate. He has failed to ask anyone where Satchmo's is, anyone who might actually know: he has failed, in other words, to ask a black person, and has instead looked for the (to him) mysterious place on his own. Still the settler, able to take control, is he. He at last finds out where Satchmo's is wholly by accident, through the black African negotiator who is trying to resolve the strike, and who has heard of a guy called Satchmo who runs a club in Soweto. Du Toit thereby discovers that black people just might be of help in situations that he himself cannot handle. This discovery, shattering to his sense of mastery, is the discovery of his dependency on the slave, of his being slave to the slave, of finding that the slave has a skill: the slave knows where things are in the wider world and knows how to negotiate the cracks between identities in ways that the master does not. It is the slave who can drive the taxis that take people between here and there.

"Only if you find out what it is like to be a worker, without enough wherewithal, can you understand what the strikers are about," the negotiator more or less tells Du Toit. His wife will make the same discovery, not in Soweto, but in front of the gate to the house of her husband's boss. Having traveled to Johannesburg, again in the ubiquitous taxi, with some wives of the men on strike, and having heard their side of the story, Jessica finds herself in the middle of the chanting and "toyi-toyi" dancing[7] they are doing outside the boss's house to attract attention to their cause, and also finds herself annoyed at the immediate police clamp-down on them. Convinced that she can talk some sense into these police officers as one Afrikaner to another, the good *Frau* goes over to explain that these women are protesting peacefully. Her expectation is that the "misunderstanding" will be cleared up and the police will go away. Instead, it is she who is taken away—to a jail cell. The unhappy couple have now both of them experienced what the other side of the fence is like. Their reversal and renewal—their new findings—are thus in part political, but they also find each other, find each other again, in the green world of the new South Africa, at Club 77, where, under the good eye of her husband, Jessica literally sings the blues as black Africans look on with a mixture of amusement, irony, and delight. The Du Toits seem to have made such new spaces their own. Forced to shed the comfortable identity of the master, they are now free to enjoy the slave, having realized that the anxiety let loose is bearable. A new capacity to take instruction from the servant robs him of his status as servant, and of one's self as master, and a new possibility of commingling, of reconciliation, becomes possible. It is the art of comedy to show that, and to show how people can actually *like* each other. Welcome to the new South Africa, to a kind of truth and reconciliation that is different from that of truth-telling and forgiveness.

At the end of the film, the couple is being driven, arm in arm, by Richard in his taxi, back to their happy home. In a country where even today few white people have been to townships and know how black people live, the couple have been there, and under the protective eye of their guardian angel, Richard, have survived the transition. In a country where 49 percent of whites voted against abolishing apartheid, to survive a transition not exactly of your own making is cause for celebration. The fantasy here is that the former slaves, now tricksters able to negotiate cities, will become your guardian angels. Occasionally it happens on the subways of New York, where, until recently, there really have been guardian angels with colorful berets, but in this country . . . ?

Taxi to Soweto is a white film, and there is no true African reversal that occurs in it. The Africans in the film are one-dimensional, and one would have to look to new films made by people of color, such as *Fools*, to see glimmers of black subjectivity at the moment of transition. *Taxi's* failure to extend comic reversal to black Africans is, I think, related to the fact that, in spite of its disruptions of norm, procedure, and law, the film does not, finally, reflect on itself (*Adam's Rib* does so—for example, through its use of the silent film within the film). Only at the end of *Taxi to Soweto* is there a moment of self-referentiality. Van Rensburg, the director, appears, a fat man like Hitchcock, and signals the final cut. This gesture of ending the film feels gratuitous; it is a wasted opportunity for self-reflection. Were there self-reflection of a more penetrating kind, the filmmaker might have realized that what self-reflection there is, is one-sided. The question of who the black Africans are, of how they react to the precipitous events of the city and the nation, of their trajectories of change, might have been more interestingly raised. A deeper sort of conversation between black and white might have happened. But that might have been too much to ask for, and too soon. In South Africa today, people remain wary when speaking outside their "group"—wary, if not sullen, if not violent. Which is also why the roads are so perilous, especially between Johannesburg and Soweto.

The utopian moment in this film (also its most classically comic) is an ending defined as happy because a painful history is resolved in people liking each other, that is, in singing the blues together in the excitement of a shebeen. "I don't know how to love you, but I want to try," Jessica warbles in Club 77, being fed the lines by the black African chanteuse who, earlier in the film, has woken her up and comically mimicked a servant by bringing tea to her. The exclamation of desire at a moment of national celebration and nation-building is fine and necessary. It is also a message with a whiff of skepticism. The madam now knows that she does not know how to do something, but wants to try. The problem with the film is that this message is also a way of avoiding tough reality by eliding the problem of *likeness* (of people becoming more alike, and recognizing their lines of similarity) with that of people *liking* each other (wanting to love each other). White madam and black chanteuse sing in mimicry—or complementarity—as if each is a color band mysteriously harmonized into a rainbow. And so the problem of communication becomes dissolved into an alchemy of complementarities in a country of human relations grown old on strife. So it is with utopian images of the Rainbow Nation, making the film's image of reconciliation enthralling but unreal. It would indeed be far easier to manage diversity and foment communication if people wanted to be with each other more than they do and if harmony could replace conversation. What is difficult, perhaps most difficult, is for people to form strategic relationships, negotiate particular forms of reconciliation, and learn to respect each other when they do not like each other and, on a related note, when they do not even have great reason to trust each other. We are talking leap of faith here. The problems both of achieving trust/desire and of achieving sufficient likeness stubbornly remain.

Those failures of achievement, in many ways the condition of post-apartheid South Africa, are not funny.

Taxi to Soweto was made before it became clear to the nation (toward the close of the 1990s) that crime, unemployment, HIV/AIDS, bad governance, lack of genuine multiparty democracy, corruption, scandal, and failure of globalization had subdued the utopianism that fuels reconciliation and, by corollary, reversal. Reversal, and the larger ambit of reconciliation, are today stalled in this mire, even if, perhaps, the work of addressing such problems just might produce a new kind of likeness between persons. After all, Voltaire's *Candide* ends with a "reconciliation" of characters in a state of extreme unhappiness—characters unhappy, until they begin to realize they share utopian and prophetic images of happy endings that must give way to the more realistic goals of producing candied fruits and pleasant drinks through cooperative hard labor. That work turns out to be the only thing that allows them to find each other bearable. It makes them more alike, almost makes them like each other, and produces its own kind of complementarity. Everything hangs on the capacity of this, perhaps any, society to address what is no longer of the domain of screwball comedy. To go, as Candide would put it, and work in the garden.

3

Afro-Medici: Thabo Mbeki's African Renaissance

Re-naissance

Semper aliquid novi ex Africa: "Always something new from Africa." The African renaissance. So many words: *indabas* and *bosberade*, i.e., meetings, conferences, discussions, pronouncements, speeches. So many words about words. In a language that everyone can understand. In English, rather than the Italian of Filippo Brunelleschi and his grand Duomo. In English, rather than the German of Jacob Burkhardt and his glorious narratives of the Italianate past. In English, rather than Zulu, language of the fierce and indomitable Shaka. In English, rather than Xhosa, in which the young Nelson Mandela spoke his first words. A renaissance in English, even if it is Zulu and Xhosa, which are apparently being reborn in this rebirth, and even if those who do not speak English cannot understand its terms of rebirth, except in translation.

Ambivalence over English and Englishness, or, more broadly, European-ness. A renaissance in English, the European language, spoken by those whose ancestors could not speak English. A renaissance by those whose ancestors, even if they could speak English, would not have been listened to by the likes of the English-speaking should they have chosen to speak, except in such stock phrases as "Yes, baas (boss)," "No, baas," "Thank you, baas." Thanks for nothing, for were these phrases but fabrications, they would have been the stuff of Hollywood comedy rather than plangent reality. A renaissance of words in English spoken by those who have not compelled such twists of language out of modernity since others before their time, living further up in West Africa or in the Americas, brought the language of negritude into being. In French and in English.

When those who talk of an African renaissance now talk in English, the others, the old English speakers, the first-language English speakers, now listen. Attentively and anxiously, lest they lose the gist and fall out of the boat of the new South Africa. Those who listen often fail to understand the gist, and it is likely that those who speak do not terribly much care, for it is the general ambience of the words that matters, an ambience that carries authority and commands attention. Attention from those who are called "white," and from others, to those who are called "black," and others. Inopportunely called so and indelibly called so. For the moment, anyway—for the postapartheid moment, anyway. One hopes that this moment will change, even if slowly, and that terms like "white" and "black" will gradually cease to serve as markers, road maps, and identity badges for the many vicissitudes of life that they currently mark. South Africans suffer from race trouble; they cannot get a sentence out without the words "black" and "white" appearing. This obviously comes from a terrible historical legacy, and continues because of ongoing inequality along racial lines. It is impossible to overcome the category of race while rampant inequality is present in a country along what have been defined as racial lines, or what Thabo Mbeki, the inventor of the African renaissance and its medici cum guru, has called the problem of "two nations." Mbeki's use of racial descriptions is as common as those of most other South Africans, who, so long as they continue to speak of black and white, will remain black and white. A shift in language is as fundamental to this project of overcoming as a shift in the distribution of goods, although certainly not more fundamental to it. The African renaissance explicitly eschews racial language while implicitly courting it. It explicitly opens South Africa to a multiplicity of citizens in the manner of the South African constitution while implicitly returning to images of a glorious black Africanist past—the past of the great decolonizing struggles and, earlier still, to that of a utopia before colonialism, which ultimately means before the white man. It is this double game, played in English, which has, as a sociological remark, generated enthusiasm for the concept on the part of certain key black South Africans in government and universities (and certain "struggelati," those building professional careers on their so-called struggle credentials) and a vague, inchoate sense of ill ease on the part of many other South Africans who find themselves unable to diagnose their combination of interest and disquiet. The nature of the double game is in this essay explored in terms of Mbeki's speeches, in terms of the legacies of those speeches in the languages of racialism, and in terms of the political purposes to which this language is now being put.

The African renaissance is meant to be a way of speaking otherwise, a phoenix language about the rising of Africa from its medieval, neocolonial, postindependence, postapartheid, postcolonial slumber to take its rightful place in the land of meganations, geopolitics, free trade, democracy, and human flourishing. So far so good. Mbeki, the president of South Africa, is proposing a vision of an Africa that is a free-trade zone in which capital may grow and human beings may be free to pursue their happiness. I almost wrote "Mbeki, the president of Africa," as if one could assume the presidency of an entity like "Africa," which is partly what Mbeki wants and what the rest of Africa fears of this new kid from the big nation down south. His hegemonic vision allies him to the likes of John F. Kennedy, the "F" in Kennedy's case standing in his case for the omnipresent unmentionable, the "Kennedy" for power through democracy, which means through the world order of the United States.

The African renaissance explicitly eschews a vision of Africa based on race and gender, that of a black fraternity. Mbeki is liberal, reaching out to women and persons "of all colors" under the sign of "the people of Africa" (in the singular and the plural). Reaching out to an Africa that is everybody's:

> The Constitution . . . constitutes an unequivocal statement that we refuse to accept that our Africanness shall be defined by our race, colour, gender or historical origins. It is a firm assertion made by ourselves that South Africa belongs to all who live in it, black and white.[1]

So far even better. But such a vision would hardly seem to require the idea of a "renaissance," for it would not be clear what the element of return, of reawakening, of rebirth would be in it. It is a magnificent, liberal vision, one with precedents in the entire history of English and French liberalism, not to mention the American version with its Lincolnesque augustness. Africa could serve as the next place where such a vision is birthed, no doubt creatively and with appropriate variation. Such would be a form of progress, a creation of new times, rather than the rebirth of old. What, then, is this "old times," this old language, this old place with the man bent over the walking stick called Africa, that makes such a liberal vision a vision of rebirthing? Why the African *re*-naissance?

"I am an African"

We begin at the beginning. "So let me begin. I am an African."[2] Thus says
Thabo Mbeki, the second head of state of the new South Africa. Mbeki
begins at the beginning when he speaks to the South African parliament
on the occasion of its adoption of the new constitution in May 1996.
Mbeki goes on to say:

> I am formed of the migrants who left Europe to find a new home on our na-
> tive land. . . . In my veins courses the blood of the Cape Malay slaves who
> came from the east. . . . I am the grandchild of the men and women that
> Hintsa and Sekhukune led. . . . My mind and my knowledge of myself is
> formed by the victories we earned from Isandhlwana to Khartoum.[3]

Mbeki's language is constitutive, befitting the moment at which a
constitution comes into being. It forms an entirety of history out of the
panoply of shards of the South African and larger African past, thus creating the history of a people, a people of which the "I" who is the African is
an exemplar. In its scope and grandeur Mbeki's speech recalls the writing
in English of the likes of Walt Whitman (who sings the body electric) and
James Joyce ("the artificer of the race"), and, in Spanish, of Octavio Paz
(with the landscape of Mexico engraved on his body in a maze of avenues
and scars). It recalls the rhetoric of Thomas Jefferson, Abraham Lincoln,
and John *"Ich bin ein Berliner"* Kennedy.[4] Through a more direct lineage,
which we will explore, it recalls the poetry of Leopold Senghor (written in
French) with its praise of Africanness, and the writing of W. E. B. DuBois.
Mbeki's is a language of authorization, of identification, of confirmation,
a language that brings into being and confirms the being of a *people*, an
African people:

> I am also able to state this fundamental truth: that I am born of a people
> who are heroes and heroines. I am born of a people who would not tolerate
> oppression. I am of a nation that would not allow that.[5]

In other places this people will be referred to as a series of peoples, but
the dominant theme is to think of it in the singular. Africa's is a people
"who are heroes . . . who would not tolerate oppression." They are South
African, but in a prior register simply African. One may note the sequence
of sentences I have just excerpted to confirm this. First sentence: "I am
born of a *people* who are heroes and heroines." Second sentence: "I am
born of a people who would not tolerate oppression." Third sentence: "I
am of a *nation* that would not allow that." Now, if one adds the sentence

that comes just before these to the quotation, a crucial ambiguity appears. With the addition, the sequence reads as follows:

> All of this I know and know to be true because I am an African! Because of that, I am also able to state this fundamental truth: that I am born of a people who are heroes and heroines. I am born of a people who would not tolerate oppression. I am of a nation that would not allow that.[6]

With the first sentence ("All of this I know and know to be true because I am an African!"), the sequence moves from Africa ("I am an African") to a people ("who are heroes," "who would not tolerate oppression"), and only then to a nation ("I am of a nation [South Africa] that would not allow that"). This leaves the semantic scope of the word "people" crucially vacillating between Africans per se and members of the South African nation. The ambiguity allows for the elision of South Africa and Africa, while also preserving some sense of separation between the two. South Africa is itself only in virtue of being a small subset of Africa. It is itself only though the expanse of Africa that is its lineage. It takes its dignity and power from the larger maternal and/or paternal ambience of Africa. And it is to Africa, rather than to itself, that this moment of constitutional celebration belongs.

The mood is one of return and rebirth. This African renaissance is a South African (re-)creation, and it is crucial to the fact of it that South Africa, formerly excluded from African identity politics on account of its apartheid separateness, is now making its geomythological move into the communalist territory of Africa by way of its language of pan-Africanism. Mbeki is a speechwriter turned politician, not a philosopher. He has an eye on a voter constituency in everything he says, and probably believes that this voter constituency will be seduced by grandiloquence. He also has his eye on the terrain of African politics, which he enters from a position of strength by speaking the name of "Africa." His political agenda will be taken up at the end of this essay, which is not for nothing called "Afro-Medici," but I will arrive at that gradually through a close examination of Mbeki's language, a language whose character of praise is finally indistinguishable from its history and politics.

During the days of struggle, pan-Africanism was firmly held by the PAC (the Pan Africanist Congress), whose mentor, Robert Sebukwe, was held for years in isolation from all other prisoners at Robbin Island, and held after his sentence had been served by special order of law. It inflamed the rhetoric of Steve Biko, the black-consciousness movement activist whose death became an icon of apartheid violence. However, the African

National Congress (Mbeki's party) was always a movement that vacillated between black power and black identity on the one hand and, on the other, a revolutionary/liberal language that was all-inclusive of Indian, colored, and white populations. The vacillation continues today, in the language of the African renaissance. Mbeki praises the diverse heroes of Africa, but his litany of heroes leaves Gandhi out, even though Gandhi's first political work took place in South Africa. It tends to delete important Indian leaders in the struggle, and in general Indian and Arabic elements in Africa are mentioned only, one feels, "because they have to be." Its stresses are—there is, unfortunately, no other word for it—"black." And by "black" is unequivocally meant "black African," not the more deracialized "persons of color" or the almost fully deracialized "historically disadvantaged."

The language awakens a renaissance by stating that it is there—there on the scene of the immediate future. It creates a people, a communal solidarity, by asserting its presence. It reverses the negative property of Africanness from its past history as the immediate badge of inferiority in a racist world (where the first thing anyone noticed about you, always to your disadvantage, was your skin) by harping on Africanness as a property conferring immediate cultural blessing. You are blessed not by skin but by cultural background. The word "African" is harped on almost to the point of obsession, as it is in the writings of the medical scientist and director of the Medical Sciences Research Council, Dr. William Makgoba. Makgoba literally enlarges the typeface of his book every time the word "African" appears, as if to visualize it as a reverse identity badge that jumps off the page.[7]

If "African" connotes a cultural property rather than a property of skin, it is nevertheless in both writers (Mbeki and Makgoba) centrally about blackness. The African renaissance empowers a formerly disenfranchised black contingency by expressing the way things are in their style, in accord with their terms of satisfaction and aesthetics of pleasure. It awakens a sense of a new Africa inclusive of *everybody* (black, white, Indian, et al.) while specially or in particular awakening the presence of *blackness* within this Africa. Black Africa, its aesthetics and cultural politics, are central in the African renaissance, while never being explicitly stated as so.

"The past no longer exists, the future belongs to us," Mbeki somewhere says. Abstracting from the unfortunate Germanic associations in these words, we have here a communalism through which South African black leaders reach out to a mythic African people who is molded in their image. The "us" to whom the "future belongs" is itself a double entendre. In one sense it refers to black Africans and/or the African National Congress; in another it refers to everybody, to all Africans/South Africans. History is always written in certain scripts and not others, and the implication of centrality depends on who is doing the talking, say, white liberals in the past or the African National Congress now. This is a script of the African National Congress, speaking, like the white liberal of the past, for everybody, but, like the white liberal of the past, in words that generalize from certain interests (their own) to others. Unlike the white liberal, it is a language of formerly disenfranchised people now glorying in their capacity to speak and write the central dialogue of the country.

One way of interpreting the double entendre of "South Africa for everybody" versus "South Africa as black Africa" is that it marks a new liberal awareness. First, the awareness is that southern Africa (sub-Saharan Africa) largely is black (in terms of variants of skin) and that it largely thinks of itself as such (blackness is a central identity construction in sub-Saharan Africa). Second, the awareness is that sub-Saharan Africa is also a place of other racial minorities who *are* in the minority, in spite of their claims (past or present) to mastery of the continent. So Mbeki knows he is largely formed by his black (so called) ancestry, but that he is also formed of the settlers who educated him and the events of the continent as a whole. "Largely formed by his black ancestry" is a phrase that is vague enough that it presents problems of interpretation. After all, Mbeki is speaking in English when he says this, and is, one must assume, largely formed by the English language, rather than by Swedish, rather than by Italian, rather than by Zulu. And he is speaking in a Shakespearean/colonial rhetoric that is very much the product of English culture (the culture of England). The language is certainly racialist because its central categories of identity are black versus other, black versus everybody, and to me it smacks of the Englishman who says, "I am formed of the entire world, as large as it, but still, finally, an Englishman." Mbeki is saying, "I lived half my life in England, but remain, finally, an African, which means, a black man, but also a man formed of the diverse currents of the continent. The *whole* continent." This continental drift is, to me, the central thing.

Again and again Mbeki speaks of the great monuments and events that have formed him, and they are always continental: from Sekhukune and Shaka to the great civilizations of West Africa. Usually they are associated with the idea of blackness. Thus Khartoum is mentioned and Moslem East Africa, or Algeria, is not.

On my reading Mbeki's language plays a double game, poses a double entendre: between the pan-Africanist desire to speak to a continent "mostly" composed and unified (he believes) by blackness and the desire to identity with and bring into being a modern, neoliberal Africa through liberal/nonracist images of *everybody* and a feel for unity through globalization. We all will be one because we all are black, cut from the same cloth. And we all will be one because we all are modern citizens of the world and ought to have the same free trade and prosperity that Asians, Europeans, and Americans have. The one language stresses blackness and appeals to the ANC and a mostly black South African constituency; the other stresses borderless openness and appeals to everybody. Indeed a goal is to bring about continental change (with South Africa at the helm) by appeal to pan-Africanist ideals, to awaken a dormant, chaotic Africa from its first-generation postcolonial slumber by appeal to images of unity through heritage. (Somewhere between Kwame Nkumrah and Ronald Reagan.) The key is that Mbeki believes words, and indeed *his* words, are capable of driving this enterprise, of kick-starting Africa into modernity. And this belief is the fantasy of an all-too-English exile, a man grown tall on the voices of the great English orators of empire.

So, finally, the reason Africa demands a *re*-naissance rather than a new form of birth (a naissance without the *re*-) is that the old languages of racial heritage may be retrieved under the illusion that by retrieving them an explicitly nonracial or multiracial new South Africa and Africa could thereby arise. The task of governance will be to negotiate this proposition in practice. But how, other than through images, spectacles, meetings in fancy hotels, with lots of media publicity? Unless the goal is not governance at all, but the achievement of power through a new rhetoric, a new language (like that of the Kennedys, who early on understood that to rule you need a good turn of phrase and who always hired the best, most moral speechwriters). Then what power exactly? (The Kennedys had arms, gross national product, and the map of the cold war; what does Mbeki have?) Perhaps power within the ANC itself, as the spokesperson of the conservative, Africanist constituent therein, almost completely composed of former exiles. (More on this later.)

An African Renaissance in English

Mbeki's conception of renaissance is part of his larger idea that reconciliation requires profound sociocultural change in a society of "two nations." The African renaissance is a prelude to true reconciliation, since it will redress the cultural wrongs imposed during the apartheid past. It is about cultural rights.

Quoting Chief Luthuli, like Desmond Tutu, Nobel peace laureate, Mbeki says that "there remains before us the building of a new land . . . a synthesis of the rich cultural strains which we have inherited. . . . It will not necessarily be all black, but it will be African."[8] The "synthesis" of "rich cultural strains" may possibly include strains from other races, yet will, as an absolute moral and cultural criterion, be "African." "Africanness" is the limit condition on the multiracialistic character of the building of the new land, which Luthuli, writing during the apartheid period, is imagining, and Mbeki, by quoting him, is doing. There may be non-black elements in the cultural synthesis, but then again, there may not be, given Luthuli's grammatically arcane phrase "not necessarily" in "It will not necessarily be all black," meaning it could well be all black. However, even if the new synthesis is not all black, it will be African—African as opposed to, one assumes, white/European dominated. But more than that: "African" meaning essentially from the rich strains of black, sub-Saharan Africa, meaning that if there is some element of Indian, colored, and even European traditions in this mix, it will be, in being African, essentially not dominated by those elements but most deeply expressive of other, more evidently black, elements. The strands of the synthesis will not merely be rich, but also, in essence, be distinctive of Africa. And that means distinctive of the cultures that sort in accord with color and are the majority cultures, the African ones. Even if "not all black," the new synthesis will mostly be so: again skin color aligns with cultural distinctiveness, so since the silent and oppressed majority is black, the culture will in the future mostly be so. Whatever that means.

The language is utterly steeped in racialism, in the thesis that skin color is the symbol of deeper heritage and that that heritage is what unifies a people, what will reemerge in the future. Luthuli is already the prophet of re-naissance. Cultural rights are cultural politics.

There is something sublime about the amorphous appeal to "Africa," a tapestry of oneness so great that South Africa recedes to a corner in its larger temperament. For (to repeat) at the very moment of South Africa's greatest moral success, on the occasion of its adoption of the most advanced constitution in the world, on the occasion of this speech, Mbeki never mentions, much less dwells on, South Africa by name. It is merely the "nation I am of":

> The thing we have done today, in this small corner of a great continent, that has contributed so decisively to the evolution of humanity, says that Africa reaffirms that she is continuing her rise from the ashes.[9]

The African renaissance and its language thus take precedence over anything specifically South African at the moment of South Africa's particular constitutional triumph. The constitution is a triumph for Africa and its "people."

Befitting the occasion of a constitution, this rhetoric carries the rhythm of a preamble to the constitution, as if of the form, "We hold these truths to be self-evident." South African constitutions have had marvelous preambles. The interim constitution of 1994 spoke of the spirit of reconciliation and of ubuntu. It could have been written by Bishop Tutu. The final constitution speaks of the need to heal divisions and is anything but Africanist. Its version of sublimity is that of the dignity in a certain perpetual questioning, a questioning that is meant to heighten the sensitivity, flexibility, and humanity of the law while constantly enforcing the rule of law. The questioning is set through Article 39 of the constitution, and in the form of a prescription. The prescription is this: each interpretation of statute must be made in the light of the spirit of the constitution as a whole. Since that spirit is everywhere about humanity and unity, but everywhere opaque, a constant reflection is required as part of constitutional judgment about what the spirit of the thing is, and how it might inform new contexts of interpretation and judgment. This internal prerequisite of questioning makes the constitution inherently philosophical. Judge Ismail Mahomed, one of the great judges of the new South Africa (now deceased), spoke in one case of ubuntu as "respecting the humanity of the other." This free-floating interpretation of an old idea in a new way is exactly the kind of thought the constitution invites. However, such sublimity pertinent to humane law is not the subject of Mbeki's sentences. His sentences are not about "we the people" and the way law tries to respect humanity by assigning the people the best rights legally possible and the most humane treatment when their traditional, cultural rights clearly and unresolvedly conflict with constitutional law.

No, Mbeki's sentences tend to begin with "I" (*I* am an African, *I* know what *I* know in virtue of this, etcetera). This is the "I" of exemplification (in me, the nation, Africa, rests). It is also the "I" of assertion, of power, of glory. It is another kind of philosophical "I," the Cartesian "I," which thinks itself into existence, or, in this case, speaks itself into existence: into existence as exemplar, as leader, as poet of praise, as symbol of the incarnate Africa to which it properly belongs. Were Mbeki of a more philosophical cast, he might have realized that he is transposing a specifically Cartesian certainty about self into the terms of pan-Africanist ubuntu: it is because of *Africa* that "I know what I know." Not "Cogito ergo sum," but "Because of Africa I think, and therefore I am." There is an epistemology in this that places Africa in the position of "first philosophy," first ethics, first condition of knowledge. "All of this I know and know to be true because I am an African!" Mbeki says, beginning the sequence of three sentences that have been occupying us. "[B]ecause I am an African," as if were he not an African, he would not know the things he knows, or know them with the same authority or in the same way. Africa, the condition of (his) first epistemology as well as moral victory, is what has taught him the lessons of reality, the language games he plays. But if Africa is the origin of (his) knowledge and identity, then what is it, this thing called Africa, other than the product of everything that has happened everywhere that has affected him? Where is *its* epistemic source located? How does its capacity for moral victory attach to its landscape? In what way is it, beyond geography, containable? How can its source be contained in itself, as if the Nile, so that its end might be envisioned from within?

A point of fact is this, and the introduction to *Africa: The Time Has Come,*[10] the collection of Thabo Mbeki's speeches that I rely on here, makes the point clear: Mbeki's speech makes it sound like everything he learned ("all that I know") was learned within the confines of Africa, which is to say, on its continent and from its people. However, he himself lived a great deal of his life in exile, having been sent by the African National Congress to study abroad at Sussex University as part of a younger generation in the struggle who would be appropriately educated when freedom came, and who would therefore be competent to assume power. Mbeki was thus formed not only by "the migrants who left Europe to find a new home on our native land," but in the Europe of his education at Sussex University, in the England where he lived for many years (working for the African National Congress in exile). His "I am an African" speech poetically deletes this fact and makes it sound as if the totality of what Mbeki thinks, the totality of his being, was created within the continent of Africa—as if in part by the settlers who came there. In virtue of the deletion, Africa becomes the universe of his training, the total field of his constitution, whose example is the (South) African constitution itself. In this language game, place, people, and the lines of education become contained within the geography of the continent and coincident with each other. Africa the continent, with its geographical inside and outside, becomes Africa the people, becomes Africa the source and causal agent of "everything that I know," as well as the source of a people who could have written this excellent constitution.

However, the African renaissance is in English. Since Mbeki writes, and has to write in English, he relies on the resources of a language whose philology and semantics outrun any concept of Africanness. The history of English is a history that ties its semantic forms to English, European, and global forms of life that are in no way specifically, much less primarily, African. In certain respects the semantics of English and the forms of life that are England are indistinguishable, if only because one can no more conceive of the English apart from their language than one can conceive of that language apart from the Englishness of the English, and the Americanisms of the Americans—and the many creative and limitless idiolects and dialects of the many who speak English throughout the globe, including in various parts of Africa. Anyone who uses the semantic resources of English, whether in one way or another, in accord with one local dialect or another, will be tied in to a semantic history that is therefore Euro-American as well as global. The English one speaks in a hodgepodge of various dialects, various histories, various forms of life. There is no ultimate way to parse them, therefore no ultimate way to begin to decide, once and for all, which inflections of English, which ways of speaking it or sets of terms within it, are *distinctively* African. One can decide this in certain respects but not in all. What the settler brought to Mbeki was a good bit of this overall history and variety called *English*. Which is not African in particular. Which Mbeki relies on when he recites and invents the African renaissance. Which the constitution relies on when it gets itself stated in English.

Thus, even for Mbeki to write and utter the sentence "I am an African" is for him to be more than an African. It is for him to be a globally produced human subject, a Homo sapiens. In stating that he is an African, Mbeki shows that he is more than an African, thus giving the lie to the myth of his epistemic origins, to the origins of "all that he knows" in the mother continent.

No doubt Mbeki knows these things. How could he not, when faced with the fact of them? Just as no doubt he would acknowledge that significant aspects of what he knows were learned abroad, since he has publicly praised his teachers at Sussex, who apparently taught him a great deal. However, this praise is deleted from his speech, to allow its Africanist metaphysics to be articulated. The dual presence of English and England in his articulation of Africa is suitably marginalized from his texts. Another kind of writer, with intentions to place the South African constitution in the global history of liberalism, might have written a speech about the history of constitutionalism from Athens to Washington (etcetera), and the fact that South Africa has now equaled and indeed bettered that history by taking the next step. Such a speech would have placed South Africa not in the field of something called "Africa," but in the history of liberalism. Mbeki does not, and this is a deliberate choice.

Decolonization and Return

The language of the African renaissance is a decolonizing language. It is crucial to the moment of postcolonial break with a neocolonial past that all signs of dependency tend to be underplayed, and cultural independence, cultural uniqueness, cultural authority are exaggerated. This is a rhetoric of self-proclamation, an act of empowerment through difference and, on a related note, through group allegiance. Here it is race that is the marker of this difference. The African renaissance must be seen in this light, especially with respect to its emphasis on the greatness of an Afro-cultural past and the transparent destiny in its resuscitation.

As Frantz Fanon states:

> Colonialism is not satisfied merely with hiding a people in its grip. . . . By a kind of perverted logic, it turns to the past of the oppressed people and distorts, disfigures and destroys it. This work of devaluing pre-colonial history takes on a dialectic significance today.[11]

One way to recover the past is to recover its *history of discourses* as well as its monuments—texts, traditions, and memories. When such discourses have already served to reinvent a past, their recovery is all the better, since it is a recovery that preaches an even deeper cycle of return and recovery. Negritude is one such discourse, hence its privileged status as the phantom trace behind Mbeki's words.

I shall seek to unfold the way in which Mbeki's words represent the renaissance of past discursive practices gradually. Note here the romanticism in Mbeki's idealization of the past:

> To perpetuate their imperial domination over the peoples of Africa, the colonizers who sought to enslave the African mind and destroy the African soul . . . in the end, they wanted us to despise ourselves, convinced that . . . we were, at least, not equal to the colonial master, were incapable of original thought and the African creativity which has endowed the world with an extraordinary treasure of masterpieces in architecture and the fine arts.[12]

Against disenfranchisement is posed return; against destruction, awakening. Hence Mbeki's harping on the gifts of past African culture and the need to rediscover these:

> We, who are our own liberators from imperial domination, cannot but be confident that our project to ensure the restoration not of empires, but the

other conditions in the sixteenth century described by Leo Africanus— of peace, stability, prosperity and intellectual creativity—will and must succeed.[13]

One finds a similar idealization of the precolonial African past in the early writings of Nelson Mandela. In Mandela's case what is idealized is the land of his forebears in the Transkei before the entry of the "white man":

> Many years ago, when I was a boy brought up in my village in the Transkei, I listened to the elders of the tribe telling stories about the good old days, before the arrival of the white man. Then our people lived peacefully, under the democratic rule of their kings and their amapakati [literally, "the middle ones," those high members of the group's regents or council], and moved freely and confidently up and down the country. . . . The structure of early African societies in this country fascinated me very much and greatly influenced the evolution of my political outlook. The land, then the main means of production, belonged to the whole tribe, and there was no individual ownership whatsoever. There were no classes, no rich or poor, and no exploitation of man by man. All men were free and equal and this was the foundation of government. Recognition of this general principle found expression in the constitution of the council . . . in such a society are contained the seeds of a revolutionary democracy in which none will be held in slavery or servitude, and in which poverty, want and insecurity shall be no more.[14]

Jacques Derrida's text on Mandela, written in praise of him in 1985 (and in praise of his praise of the laws of Kantian democracy), makes much of Mandela's praising of this old society, which, in Mandela's idealizing imagination, contains all the seeds of the future that the struggle is trying to make happen. Utopia is but a return to and exfoliation of these seeds from the past. Derrida's text does not take up the full brunt of Mandela's retrospective idealization, but the point is that for Mandela to idealize the past as the seeds of the future, as a utopia that reflects the utopia that will come, and which is reflected by it, he must project the categories according to which the future is currently being imagined back onto the past, thus rewriting it. The old society of the Transkei ends up looking like a figment from Mandela's own Marxist radical democracy: "There were no classes, no rich and no poor"; "The land, then the main means of production, belonged to the whole tribe, and there was no individual ownership whatsoever"; "All men were free and equal." These are abstractions culled from Marx's writings on the final moment of history, that moment at which the struggle is over, the state has withered away, and the aesthetics of Rousseau shine like a rainbow—although not quite like the current version of the Rainbow Nation. In this kingdom of ends, each will be equal to all others and each will inherit everything by owning nothing.

In this story, it is with the arrival of the "white man" that corruption has taken root in paradise. This too is Rousseauist: the time of the elders was the time before civilization, when all was good and everything belonged to all the people—the moment before, as Rousseau put it, one man got up and said, "This is all mine," and civil society was born. In Mandela's story, that moment when "civilization" was born in the form of inequality is datable to the arrival of the European. The great legacy of African communalism (shed of its own historical inequalities by the storyteller) is retold by Mandela from the perspective of Rousseau and Marx.

This is the point: Mandela inherits a past that consists of stories and nothing but stories. It is the past recast as a story told by the elders about their elders; it is not the past as a set of events or a set of facts. Mandela contributes to this oral history (writing the story of his life) by retelling the story in accord with his own categories and concerns. By doing so, the struggle becomes an African struggle, posed in the image of ancient Africa.

(African communalisms might well have significant features in common with the communitarian image of utopia favored in the strand of political theory that runs from Rousseau to Marx and through Marx to the present. It is the myth of their superimposition that is of concern here.)

My point is that Mandela's idealization of his own particular fragment of the African past (the society of his forefathers) is, finally, an idealization couched in the general terms of Africa. Mandela speaks of his fascination with "African societies," as if his is but an example of "African societies in general," or, more simply, of "Africa before colonialism, an Africa that reflects the future." "Everything that I know of the future," Mandela might have said, "comes from the Transkei." Which is to say, "From the stories about the Transkei that I heard from the elders." Mandela does not say this, but his words certainly suggest it. Insofar as they suggest it, the struggle that is his life is then a struggle for something to be reborn: a renaissance, indeed a renaissance of Africa taken as an abstracted and unified precolonial whole. The renaissance is a renaissance of what was already contained in "African societies in general," in their common lineage.

The question of lineage figures centrally in Mbeki's speeches. Indeed, my view is that, while an absent lineage of monuments and heroes is called upon again and again, the real heritage is *discursive*: in the history of the idea of Africa that runs from African American writings of the late nineteenth century through the long discourse of negritude. Thus the African renais sance is about a heritage of *words* more than a heritage of things. Africa is certainly a place of monuments, but it is also less monumental in structure than the Italian form or the Asiatic ones (Indian, Chinese, Cambodian), or even the Mayan. Crucial to its past are stories, oral inheritances, words. Since colonialism chronically pathologized Africa as "lacking in the monumental stuff of culture," even while relying on African artifacts to invent its modern art, one understands Mbeki's desire to harp on a monumental past. Indeed he is monumentalizing his own words, dignifying them with the power of first-generation Africanist leaders (Nkumrah, Kenyatta), but also with the depth of "the stories of the forefathers." The African renaissance monumentalizes language by speaking under the illusion that it is about an Africa of physical monuments.

The Genealogy of Race

The genealogy of the African renaissance leads from the Italian. From Italian humanism to the history of racialism to negritude, the genealogy follows.

That character and culture were specific attributes that made the peoples of the world into a humanist diversity of *peoples* was an idea as old and long-standing as the ancient Roman humanism of Seneca ("Nothing human is foreign to me") and that of the Italian renaissance. Vico and Montaigne, the two masters of renaissance humanism, had appreciated human difference with sympathy and interest (see chapter 2, "Soweto's *Taxi, America's Rib*"). Explaining human difference in terms of linguistic and cultural diversity, and by recourse to the collective histories of groups, Vico had already prepared the ground for the nineteenth-century fascination with philology. Different peoples became peoples—each with its power and glory—through their cultural trees and trees of language. The eighteenth-century thinker of nations, Gottfried Herder, believed that what lent a people its genius was its shared language. By "language" was meant the texts, artifacts, arts, stories, and language games that generally comprised their culture in its broadest sense. Language embraced the panoply of culture. It remained for the nineteenth century to interpret this through the discovery of philology, according to which languages were arranged in systematic groups along lines of broad inheritance. And so, culture became racialist at the moment when colonialism was at its apogee and people were generally being thought of as divided into "the races."

The concept of race is a complex construction, also involving the work of philosophy, biology, medicine, and other areas of thought. It has been much discussed in recent years, and I do not wish to spend time going over well-known ground. Racialism, the thesis that human difference aligns itself along the lines of the broad physical characteristics of "the races," was widely believed in the nineteenth century. By the races was meant the "yellow" or east Asian race, the "brown" or "oriental" race, the "white" or European race, the "red" or Native American race (which would have been called "Indian" at the time), and the "black" or African race.

The nineteenth century's invention of racialism sorted persons into races on cultural and linguistic grounds: in terms of lineages associated with color of skin and shape of bone. But the nineteenth century also invented modern racism of the physical type, the type that defined character directly on the basis of physical characteristic or phenotype. And the races were never thought equal, even if orientalism and Africanism might praise certain specific characteristics (cultural or physical) of brown or black peoples.

Racism in Africa was largely directed to the body of the African—the body's color, its shape, contour, size, posture, expressive gestures. In other regions of the colonial world, specifically in the Orient and the Far East, racial difference was explained through recourse to civilization: the world of monuments and scripts of the Indians and Chinese that were alternately taken as exotic monstrosities and frozen glories. However, Africa (like native America) was believed to lack any kind of civilization and was instead taken to be what Hegel called a "land of childhood."[15] Since neither scripts nor monuments were found, the African's racial difference was obsessively demarcated in terms of the modifications of the body. His body merged with the intensity of the African landscape (as if this too were a homogenous thing). And so he was constructed as a type, and the concept "African" was born. There had been no such concept until colonialism and the racialist/racist concepts it developed came along. Africa is, it is well known, the invention of the colonizer. From the first, person and landscape were merged in a syncretism of body and climate, physique and soil, brain and geography. The liminal character of much of the African continent (its deserts, heat, jungles, mountains, harshness, brilliance of sun) and the tough, angular body of the African became homogenized in European thought. It was all sweat and dust, Marlow traveling down the river, febrile and hallucinogenic. The African's body and his landscape—at once childlike and monstrous, innocent and overeroticized, gorgeous and deformed, a field of impossible resistance and uncontainment and a home of untrammeled openness to mastery—became the locus of attraction, repulsion, and definition by the epistemic regimes of colonialism. The African is an African in virtue of his physical marks and in virtue of his setting in the landscape. Getting ahead of the story, one can see how natural it seems to Mbeki that African is at once land mass (a continent) and point of origin (a human-scape).

It is easy to imagine the terrible pressure such a view had on the African and African American intellectuals of the nineteenth century, intellectuals who were usually Christian, usually believers in modernity and its canons of progress, and also suscribers (how could they not be?) to the broad outlines of racialism. Hence the importance for a writer like W. E. B. DuBois in converting the racist image of the blackness defined in terms of "the black body" into a cultural type, thus dignifying his race with its own special je ne sais quoi, its own poetic and cultural essence, in this case one that requires the *landscape of Africa* to thrive. As Kwame Anthony Appiah says in his well-known book, *In My Father's House,*[16] the move by DuBois from a physical conception of an African to a cultural conception is meant as a way of retrieving black people from racism, while also descrying their unity in a way that could include African Americans like himself. Writing as an African American implacably alienated from American life (his book *The Souls of Black Folk* came out the decade before the massively racist film *Birth of a Nation,* which was also, by the way, the year of the Russian revolution), writing and in the name of a people who are, in his time, neither free nor clear as to who they are, DuBois's project is to write African Americans into the larger scope of the "African lineage." Their home is with their people, whose culture can only thrive in its geographico-cultural location, namely, the mythological place "Africa." They are one of the ten lost tribes of the Bible, in search of their own River Jordan, somewhere between the Nile and the Zambizi. African Americans are understood to exist in a diasporic condition that can be overcome only through return to that couplet that is their origin: Africa as landscape/Africa as people. Descent means return.

Appiah notes well that the African Americans who developed the racialist theory of Africa also viewed their return to the homeland with ambivalence, since as western Christians they believed Africa to be backward, primitive, and in need of the good medicine of western modernity. Africa itself was in a great slumber that would awaken only with their return and exportation of western modernity to the slumbering colony. Thus, on the one hand, African Americans must return to the space where the great race had its place; on the other, their return will mean progress for Africa, an awakening of the race with haste to its space.

Appiah has argued with considerable conviction that DuBois's cultural racialism could not hold water—at least in anything like the way it was formulated. DuBois's theory depends on the assumption that African Americans and Africans are all "from the same racial source" to which they can be traced back. And this assumption in turn depends on the claim that their lines of lineage are everywhere clear, which they are not. The criterion of the unity of the race—the unity of *being* betwixt and between African Americans and Africans—is common lineage, for it is through the lines of lineage that cultural identity is transferred from generation to generation. However, many African Americans are the product of complex and variegated lineages, descending, for example, from West Africans and Euro-Americans (at least). Since lineage is the criterion of racial identity, these complex lines of lineage would allow African Americans to be considered as "white" or "Hispanic" or "Native American" as they are "black." Dutch "blood" would make one "white," Ghanian "blood" would make one "black." Complex lineage produces an undecidable situation, for the criterion of racial identity can go one of three ways. As Appiah says, one would therefore need another criterion to decide how to apply the criterion of lineage.

Nor are Africans immune from this problem of multiple lineage. It might be thought that Zulus have remained "pure," but how "by and large" pure must one remain to remain "pure"? According to what criterion of racial purity can this question be decided? When a Zulu culture has historically intermingled with its neighbor culture, does that disqualify it from the criterion of its racial purity or not? And who is to decide? Moreover, cultural diversity occurs in modernity even within groups that have, for all intents and purposes, remained pure, since they become urbanized, industrialized, culturally intermingled, etcetera, leading to the hybridity of Sophiatown, which the apartheid state found intolerable. Anyway, there are many kinds of blackness in Africa, with overall physical differences as great as, for example, between Jews and Russians, Italians and Egyptians. There is no one blackness; even considered physically there are many. Even if one assumes a homogenizing sweep within the "black African races of the south" (which is to assume a racialist/racist standpoint to begin with that could not, finally, be justified), one will have to encounter the Muslimization of Africa in the central and northern regions.

In point of fact, the criterion for unity of descent that turns a DuBois into a black person rather than a Dutch person has been uniformly supplied by the history of racism. The criterion has not been consistent. In the America of Jim Crow, a single drop of "black blood" was enough to ensure that one was not white. But in South Africa, mixed blood was considered "colored" rather than black or "African." A person who would be black in America might not be in South Africa. And in Brazil, that person, if "light enough," might be white ("with a little salsa"). For Jews, the criterion of membership in the set has been equally notorious, with Nazi formulae (one grandparent is enough) vastly differing from the maternal criteria that Jews themselves have set for group membership. South Africa, in a fit of expediency, declared Chinese people to be "honorary whites" during the reign of apartheid (here, racist policy was overridden on economic grounds).

For DuBois, race becomes the master concept that links a wide variety of historical identifications through an essentialist definition. His is a philosophical position on language as well as humanity: the right language for speaking of people is that of race. Race is the master language for characterizing people within peoples. It is a language capable of including all other ways we need to speak of human character and subjectivity: lines of cultural memory and cultural belonging, of creativity and depth, of similarity of belief, thought and action, of language, art, and morals—these are all sorted in terms of race. Then what of his own Christian language? Is that white or black? Is the song about the crossing of the River Jordan African or European? In this regard, he brings his Christian ambivalence to his thinking about Africa, and it is an ambivalence central to the very idea of *renaissance*. For, to repeat, Africa will engage in a renaissance only if the modern African American returns there. He is an African but also a Christian, and both are required for the rebirth of Africa. Returning to his true homeland, the African American will find himself for the first time in his right landscape (the African soil) and with his true family (Africans like himself). And, conversely, this modern Christian will bring to Africa Christian modernity (not to mention piety). Hence, the cultural baggage that the African American will bring is one that is *at odds* with his lines of descent, for it is Dutch, American, French, English, Hebrew, Greek. The African American's race is that of *modernity*, not simply "blackness," which means that his race is not essentialist, not containable through lines of descent.

A renaissance can never be explained through lines of descent, because in its very nature it always brings something new from elsewhere back to the past—like the Italian regard on the classical Greek past.

We have seen that this is exactly the problem in Mbeki's attempt to contain the English language he speaks and the English education he has within the confines of pan-Africanism, and this is, I think, the central contradiction in the construction of the idea of the African renaissance, from its inception in the African-American writings of people like DuBois. It is very close to the philosophical problem that Appiah has noted: that of the impossibility of containing lines of descent, given intermingling, which can now be called modernity.

To sum up this sketch of a genealogy: DuBois wishes to retrieve something of the broadly tolerant and capacious humanism of the Italian renaissance but can do so only through the rigid racialism of his day. Seeking a reversal of the way in which Africans have been conceived, his concept of the African race responds to their degradation while also playing out a specifically African American drama of return to the promised land. DuBois, writing from the diaspora, thus articulates a theory of race that requires return to that landscape where his race can flourish; his Africa is a romantic mythology of origins. Since return will produce rebirth—of African Americans and Africans alike, both of whom have been languishing—the idea of the African renaissance has its seeds already present in this dual picture of Africa as disease and cure, place of sleep and place of flourishing, past and destiny. The idea of a renaissance is thus articulated in terms of the concept of race, upon which it hinges. It is a picture formulated from the diaspora, which then filtrates back into Africa through the usual routes of solidarity and north-south dependency.

This racialist conception continues into the writings of negritude, which recruited the thinking of DuBois and company and put it to the task of nationalism and decolonization. The claim of a special property of Africanness, a common set of expressive forms, a poetic je ne sais quoi shared by all black people and definitive of "blackness," becomes the call to awaken a pan-African claim to sovereignty, for it is in virtue of this shared essence that difference from the colonizer is assured and the claim of communal "African" sovereignty gestates. Race is therefore central to the "aesthetics" (the poetry) of nationalist African politics.

It is not for nothing that poets are crucial to its formulation of terms, that is, of spirit. These poets speak in praise of an essential repository of expressive forms—found in the African museum, the African oral tradition, and on the African street corner—which "prove" the lineage of the race and make the spirit tremble. Senghor, the poet and statesman of negritude, is certain of such a *presence Africaine:*

> Who would deny that Africans too have a certain way of conceiving life and living it? A certain way of speaking, singing and dancing: of painting and sculpting, and even laughing and crying?[17]

It is possible to argue that this vision of a common expressive form in the diversity manifestations of African monuments and African lives is itself the clearest legacy of all from colonialism, even if uttered as an awakening from the shackles of colonialism. For it was central to the homogenizing gaze of the colonizer that he saw the colonial world of Africa as a single entity, a vast, unmodulated museum of peoples and artifacts, each of whom did the same as the other and meant the same as the other. When negritude takes over the mentality of nineteenth-century racialism and converts it into a communally reinforcing image of African brotherhood and motherhood, it cannot help but take over the homogenizing gaze that the colonizer addressed to something called "Africa." In the presumption resides the assumption, and through this mechanism of takeover, through which race becomes one's own for one's self, dependency on the concepts of the other are clear. So from the disdain for the black body in all of its modifications arises a compensatory adulation of it, with its special gestural properties, its "ways of laughing and crying."

The legacy of negritude is everywhere the phantom presence in Mbeki's language, everywhere its link to the lineage of *presence Africaine*. Since the legacy is that of an ambience, a phantom, a background, Mbeki remains vague about the extent to which 1) his image of cultural return is that of a return to the tapestry of African differences, which would have to be nonracial, or 2) a return to a single set of expressive forms. This is to his purpose, for, in being vague, his language can suggest both views while asserting neither:

> The beginning of our rebirth as a continent must be our own rediscovery
> of our soul, captured and made permanently available in the great worlds
> of creativity represented by the pyramids and sphinxes of Egypt, the stone
> buildings of Axum and the ruins of Carthage and Zimbabwe.[18]

The legacy is plural (pyramids, sphinxes, Carthage, Zimbabwe), but the "rediscovery of *our soul*" (my italics) suggests a common entity, a single "soul"—that is, a *presence Africaine*.

One can only applaud the urge toward rediscovery, granted the forced removal of African treasures to the great museums of Europe and America and the museumification of the entire continent. Indeed, yet another strategy for the disparagement of Africa was to harp on its so-called paucity, its cultural thinness. To assemble a variety of monuments and civilizations before the gaze of the world to show how much has been done there would be to go a long way toward shedding the light of ebullience on the formerly dark continent. But such a presentation would hardly present the *presence Africaine.* Rather, what would stand before the eyes of all would be a multiplicity that is, finally, "ours," only in the sense of "no longer being the property of the colonial other"—and in the sense of being a treasure trove that all Africans can share in, each in his or her own way. From one perspective, this is what Mbeki means to happen, and it is an admirable thing to mean to have happen, while from the other, this multiplicity is meant as the patrimony of a singular collective, a "we" that is unequivocally that of African nationalism.

Afro-Medici and the State

Mbeki's agenda is about the assumption and exercise of power. It is clearly a *political* one. A new president of a weak state like the South African state, which has difficulty getting things implemented, needs a rhetoric. It is part of the way weak states try to concentrate authority: through spectacle, ideology, language, gesture, and the tightening of controls. The state is weak with respect to business, with respect to its capacity to govern at regional levels, with respect to bureaucratic efficiency (in spite of/because of the size of the bureaucracy), with respect to "delivery" (of civil as well as economic rights).[19] On the other hand, the South African postapartheid state has a huge "legitimation capital." All Mandela had to do was throw the football into the stadium and the entire world cheered. The African National Congress has earned a significant degree of international approval and money in virtue of its struggle past. So the language of the African renaissance is required for two reasons: because the state is weak and because its "legitimation capital" is strong (or was, in the middle to late 1990s, when the language of the African renaissance was at its apogee). And this is a language of legitimation. In terms of politics, it is a brilliant stroke, for it accomplishes three things: First, it is a neoliberal language about facilitating free trade within the African continent, a kind of European Union language about making the flow of capital within Africa expand (through free-trade borders, stable governments, etcetera). Insofar as Africa has been deleted from globalization, it is a language about speaking to the world as a bloc power, thus gaining greater purchase over world affairs. Second, it is a language about pan-Africanist power, appealing to racialist/political sentiments widely held within the African continent that hark back to the days of Kenyatta, Nkumrah, and Luthuli, which is Mbeki's own self-idealized formation. Third, it is a stroke of the knife, appealing to Mbeki's own Africanist faction within the African National Congress at the expense of others.

The first two features of the language announce Mbeki's own centrality to the entire political field of Africa. The third sidelines competitors within South Africa, such as the more brilliant and independent Ramaphosa, who is never even mentioned during the Mbeki speech on the constitution, which Ramaphosa more than anyone else helped to negotiate into being. The language of the African renaissance prepares Mbeki's own entrance onto the continental African stage with the thrust of a Kennedy. Mbeki is the new kid on the block (from 1995 to 2000), taking control in what is currently the most powerful country on the continent, and his invention of terms of renaissance is a way of asserting his hegemony. He is the Afro-Medici, the one whose city-state aims to become hegemonic in the continual barrage of alliances—the wheeling, dealing, and violence that currently engulfs much of Africa. Recall the ambiguity in the three sentences with which this paper began, the ambiguity of a South Africa properly belonging to Africa and of a South Africa that is its own nation. In that vacillation between African communalism and national distinctiveness, a rhetoric of hegemony announces itself. Mbeki, in stating that South Africa is nothing but a variant of the larger domain of Africa, engorges and engulfs that domain.

As for the first goal of the language:

> What we have been talking about is the establishment of genuine and stable democracies in Africa, in which systems of governance will flourish because they derive their authority and legitimacy from the will of the people.
>
> The point must be made that the new political order owes its existence to the African experience of many decades which teaches us, as Africans, that what we tried did not work, that one party states and the military governments will not work.[20]

The renaissance is here stated to be an overcoming of the postindependence days of one-party regimes and rank corruption that still beset many African states, days that were encapsulated in the joke that was often told in Guinea: "We used to say plaintively, 'When will the colonization end?' But now we say, equally plaintively, 'When will the independence end?'" Mbeki, ever vigilant of this complaint, is of two minds:

> The African renaissance is upon us. As we peer through the looking glass darkly, this may not be obvious. But it is upon us.[21]

versus

> If there weren't problems there would be no need for a renaissance . . . there are problems, there will be problems.[22]

Here or in need of being here, or both, the African renaissance is a concept that converts disaster into possibility. Who could argue against the need for free trade and good governance? Who could argue against Mbeki's right to dream these ideals and to place them on the political agenda? My point is that through these words about "justice and the little people" (that is, the "Africans who are heroes"), he asserts his own, and South Africa's, hegemony.

As for the second goal of the language: what these words are certainly is an announcement of Mbeki's own appearance on the scene, and that of South Africa, as the Kennedy of the world order, with Zimbabwean leader/dictator Robert Mugabe in the role of Castro. Which is why Mbeki's words are greeted with a mixture of enthusiasm and suspicion throughout Africa, and why Mugabe has immediately seen fit to oppose Mbeki in almost every matter of state. (No doubt Mugabe has his own agenda, but that is another matter.)

As for the third goal of the language, there has been a power struggle between exiles and those who remained in the transition period, and the exiles, with Mbeki, won out. They are a cadre of persons grown up on the oaths of loyalty, the closed circle of power, the paranoia, the Stalinism of struggle movements during the second half of the twentieth century. They all lived far away from their own country for many, many years (one can blame apartheid for that, as for so much else). They developed, in the course of this, fantasies about "Africa" that naturally grow strong in those for whom distance makes the heart grow fonder and removal from the grass roots of the country breeds the incursion of fantasies. Mbeki's fantasy is the language of the African renaissance, which is also a way of replacing grass-roots action by ideology. You would never have found such a language in Ramaphosa, the acute negotiator of the constitutional process and, before that, trade unionist. His is a world of genuine reality. Mbeki's language is an exile language, like DuBois's, a language of *elsewhere.*

Certainly the language is also a smoke screen for the little that has in fact been done by the African National Congress (as of 2001), which is a weak state. Through the pomp and circumstance of highfalutin words in nothing but English the spectacle of action is conveyed. As for the smoke screen, one wonders why the retrieval of the glories of Khartoum should serve to alleviate the sufferings in Rwanda and the wars in the Congo, Rwanda, Eritrea, Angola. The thought is an aestheticization of politics worthy of the Christianity of the Italian renaissance, or better, the Baroque, which dedicated churches to the mass slaughter of infidels (which means opponents) and which had the likes of Bernini design their glorious interiors so that violence could be converted into the heights of civilization, and civilization into the symbol of triumph.

Clearly a new language, along with a new set of terms of reference, *is* politically necessary for the reentry of South Africa into the global market of supply and demand, and in postmodern times one could not find a better marketing idea than Mbeki's. Mandela could depend on his image alone to charm the world and bring dollars into South Africa, but after the passing of this saint from politics, others will need a new language, a language also well understood by those Africans who are in power and who control the fates of African affairs. When the *icon* (Mandela) fades, politics finds itself already behind the eight ball and requires compensation for its lost power to compel a nation—which the language of the African renaissance is meant to supply. Indeed, it is a language that aptly converts weakness into strength, as it does difference into solidarity, for it is one thing to go to China and beg for money (as Mbeki recently did) and quite another to go "in the name of the African renaissance" (as Mbeki recently did). This is an excellent marketing image, if not too ludicrously out of sync with the African chaos and despair that is shown every day on CNN in Hong Kong. Indeed, Mbeki's language has been picked up globally; President Clinton refers to the African renaissance. The language is also an excellent electioneering strategy as the May 1999 elections approach (see above). From this perspective, the harping on the past that one finds in the African renaissance, its mush-making of African differences into homogenized unities, its neoliberal, self-advertising agenda makes it an artifact that might have been invented by Saul Kersner. The African renaissance is the high-concept *Lost City* of politics, with its Africa created by Hollywood artisans along the lines of a Rider Haggard novel cum Disneyland.

The problem with this language is that it seeks to be the umbrella language containing all others, the *Ursprache* to which all others will be referred. And when one language rules a country, that country inherently excludes certain of its voices and reduces its capacity to respect diversity and, on a related note, to acknowledge the complexity of social reality—as the previous history of South Africa has illustrated with fatal accuracy. At present there are a number of languages and images extant in South Africa: images of rainbow nations, of a culture of reconciliation, of the need for redistribution, and of the politics of recognition. The liberal health of the nation is a matter of all of these being in play, so that each may limit the rule of the others, so that none may take on the public illusion of totality in scope. For each language is finally one that asserts the posture of one group over others, the closure of one reality vis-à-vis another, even while it claims to include that which it marginalizes. The critique of liberalism in South Africa proves that its history was not free of colonial images of natives requiring white guidance and slow improvement; liberalism was a language that reasserted the hegemony of the colonizer over his children and her pupils. The African renaissance is, similarly, not free of its own hegemonies.

(Let us remember that, up close and personal, the Italian renaissance was about power and was highly violent. Europe idealizes its own past when it thinks of the Italian renaissance apart from these terms. Where there is a monument there is beauty, but always also oppression. Who built it? How were they taxed? Who lived in it and how did they rule? Should the Italian renaissance really be the model for Africa, even in name?)

The hegemony exists at the level of the state. While preaching the African renaissance as a prelude or condition of reconciliation, it ends up looking highly communalist, and, on black lines, a fact exhibited in Mbeki's increasingly black-appointed governments. In the light of the white tribes of the past, which simply took all positions for themselves—English or Afrikaans, Afrikaans against English, English against Afrikaans—this behavior is well prepared, and can be seen from one perspective as a redress of the past (in the name of ultimate reconciliation). But given the language of the African renaissance, this modus operandi must be watched for its operatic character, the character of the black nation opposed to the liberal one. Communalism inevitably comes into conflict with liberalism at one point or another. It has already done so in the English of the African renaissance.

And the language has, in recent times, served the purpose of an absurd and horrifying attempt to concentrate state power and authority even over knowledge practices. This can be seen in the stand President Mbeki has taken in the early months of the year 2000 on HIV/AIDS. Here, I rely on work I have done with Professor Ahmed Bawa, physicist and director of the Ford Foundation Africa, and Professor Jerry Coovadia, prominent AIDS researcher and organizer of the International AIDS Conference in Durban, in July 2000. And I refer to Mbeki's astonishing proclamations that HIV does not cause AIDS, and his open letter to President Clinton to the effect that those few scientists who do not concur with scientific consensus have been politically censored by the American scientific community, and to the further effect that Africa will no longer bow down before the domination of western science, all of which have come in for considerable criticism in newsprint. Now why should Mbeki have chosen to turn the debate from implementation policy to the nature of scientific explanation per se? What was behind his adamant claims that western science is in danger of imposing its findings upon Africa in some neocolonial gesture? The former minister of health, Nkosasana Zuma, had never chosen to pronounce on scientific theory. Her claims were about the specific details of treatment: that despite the AIDS crisis in South Africa, there was insufficient evidence that AZT works well enough to justify the expense of providing it for pregnant women and rape victims (who are, in South Africa, invariably women). Zuma's decision was itself rightly the object of public furor, and was made in spite of considerable evidence from the international medical community that AZT does work—well enough, if not perfectly, to more than justify its expense, especially given the epidemiological figures about the spread of the disease in South Africa. However, it is unlikely that Zuma, who is, after all, a medical doctor, would have followed Mbeki in claiming that the so-called dissidents are correct. During the moment of the debate, she was uncharacteristically silent. Mbeki was on his own—or nearly so, for he did consult a professor of African history in the United States, Charles Geschekter, about the relationship between scientific practice, scientific truth, African history, and colonialism. The result was Mbeki's belief that, since science has deeply perpetrated itself into the history of colonialism, scientific practice and scientific truth therefore are nothing other than cultural constructions—at the same level as other representations and signs of western history. Africa would have, he came to think, to find its own scientific cures, since its diseases were different (distinctively African in symptomatic configuration) and its knowledge systems were different.

Mbeki's position is part of his larger economic agenda, an important aspect of the African renaissance. By discovering specific forms of African symptomatology, Mbeki would have shown, he believed, that HIV is caused by poverty, thus assimilating science to development theory. For those symptoms of what would be classified as a specifically African form of AIDS would be the classic symptoms of the poor—tuberculosis, sexually transmitted diseases, etcetera. This discovery would have empowered his economic goal of relating all social problems to larger issues of development and globalization, the same desires that caused him to quite eloquently confront the G8 nations in Geneva about the need for economic justice in Africa and to try to take hold of the World Conference against Racism in Durban in 2001, and discipline its anti-Zionist virulence into a detailed economic claim about "reparation for racism through increased foreign investment on the continent of Africa."

To state the obvious—about western science being trustworthy—it cannot follow from the fact that the history of science has articulated doctrines that have indeed served the purposes of racism and colonialism, that a *general* skepticism about scientific practice per se is in order, one that identifies theory in physics or medicine as "western" or "eastern" and refuses its claims in other continents like Africa. This is to reduce science to any other sort of cultural representation, which it is not. That scientific communities have accepted theories on racist or other grounds cannot be a reason to refuse or revile the process by which communities accept theories, based on mounting empirical evidence and theory construction, if only because such a refusal would render incoherent the very processes of science per se. Few would argue that, because the same medical practices that gave rise to modern surgery also contributed to the making of modern "scientific" racism, therefore surgery is a purely western imposition on the colonial world in the way that medical stereotyping of the Hottentot was. Were the president to have a kidney stone, he would no doubt trust in surgery in spite of the problematic conditions by which the nineteenth-century medical community accepted racist notions and pursued racist research programs.

What Mbeki seemed to want was a pure reduction of theory acceptance to cultural values and communities, a regionalization of science both in terms of the specifically African disease types and specifically African solutions. Since theory acceptance was a cultural matter, it would become possible for the state to broker an "agreement" between disputing theories and practitioners, which is exactly what it tried to do when it invited the dissidents and the scientific community to Pretoria to "work things out." Naturally, these groups had nothing to say to each other (debate was impossible), but the presumption was that the state could assert negotiation power over knowledge production, which would then be called "African."

The African renaissance, carried to its extreme, is evident here. For the goal is that the state, with Mbeki at the helm, assume control over knowledge production in ways that push Africanist ways of knowing beyond all limits, even those of scientific rationality ("All of this I know and know to be true because I am an African!"). The rhetoric must be understood as a call to refuse all limits on Africa as a distinctive source of knowledge.

No doubt the diverse peoples of South Africa have all kinds of local knowledge that has been repressed by master discourses of colonialism, and their relations to science are fertile topics for research. However, the reduction of science to cultural knowledge and state power is its destruction.

Hence, the African renaissance is behind the Mbeki stance in three related ways: 1) in terms of cultural politics and the desire for postcolonial, uniquely African solutions; 2) in the desire for the state to assume control over socially relevant knowledge production; and 3) in the desire to assimilate the HIV pandemic to the need for developmental and globalization agendas.

It is an irony that at the very moment when the president was telling the world that HIV does not cause AIDS and accusing America in particular of scientific censorship, his own government was heavily invested (through Professor Makgoba and the Medical Research Councils) in the search for a vaccine to prevent the spread of HIV. This harks back to the uneasy relationship the state has with decentralized research, of which I spoke in this book's introduction, for it allows science to progress within South Africa in decentralized form while according the state ideological prestige (so Mbeki thought) and the capacity to broker scientific truth in the manner of political negotiation. Only when the negotiation failed, and failed publicly, did the state become openly antagonistic to the Medical Research Council, which it now viewed as a competitive threat.

Bawa, Coovadia, and I wrote an article for the *Sunday Independent* in which these themes were developed, and received a blistering response from the minister of health, Dr. Tshabalala-Msimang, and associate, whose most interesting remarks were to call Bawa and Coovadia important indigenous South African intellectuals who had gone astray (presumably from their inherent "indigeneity"). I was left out, being on no one's count, not even my own, an African, nor anyone who had had any role in the struggle. However, it *was* crucial to the minister that Bawa and Coovadia, both of whom are fourth-generation Muslim immigrants (from the same area of Gujarat in India, it so happens), should be called "indigenous." For there was little more to the concept of "indigeneity" used by the minister than "person of color with excellent struggle credentials." It is all part of the Africanist rhetoric: distinctively African persons are communalized through the antiapartheid struggle, and then in virtue of the property of Africanness, agree on matters of knowledge. When disagreement is shown, as it was by Bawa and Coovadia, this means they are compromising their indigeneity. Behind the virulence of the minister's response was a call to bring them back into the fold. By their remarks, they had challenged their own place in the African renaissance.

Many people spoke out strongly against the Mbeki position during the Durban 2000 conference, most significantly Nelson Mandela, who gave a moving speech about decency, delivery, and negotiation, specifically targeting the need to cut down on infant-mother transmissions of the disease through the use of the drugs AZT and nevirapine. The effects have so far been nil. The government has reneged on its position about the causal question, but with enough hedging to leave it all unclear. "Yes, HIV is a cause of AIDS," it now admits, "but so is poverty, unemployment, etcetera." These are claims that, taken correctly, are true, but their point is to obscure the issue that HIV is *the* medical cause—the virus itself, producing the fatal condition known as full-blown AIDS within five to seven years (as a norm and without the preventive help of antiviral cocktails)—while poverty and unemployment do not of themselves cause AIDS. The point of this obfuscation is (1) to avoid the intervention of a program of drugs to reduce infant-mother transmission; (2) to avoid the interrogation of black African sexual practices, which profoundly contribute to the high rates of transmission (practices like multiple sexual partnerships without the use of condoms, and "dry sex," in which the woman uses herbs to dry out her vagina); and (3) to avoid health interventions that would reduce the spread of sexually transmitted diseases, which in turn produce lesions that increase probability of infection during intercourse.

It may well be that the knowledge issue, posed by the African renaissance, was in part a disguise for a more insidious, problematical agenda, a Malthusian one. Let us assume that the state will, it believes, not be able to provide for the millions of orphaned children who, in ten years time, will be on the streets of South Africa, given the deaths of their mothers and other relatives. The choice is therefore horrible in its starkness: either one denies anti-retrovirals to pregnant mothers to prevent these millions of orphans from coming into being, or one floods the society with them and their terrible lives. Now, if this is the choice—millions of orphans living degraded, suffering lives and causing social havoc, or their quicker deaths—*and* you choose the latter, you had better never say so in public. (In any event, there will be, according to the most recent report of the Medical Research Council, two million orphans by the year 2010.) Transparent debate about the Malthusian issue is virtually impossible in a culture genuinely committed to human rights and dependent upon legitimations concocted in terms of the language of rights. This is because the choices are so stark: the unaffordable (drugs for pregnant women with the disease to cut transmission) or the condemnation of a million children to die of the disease. So what you do instead is create a smoke screen, and the knowledge question is a perfect subterfuge. Instead of facing the terrible moral issue (Is it better to try to offer life to the unborn, even if it may be precarious? Can the society try to invent ways of making these orphans part of a sustainable world? Is it always better to allow life to happen, or is it sometimes better to kill it off?), you create havoc in the halls of science by denying that HIV causes AIDS.

I am not saying this is the government's position; I am saying I *suspect* it probably is. I suspect it on the basis of its unequivocal refusal to even entertain the use of anti-retrovirals, and on the basis of its general hostility to allowing debate on the subject in public. The government's refusal of transparency means that the options are never adequately considered by relevant health stakeholders, including citizens affected with the disease. Drugs *are* affordable, mass death *is* preventable. The absorption of a million orphans may be sustainable (it is hard to tell, apart from scenario planning, which is highly suspect). Even if it were not, a commitment to saving the lives of the as yet unborn could be placed on the table of foreign-aid negotiations; foreign nations might respond in a crisis, especially if South Africa were to ally itself with the current "campaign against terrorism," thus earning "points."

It needs to be said that it is hard to make sense of the ongoing antagonism of the government to HIV/AIDS work. We all scratch our heads at the ostensible irrationality of it. As recently as September 2001, the Medical Research Council presented a factual report dramatizing the current landscape of the disease in South Africa, which the government, yet again, waffled over. The Sunday, September 29, 2001, newspapers were full of charges that Mbeki is trying to reduce the AIDS budget even now. Some say this is in the name of his young African male constituency, which sees the regulation of their sexual practices as a deep insult to the freedom of the African male body. This perceived threat runs deep in the country, and is associated with the failure of the society to address gender issues (in spite of constitutional directives). However, since half of the ANC constituency is women, it is hard to see how this is a deciding factor on political grounds. It reduces to a refusal of men in power to accept limitations on their own sexual practices, limitations that arrive, ironically, just at the postcolonial moment when the black body is meant to be freed from former racist degradation. There is little worse than finding your sexuality a harbinger of disease and degradation just at the moment it is meant to be freed from the castigating gaze of colonial, apartheid power. Mbeki himself claims that he wishes to reduce the AIDS budget for another reason: because he believes in the privatization of health care. This would make sense, given the neoliberal agenda of the ANC, but it is socially mad. You do not suddenly privatize health care in the middle of a disease crisis any more than you suddenly privatize the military in the middle of a war. One suspects that the government wishes to be rid of what it sees as a hopeless drain on its state resources, and that it has made, yet again, a non-transparent decision that sustainability is a matter of cutting losses: those employed by big business will get anti-retrovirals because big business will (or already has) instituted its own health-care programs to keep its work force going. The poor will, meanwhile, die fast.

As of October 7, 2001, there is opening up a split in the African National Congress about the HIV/AIDS issue, with many challenging Mbeki and working behind the scenes to "deliver" on the AIDS issue (as the newspapers put it). One hopes it continues, for the effect of Mbeki's persistent antagonism to state intervention, and to the research agendas of the Medical Research Council and other decentralized bodies, has been to undermine health clinics, social programs, and NGOs within the South African provinces and cities. These are finding decreased participation by local populations in their projects. People seem to be thinking, "It is all a hopeless matter, and the HIV question is so vague that we do not know, we are not sure, anyway, if it is all a matter of poverty." And then they do not come anymore to the clinics. In a context of crisis—mounting rates of infection of at least 15 percent (39 percent of the overall population of KwaZulu-Natal is infected) and increasing numbers of patients exhibiting full-blown AIDS—this message is disastrous, cataclysmic. Some say the bell curve of increasing infection rates had topped out. Others say it has not. We do not know (as of July 2001).

Finally, what the government's position does is make it impossible for South Africa to truly investigate ways in which indigenous health systems (sangomas, herbal medicines, etcetera) and, especially, the authority invested in them by local populations, could become used in partnership with modern medical and sociological techniques for better prevention and management of the disease. The African renaissance, so formulated, radically separates the indigenous from the modern, the Africanist from the global, and so prevents hybridization of both in creative ways. This is no renaissance; it is pure authoritarian doctrine by a state that increasingly defines itself in monolithic, hegemonic terms of leadership and submission.

The position substitutes cultural politics for good governance. It shows the dangers of the African renaissance, which is exactly a form of cultural politics. It shows how the assertion of what look like cultural rights turns out to violate human rights in other respects. It also shows how the language contains the deep desire for Mbeki to concentrate state authority, here by actually brokering scientific truth.

The African renaissance must instead be about building partnerships between communities and the generation of new knowledge. It must be about the exploration of a diversity of ways of knowing, each in the light of the other, all in the light of context. None of these ways of knowing is the same, or has the same criteria of truth. None is free of complication. But to reduce them all to a single concept of state arbitration is to fail to understand what an expert system is, and, on a related note, what a local system of knowing, with its own kind of authority, is.

What is at stake in the African renaissance is a debate about concepts of race and racially constructed practices in South African life. These are problematical because they are about constituent power based in race and because they repeat ideologies that make it impossible to generate new knowledge to solve new problems. The African National Congress may be analyzed as (1) committed to a nonracialist liberalism, which is reflected in the constitutional structure of South Africa, and (2) committed to a black-consciousness position about black identities. It is the unstable and unholy alliance between these positions (both of which must be held, and each of which is finally inconsistent with the other) that defines its ideological scope, and has always defined its ideological scope. It is an irony that the constitution Mbeki praises bends over backward to deracialize its language and speaks of "healing divisions" in its preamble, while Mbeki, its praise poet, talks a language at odds with this spirit of liberalism. The Equity Bill, which mandates that persons of color and women be appointed to jobs if "appointable" according to the job description, even if there is a "white person" who might be "better," mandates this explicitly because such groups have been historically disadvantaged. This bill, whose far-reaching economic implications further state that such persons be appointed if "trainable within a reasonable amount of time and given a reasonable amount of resources," even if they can't do the job at the time of their appointment, also acknowledges that if and when redress is achieved (let us hope it can be), the bill falls away. For were it not to fall away, it would end up producing a new version of inequality, favoring "persons of color and women" and continuing a version of racism.

Semper aliquid novi ex Africa? Since the AIDS debacle has become explicit, like a looming cataclysm, there has been little talk about the African renaissance, which would be, to say the least, insensitive as people (citizens) begin to die in droves.

And yet the dialogue remains as a cultural politics. The explicit nonracialism of the South African constitution and the new liberal society require Mbeki to speak the language of racialism in a secret code. This underground dialect empowers a new black constituency and is part of the power politics of his increasingly racialized administration. But what

Mbeki's secret dialect raises is the larger issue of the role of race, racialism, and racism more generally in the new South Africa: of how people want to see themselves in terms of racial categories, of what they mean, of debates around them, and of what nonracialism is in South Africa today. And what the proper language of good governance is in the light of these concerns.

4

Racial and Nonracial States and Estates

The Persistence of Race in the New South Africa

Presenting a paper to the University of Natal History Seminar in April 2000, the South African sociologist Gerry Mare began in this way:

> In 1985 acting president of the then-banned and exiled African National Congress, Oliver Tambo, was asked, at a press conference, what was meant by the liberation organisation's commitment to "non-racialism" rather than "multi-racialism." His rambling answer was reproduced in the ANC journal *Mayibuye*, in one of the extremely rare references to race or even to "non-racialism" in that publication:
>
>> "There must be a difference. That is why we say non-racial. We could have said multi-racial if we had wanted to. There is a difference. We mean non-racial, rather than multi-racial. We mean non-racial [because it implies the refusal of] . . . racism. Multi-racial does not address the question of racism. Non-racial does. There will be no racism of any kind therefore no discrimination that proceeds *from the fact that people happen to be members of different races.* That is what we understand by non-racial."
>
> Such a clearly unthought out answer comes as a surprise from the leader of a movement which has prided itself on its commitment to non-racialism, during the years of struggle against apartheid, and in the process of subse-

quent reconstruction; as, must be said, is the reproduction of the statement. The ANC has used such a commitment as a feature to distinguish it from other anti-apartheid organisations.[1]

Mare's words may be complemented by a remark made at the seminar by another academic, who also, like Mare, had been deeply involved in the struggle against the system of racial estates called apartheid, and who almost blurted out (according to my reconstruction):

"I spent twenty years of my life fighting for the ideal of a non-racial society, and it isn't going to happen. If I could take back those twenty years I would do so, for those in power, and indeed most South Africans do not want such a society."[2]

This is a man who was deeply involved in trade-union organizations, and spent time, like Mare, in jail. So for him, like Mare, the stakes are huge. He finds himself suddenly in a category as otiose as that which he was in before: the white category, a whitey, a guy who is still of a type, now a marginalized type, a type with economic power still, but little strong political identity. He hates this, knows it is wrong, knows in his bones it does not do the society any good, knows that things would be better were it not so: that was what he did the work for, that is what he went to jail for.

Oliver Tambo's remarks were about the overriding importance of abolishing the system of racial estates that structured, and whose legacy continues to inflect, every aspect of South African society. Tambo writes from the struggle, and it is not clear how *he* envisions the future (what *he* knows in his bones). We do not, unfortunately, know what Tambo would have said, were he alive and part of that seminar in the year 2000. What, then, is race today, in South Africa, and perhaps elsewhere? How should racial labels best play themselves out now, in our current modes of life, if not "metaphysically and for eternity"? And for whom? Is belonging to a race, after the end of racism, meant to mean nothing more than having a certain skin color and bone structure, or is it meant to imply the continuation of human racialism—between the African, the Indian, the San (formerly described by the politically incorrect term of "bushman"), and the White—on deeper cultural and linguistic grounds, but in a new system of estates based on racialistic equality?

The constitution speaks of race purely in terms of historical inequality. Protective of diversity, the constitution mandates instruction in all the eleven official languages, as if taking a page out of work by the philosopher Charles Taylor, who has argued that liberal commitments to equality and autonomy must in at least some instances defer to the proposition that sometimes individual liberty can flourish only when group identity is preserved, and group identity may mean building special rights into the constitution of the state for such groups. His example is French instruction by Quebecois instructors in Quebec, which, he argues, is needed to preserve group identity, which is in turn the prerequisite for individual liberty.[3] Whether his individual case is reasonable or not is less important than the principle of his reasoning: that there may be (and indeed are) certain cases for which liberty requires special minority rights codified in law. In this vein the South African constitution also mandates that the flow of information take place in all the eleven official languages. This is an impossible mandate to adequately fulfill, given the limited funding for state broadcasting, but it is, in my view, a just mandate from the conceptual point of view. What the constitution emphatically refuses to mandate are special rights based in race: from the constitutional perspective, such special rights would be as otiose as the apartheid state itself was. I have said earlier that the Equity Bill—not part of the constitution, but a law clearly in its spirit—is about redress on the basis of historical disadvantage. Since historical disadvantage is clearly the result of a racist past, and everybody knows it, blackness (understood as about people of color rather than black Africanness) is favored from the perspective of redress. However, once target goals for equality of employment are reached, the bill will, in the fullness of time, become obsolete. The important point is that there is no equivalent idea about ultimate obsolescence for cultural rights, linguistic rights, even certain "traditional" rights. No one is saying that instruction or broadcasting take place in all the eleven languages *only* until everyone learns good English. On the contrary, it is partially against the fact that everyone knows that English is increasingly the universal medium for communication and economic advancement that protection of other languages is mandated. Again, the actual problems are real: what often happens is that the good schools teach in English while poor rural schools teach in Zulu or Xhosa, thus perpetuating Thabo Mbeki's "two nations." However, my point is that the difference between cultural rights and racial preference is, from the constitutional perspective, one of a *right* on the one hand and an unfortunate historical necessity on the other. No one is saying—no one should say—that instruction should allow people with black skins to learn exclusively with others of black skin, or worse, white with white.

Constitutional liberalism is about liberty and autonomy, and it is a matter of autonomy and liberty how, within the guidelines set forth in that document, race is to be reconceived and reconstructed. Whether black nationalism, nonracialism, or something new are options in civil and political society as ideas, modes of allegiance, forms of social bonding—*these* are the things about which democracy must converse. They are things of such sensitivity and historical legacy that one could hardly expect consensus, now or in the immediate future. So the first feature of the new racial estate is that it is an estate of dissensus guided by constitutional laws about racism, redress, and the like. This is a principle every citizen must assent to, although whether they do, and what the constitution even means to them, is highly opaque.

The second feature is that, whatever else anyone may say, South Africa is a profoundly overracialized society. It could hardly be expected to be otherwise, given the past. When race becomes a marker of every aspect of life, the rich languages, concepts, ideals, affiliations, and emotions people have about things are straitjacketed—as they would be by any singularity that cannibalizes the human mind, encroaching itself in our every thought and action. South Africa is racially obsessed. When the philosopher Jacques Derrida gave a lecture at the University of Natal in August 1998, the *Natal Witness*, a left-liberal newspaper of impeccable credentials, reported the lecture with a description beginning, "Derrida's lecture . . . attended mostly by white people . . . ,"[4] as if this categorization of it was crucial to how people ought to think about it and, indeed, understand its relevance to "the new South Africa." Race, a virtual fetish item in South Africa, veers between being an item of direct confrontation and one of hostile silence. It is something that every South African lives with every day, although not in the same way; something every South African learns to ignore, subdue, maintain, resist, subvert, capitalize upon, identify with, refuse, displace, proclaim, split off. Every kind of illusion, false consciousness, hardening of the arteries, nervous breakdown, shame, guilt, and pleasure has been taken in its wake, for race, along with the class structure it has been so closely associated with (and remains so closely associated with, in spite of changes), is something you cannot, finally, avoid: it is part of every inflection in the South African form of life.

The third feature of race in the new South Africa is its direct connection to economic inequality. So long as economic inequality continues to stratify the country along racial lines, there can be no solution to the race problem. The solution, it follows, is not simply internal redress, for redress is all well and good in a contained way; but when a country loses a million jobs in a year, its fate is not in its own hands. Globalization, foreign investment—these things will be crucial in the buildup of a middle class that will, finally, lead to a gradual process of integration in ways no one can predict, thus changing the concepts people have about race, again in ways no one can predict. Mbeki is right to pressure the G8 Summits to deal with the African problem. In this regard he is speaking both as a black Africanist, and hence a racialist/communitarian, but also as a genuine liberal. No one said historical actions could always be analyzed as rational or consistent.

There is no question that the history of racism has helped to produce and sustain global economic inequality. However, if the World Conference against Racism (Durban, September 2001) is any kind of bellwether, the topic of racism has become in the "south" so overwrought with multiple political, social, moral, cultural, and economic agendas that it has collapsed as a delineable subject into a mass of rantings and ravings. Needless to say, this is not the best tactic for any particular improvements in the instances of racism that remain throughout the world, nor for addressing the systemic implications of racism, past and present, for global economic justice. Moreover, racism has become the rallying point for fundamentalist identity politics, which are themselves inevitably racist, simply using the language of racism (anti-Zionism) to achieve mass fundamentalist aims.

South African public responses to the horrific destruction of the World Trade Center have, according to an article in the *Sunday Independent* (September 23, 2001), also divided to an extent along racial lines. A significant percentage of black African students at Wits University who were polled believe South Africa should not stand in solidarity with the United States because it is a "white country." White students stand in solidarity with the United States (because they are "white"?). The point is that the poll has once again to assume that racial categories are the relevant ones for the polling process. And, unfortunately, they remain so. Racialism in South Africa approaches the preposterous.

There is presently little consensus in South Africa about race, nor about how it should be understood in the fight against racism.

More particular to South African politics is the fourth feature of race: race has become the new currency of political infighting, just as it was in the past. This transfer of the template of the past into the current arena is a "gloves off" situation in which, when the current government is criticized, it responds by claiming that the criticizing parties are (if white, Indian, or even colored) racist. The new strategy is to blame your opponent for racism when you are losing the argument. And this is hardly a way to overcome "the race problem." It is a reracialization of the country, which—whether one's proclivity is, finally, for a multiracial society, a nonracial society, or a reracialization of society along, for example, the lines of the African renaissance—cannot be deemed acceptable. There are moral as well as constitutional guidelines for racial practices. On a related note, state power is being concentrated by racialist discourses. Thus, the Human Rights Commission went at the South African media in a most virulent way, accusing them of racism and interrogating them, while business was left to its own devices. This is not only a strategy for attacking the weak (when, perhaps, you are too weak to attack the strong, or the substance of your state authority is in a situation of Gramscian weak revolution to facilitate the growth of capital). It is also an attack on the autonomy and robustness of civil society per se. So racialization cannot happen at the expense of civil society, since the freedom and liberty of individuals and groups, mandated by the constitution to come to new thoughts and attitudes about race, depend on there being a civil society robustly in place where this crucial aspect of the conversation of democracy can take place. (In newspapers and on television, for example.)

Skepticism about Race

The question of how to deal with current race ideas and practices is not at all identical with the more abstract, philosophical question about whether there are, in fact, any races. If there aren't any, it might still be important to speak the language of race for a variety of specific historical reasons. Conversely, even if there are races, it might be the better part of practical wisdom and justice to deracialize racial language and practice, following, for example, the language of the South African constitution. However, the abstract philosophical question turns out to inflect practical issues about race in surprising ways. I will therefore turn to it, with the expectation of returning to the South African moment in the light of its results.

Are there races? From the philosophico-cultural perspective, race has formed a heterogeneous class of items. But it has been a kind of master concept of modernity to have had the presumption to claim that this class of racially diverse items can be known, understood, and, importantly, evaluated in terms of an overall concept of "the races." Naturally, the right concept was one's own, and one owned the license to use it like a gun. My point is that the epistemology of race specified a master concept that could sort everything we wanted to know about race into a single systematic arrangement. And so the peoples of the world became knowable. Horribly so. The role of philosophy in the production of the illusion of a single perspective or master concept has been as important as that of medicine or anthropology: when Conrad states that "all Europe contributed to the making of Kurtz," he really means it, and he is absolutely right, since such fundamental epistemologies are the result of synergies between all quarters. Even those philosophers who argued in the nineteenth century against (then) current racial norms tended to do so on racialized grounds, as DuBois did of racism, and Nietzsche, whom DuBois had probably read as a student of philosophy at the University of Berlin, did of contemporary German anti-Semitism, which he deplored as the expression of cultural weakness and self-immolation, but which he deplored on *racialized* grounds. The German character had become, in Nietzsche's own mind, a debased racial type, a pale image of its great and noble Aryan forebears from the days of early Greek culture. Preaching a European renaissance, if you will, Nietzsche did so through lines of philological descent. To overcome its mortified condition, language would have to return to its authentic and noble past, a past before the time of the fatal Judeo-Christian religious cocktail (that of the wine and the wafer), a time in which language was the guardian of nobility. This return would partly drive self-overcoming individuality, whose creativity the modern world needed. This racialistic construction is that of the African renaissance today, which remains, if uncomfortably, within the system of concepts set by the nineteenth century and its overriding ideas of race. As does the white liberal, again so called in racial terms, whose enlightenment images of equality beyond all stereotypes, including the racial ones, themselves depend on the idea that race is "only skin deep" once the history of prejudice is swept away. Such ideas remain wedded to master concepts that are unexplored.

In contrast to this presumption of power and authority, perhaps the most illustrious recent philosophical position taken about race is the liberal one (with which I have much sympathy and from which I have learned much). It is Appiah's. There are, Appiah concludes, no races. Race is an illusion. Appiah's conclusion, which is a philosophical conclusion to a philosophical argument, is connected to his larger vision of humanity in terms of nonexclusivity, diversity, multiple identity, cosmopolitanism, and anti-essentialism. These attributes of Appiah's vision of modernity are also a plea to Africa to liberalize itself, to get itself off the hobbyhorse of negritude, pan-Africanism, and black consciousness and to revitalize itself through a truly liberal self-conception, which would respect its own internal diversity. Naturally, the exigencies of political states to hold onto power in a context of massive social chaos and poor economic circulation—along with the ascendancy of state tribalism, favoritism, and corruption (what Claude Ake calls the privatization of the state for a small elite at the expense of civil society) in many first-generation postcolonial African states—is very much on Appiah's mind.

My view is that the liberal cosmopolitanism and the critique of first-generation African politics stand, even if Appiah's philosophical conclusion—there are no races—is a bit too pat. Whether Appiah's work fails to consider the importance of those rights that go beyond constitutionalism (economic rights, for example) is something I do not wish to discuss here. He is a philosopher, not a political scientist. It is with the conclusion "there are no races" that I am exclusively concerned.

We have already encountered the first part of his argument earlier in this book. It is the argument against DuBois's claim that race can be given cultural definition in terms of heritage. Appiah's argument is, recall, that given the hybridity of so many African-Americans like DuBois himself, heritage could, considered abstractly, be decided in a number of contradictory ways. DuBois could be Dutch, European, white, black, etcetera. A further criterion is needed to decide in favor of his belonging to the black, or African, race, and this criterion cannot be found in heritage itself. (I would add that such criteria usually come from the history of racism.)

The second part of his argument is about genetics, that is, about the claim that race can be given a physiological definition in terms of genetic difference. Appiah writes before the conclusion of the Human Genome Project, which strongly supports his views, since whatever else is true, racial differences, if there are any (and I leave this open), will be far smaller than differences running betwixt and between human populations at large. That is totally clear. There is no overall concept of race that will mark differences in ways greater than general differences between any population groups, taken as a random sample, in a place like America or South Africa. End of story.

Appiah's argument that there are no races requires a bit of stage-setting. Genetic differences are marked by different sequences of DNA in the chromosome. Certain loci, or gene markers in a sequence of genes comprising a certain chromosome, admit of such differences, while others are invariant among all humans. Those sites where different genes can be found in different persons are called alleles. According to Appiah's stage-setting, research has shown that the chances of any two humans having the same gene at a given locus is 85.2 percent. In other words, humans have genetic codes that are largely alike—a not unexpected result. The chances, by contrast, of Caucasian Britishers (which may or may not be the same as Caucasians generally) having the same genes at the same loci are 85.7 percent, suggesting that racial difference (between Caucasians and other "races") increases genetic differences by 0.5 percent. Which seems like a small amount.

The significance of this small percentage figure becomes less clear when it is pointed out that the overall difference between the genetic codes of humans, taken as a whole, and apes is less than 2.0 percent, or, at most, four times the difference between the races. Such a figure, taken by itself, suggests that within the range of 0.5 percent, massive human difference at both higher and lower levels could be found, which is why genetics can so easily be taken to imply results that are, in fact, uncertain. However, in principle, 0.5 percent could mark large differences between the races, and it could mark small ones. In itself, there is no implication that the absolute differences marked would be small.

Having set the stage, Appiah's argument has two parts. First:

> To establish that . . . race is relatively unimportant in explaining proportion of differences in loci on the chromosome, is not yet to show that race is unimportant in explaining cultural difference. It could be that large differences in intellectual or moral capacity are caused by differences at very few loci, and that at these loci, all (or most) black-skinned people differ from all (or most) white-skinned or yellow-skinned ones. As it happens, there is little evidence for any such proposition and much against it.[5]

And second:

> But suppose we had reason to believe . . . [the above assumption]. In the biological conception of the human organism, in which characteristics are determined by the pattern of genes in interaction with environments, it is the presence of the alleles (which give rise to these moral and intellectual capacities) that accounts for the observed differences in those capacities in people of similar environments. So the characteristic racial morphology— skin and hair and bone—could be a sign of those differences only if it were (highly) correlated with those alleles [loci where one finds different genes in the different groups of people]. Since there are no such strong correlations, even those who think that intellectual and moral character are genetically determined must accept that *race* is at best a poor indicator of capacity.[6]

Thus there are two points at which evidence is lacking for racial differences (biogenetically given) at the higher levels. First, one would have to assume that a small number of loci would produce significant differences in higher functions, and furthermore that at these sites there are alleles (different genes in different human subgroups). There can be little doubt that within the human species there are all kinds of significant differences, biogenetically given, with respect to the many significant capacities that comprise intelligence. Some people are evidently so far more creative than others with respect to this capacity, or some are so markedly more facile at analytical thinking, logic, interpretative thinking, twists of language, etcetera, that it is unreasonable to think that all such differences are due to environment. Especially since within almost identical environments, one finds the same level of difference (between, say, people who can draw and people who can't) that one finds between people of markedly different environments. So Appiah cannot be disputing the brute fact of difference, biogenetically given, between various humans. At best, he is disputing that these differences are due to a small number of loci. About this, even at the close of the human-genome project, with every bit of DNA mapped, it is highly unclear how many loci control what aspects of higher difference, nor how to divide human intelligence into "aspects" (nor—beyond a certain point—what is "higher" and what "lower" across the immense range of human abilities and their varying contexts of application).

So far nothing has been said about race per se, since such differences could be randomly spread throughout the human population (which is likely for many such differences). This brings us to the second part of the argument, namely that the differences under consideration would have to be "strongly correlated" with what we take to be the races. And this means that they would have to be strongly correlated with those genes in the human population that define this race or that race on the basis of "the grosser features" of skin color and the like—for which there is no evidence. Hence the conclusion: "Since there are no such strong correlations, even those who think that intellectual and moral character are genetically determined must accept that race is at best a poor indicator of capacity."

This argument is convincing against the racialist/racist who believes (assumes) there *is such strong evidence.* However, it is less convincing if taken to argue for its conclusion, namely that there are no races (the argument being that biology is a "poor indicator" of race). Appiah's assumption that there must be a "strong correlation" between the relevant loci (controlling differences in intelligence) and those controlling gross differences in racial anatomy is too strong. It remains within the framework of the old racial stereotypes, according to which either blacks (or Jews or Chinese) all (or mostly) share the same properties (as in: they are all so musically talented/funny/clever/stupid by nature). What is a more likely scenario of racial difference at the higher level is a weak correlation between anatomy and higher properties, with, say, 20 percent of group X having the relevant alleles for property Y, or, alternately, group X having 20 percent more chance, statistically, of exhibiting these alleles than other groups. Weak correlation must be enough of a correlation to be significant (0.0003 percent is probably not enough, 20 percent probably is). Alternately, weak correlation means a larger percentage of correlation than that of other groups, where again, how much larger the percentage must be remains vague. Scenarios for weakly correlated higher differences might well be, as Lucius Outlaw elsewhere puts it,[7] inviting on grounds of biodiversity. They would also concur with expectations regarding small differentials in natural selection that different human subgroups have accreted in the light of their different histories (assuming sufficiently clear lines of descent, which, in some cases, I think, can be assumed in broad terms). Within the huge range of abilities and their interrelations that constitute the family of things called human intelligence or intelligent behavior, these differences would not, one supposes, be confined to the four broad racial grounds that the nineteenth century fetishized, but throughout many human subgroups. Would such biodiversity be so terrible? Would it be grounds for racism? I think not. The key would be to reclaim biodiversity from its legacy of racist "implication" were such differences established.

The issue of correlation is connected to the way in which Appiah sets forth the kind of genetic scenario he believes relevant to the racial question. His starting point, we have seen, is a scenario according to which a small number of loci controlling significant aspects of intelligence must then be correlated to genes for differences in skin and bone. He says strongly correlated; I suggest, more likely, weakly. However, the issue of strong or weak correlation may be posed regarding another kind of genetic scenario that would be equally likely, and for which the evidence is less clear. Consider what Appiah means by a "small number of loci." One way to understand this is as a percentage figure. Since the total percentage of difference between Caucasoid and non-Caucasoid gene pools is 0.5 percent, and since some, if not all, of that 0.5 percent has to control differences in skin and bone, that would leave less than 0.5 percent of the loci available to mark higher differences, which is a small percentage overall. But it is less small if understood not as a percentage figure, but as an absolute number (the number of actual loci that would be available), since it is a small percentage of a very large number. The total number of genes that make up a human being and that are contained in human cells was thought at the time Appiah was writing to equal one hundred thousand. It turns out to be far less, but let us carry through the argument, based on his figures, for thought purposes. The lesser number is not crucial here.

So 0.5 percent of this number is five hundred, leaving five hundred genes to mark whatever differences there are between "the races": lower and/or higher. Clearly some (if not all) of those genes have to mark the obvious differences of skin and bone, which no one denies. So five hundred is an outer limit on the number of genes that might mark higher racial differences, if there are any. This limit figure occasions the following possible scenario: of the total number of genes that would be potentially available to control differences in higher functions between the races (less than five hundred), it is not a few at a "small number of loci" that do the controlling (Appiah's scenario), but instead a fair number of them (say, 250) that mark higher differences. These are, moreover, distributed throughout the chromosomes in some obscure pattern, the key being that a human must have all of them (the whole pattern) for that difference to be marked, rather than merely *some* of them. Such would be a kind of interactionist picture of the genes (one requires them all as a system in order for the specific characteristic to result). Now, this scenario might well be very hard, if not impossible, to discover, for outside of the racially relevant population, all of the relevant genes would be found. It is simply that they would seldom, if ever, be found as a *complete pattern*. Person A would have 70 percent of them, person B another 30 percent, person C 10 percent, person D none at all. The relevant race alone would exhibit all of them, in some strong or, more likely, weak correlation to its markings for skin and bone. Indeed, taken gene by gene, the racial group might have no greater likelihood to have any particular gene than at least one other human subgroup. It is only that no other human subgroup will have *all of them* in the same degree as the race in question. I call this indirect correlation between higher and lower functions, since it is the correlation of an interactive pattern with racial anatomy.

The detection of this pattern would be made more difficult still if it is assumed that the pattern is weakly correlated with racial anatomy. Imagine about 25 percent of the population having the complete pattern, as opposed to, say, 10 percent of another group. We now have the scenario in which each of the individual genes comprising the pattern is found in equal percentage among at least one other group, the complete pattern is found in only 25 percent of the relevant group, and it is found in 10 percent of at least one other racial group. This is the question: how will we know what the pattern is, so that we can identify if and whether it is racially distributed? Only if the pattern is already identified as an interactive set can it be correlated, or not correlated, with racial groups. How can the pattern be determined? To determine it from behavioral evidence, reading back from the social behavior of people to their genes, is fraught with the usual perils that have to do with reading biology as the inner script of environment, with no gaps in between. To determine it by first isolating the five hundred genes (the 0.5 percent) that are distinctive of the race, subtracting those that control anatomy, and, if lucky, working from there, assumes that these five hundred genes are transparently determinable as the racially distinctive ones, when in fact the scenario I have set out precludes this (given the distribution of the genes that control the pattern throughout other populations, and the genes' weak correlation with the race).

Alternately, the route would be to identify the pattern independently of any racial group (any human who has it is marked in the relevant way), and then work up a picture of its distribution throughout human subgroups, racial and/or other. Given the results of the Human Genome Project, it might be the case that further research would be able to detect such a specific gene set, and it might not, given the potentially subtle interactive quality of the relevant genetic "subsystem." Even if detected, the evidence might be so general as to allow for massive environmental influence in the causal chain between having the genes and expressing the characteristic.

Such problems in detection make it possible that patterns exist, which may or may not be racially correlated, and which science, as it is currently practiced, may or may not be able to detect. Alternately, science as it is currently practiced may identify genuine patterns, but at levels of generality that allow for huge environmental input in the causal chain between genes and overt behavior. One scenario is therefore that there may be races whose characteristics may never be scientifically determinable: we await the results of science, but also with a certain sanguinity about what even science can tell us about racial composition. Another scenario is that patterns that science does manage to find are insufficiently informative about the race question because they lack enough direct causal correlation with overt behavior. These scenarios together suggest that, at best, we are somewhat in the dark about the race question and may always be so.

This conclusion is reinforced by more recent remarks by the paleontologist and cultural theorist Stephen Jay Gould:

> The fruit fly Drosophila, the staple of laboratory genetics, possesses between 13,000 and 14,000 genes. The roundworm C. Elegans, the staple of laboratory studies in development, contains only 959 cells, looks like a tiny, formless squib with virtually no complex anatomy beyond its genitalia, and possesses just over 19,000 genes.

The general estimate for Homo sapiens—sufficiently large to account for the vastly greater complexity of humans under conventional views—had stood at well over 100,000, with a more precise figure of 142,634 widely advertised and considered well within the range of reasonable expectation. Homo sapiens possesses between 30,000 and 40,000 genes, with the final tally almost sure to lie nearer the lower figure. . . .

Human complexity cannot be generated by 30,000 genes under the old view of life embodied in what geneticists literally called . . . their "central dogma": DNA makes RNA makes protein—in other words, one direction of causal flow from code to message to assembly of substance, with one item of code (a gene) ultimately making one item of substance (a protein), and the congeries of proteins making a body. Those 142,000 messages no doubt exist, as they must to build our bodies' complexity, with our previous error now exposed as the assumption that each message came from a distinct gene.

We may envision several kinds of solutions for generating many times more messages (and proteins) than genes, and future research will target this issue. In the most reasonable and widely discussed mechanism, a single gene can make several messages because genes of multicellular organisms are not discrete strings, but composed of coding segments (exons) separated by noncoding regions (introns). The resulting signal that eventually assembles the protein consists only of exons spliced together after elimination of introns. If some exons are omitted, or if the order of splicing changes, then several distinct messages can be generated by each gene.

The implications of this finding cascade across several realms. . . .

The social meaning may finally liberate us from the simplistic and harmful idea . . . that each aspect of our being, either physical or behavioral, may be ascribed to the action of a particular gene "for" the trait in question.

But the deepest ramifications will be scientific or philosophical. . . . The collapse of the doctrine of one gene for one protein, and one direction of causal flow from basic codes to elaborate totality, marks the failure of reductionism for the complex system that we call biology. . . .

First the key to complexity is not more genes but more combinations and interactions generated by fewer units of code—and many of these interactions (as emergent properties, to use the technical jargon) must be explained at the level of their appearance, for they cannot be predicted from the separate underlying parts alone. So organisms must be explained as organisms, and not as a summation of genes.[8]

Since a small number of differences in genetic makeup can potentially deliver large differences in "expression" on account of what is likely, to Gould, a matter of "combination and interaction," the thesis that small genetic differences, measured in terms of alleles and the like, cannot in principle produce significant differences in expression, is undercut. This is not to argue *for* significant racial differences; it is simply to undercut the watertight conclusion that there is no basis in the current state of science for the *possibility* of significant differences.

I repeat, what is totally clear from the results of the Human Genome Project is what the best liberal imagination has always reasonably and humanely suspected: genetic difference cuts across race far more strongly than it cuts between the races. Human difference is not, at basis, racially marked, but marked between the entire pool of the human species in all kinds of ways (intelligence, higher motor coordination, disease, etcetera). The days of ascribing the "big" terms of difference on racial grounds are over.

However, I must also repeat that this still leaves a certain skepticism about the extent to which race (differences in skin and bone) does correlate with some higher differences, and by race is here not simply meant the races as DuBois thought of them, but also the host of other ethnicities, which, up to this degree or that, do evidence this or that anatomical unity: the Finn by size, the German by forehead, the Semite by originally darker skin, the Roman by hair, eye, and nose, the Japanese . . . I am certain that between all such groups or races, anatomically defined, there are no large overall human differences, so any given biodiversity will likely remain at small, perhaps even minute levels, unequally distributed between groups according to various levels of correlation. Which means the idea of huge overall differences between races sufficient to prove the Kipling remark that East is East and West is West, on biogenetic grounds, would give way to a racialism of many races and microdifferences that would be more in keeping with contemporary notions of biodiversity. And the more luminous cultural differences between such groups (as well as within them) would remain a matter of sociohistory (of environment rather than gene pools). And so the concept of racialism would be partially resuscitated as a naturally given system of differences. Note that as races multiply, the lines between race and ethnicity become almost indistinguishable (Finns, Japanese, etcetera), so race also begins to evaporate as a concept.

So less and less is at stake, biologically, with the concept of race. What I am arguing is, therefore, that the proposition "There are races" is as uncertain as the proposition "There are not races." But I am also tempering that argument with the claim that far less is at stake in the potential differences between the races, if there are any, than one would have thought. From this kind of modest skepticism about race (which is to say, about *both* propositions) and from this relative devaluing of the biological question, there follows a kind of postmodern conclusion: one cannot hope to find a firm conceptual standpoint from which all the heterogeneous ways in which race enters the fabric of human language and practice can be arbitrated. No longer can racialism be accepted, much less racism. Skepticism on biological grounds prohibits any decisive role for the natural argument. Put that together with Appiah's work on the inadequacy of cultural explanations of race in terms of heritage and descent, and the conclusion follows: debates about the relevance of this or that concept of race in social life cannot be arbitrated by appealing to the high court of theory.

Race and Ethnicity: The Work of Lucius Outlaw

There is a telling corollary to this: the line between race and ethnicity is impossible to define by recourse to any general theory of "race and the races." Neither appeal to DuBois's lines of heritage and descent nor appeal to biology can spell out the difference. Whether belonging to a race (in one's own or in the eyes of others) is the same as belonging to an ethnicity becomes a *practical* question for social and cultural analysis rather than one to be sorted out in terms of such grand theory.

Nothing could be more obvious than the difference, one might say. A black man is known by his skin, and that marker causes visual havoc in his life in a way being known by food habits, religious rituals, or even language may mark a man as being part of an ethnic group. Everything, it might be said, starts from the body, rather than from these other kinds of markers. It is simply different to live a life that imposes categories of race on your gross features of skin and bone than it is to live a life where your accent, your cultural habits, and the like count first.

And yet nothing follows from construction of the body apart from the deep categories that reside behind it. Race is underdetermined by the body: only with the larger system of meanings into which the body is placed does the body become a racial one. This is especially evident because many groups have at one time in their histories been racially constructed and then, gradually, this construction of their bodies in relation to group categories of a racialistic/racist kind have ameliorated, giving way to broader ethnic constructions that are less tied to the body, less strict in their implications, and less virulent. When ethnicity becomes fundamentalist, it almost always reracializes itself, and on a related note, almost invariably turns racist, since it is about the other now defined as an implacable alien type, as your enemy in principle.

This suggests that the more racial constructions can commute into the more variegated and diversified categories of ethnicity, the freer people defined by the category become, and similarly, the more free they become to conceive of others in relation to themselves. It is for this reason that many African Americans have argued that rethinking blackness as ethnicity (as "Africanness") is an improvement in the quality and character of their lives, while remaining firmly aware of how much their skin still counts as a marker of race in the racist sense.

The *practical* question of the most just constructions of a person or group would remain unsolved by grand theory even if there *were* knockdown, beyond-the-shadow-of-a-doubt-type arguments against both the cultural and the biological basis for the races, as Appiah believes. For if it could confidently be stated that there are no races, then belonging to a race or being placed in one would clearly be a historical/cultural construction rather than a metaphysical reality or a fact of science. Naturally the social aptitude of race as opposed to ethnicity would remain an issue for practical justice. Fictions, Don Quixote showed, become part of the scripts by which we live our lives, if believed with sufficient fervor. To change them is to change the nature of human life, even if it is not to change human nature. However, were Appiah's view the correct one, there would remain no possibility that even a *partly* biological difference could be part of what differentiates race from ethnicity in some, if not all, situations. I believe that such a possibility must remain open—open in the sense of an open question. This is the result of skepticism, of "I-do-not-know."

Lucius Outlaw has argued that the possibility of racial difference on biological grounds should not only be kept open but celebrated. His purpose is to suggest a notion of raciality that (1) involves no notion of superiority or inferiority but simply of difference, (2) is biologically based, (3) allows for variation within the racial group, but that (4) also is "contingent" in the usual socio-historical ways. There *may* be natural differences above and beyond those of skin and bone that biology can (that is, will eventually) discover, and that might just be part of the biodiversity of the human species and therefore worthy of celebration (from the biogenetic standpoint, anyway). Such differences need not, the suggestion is, be cause for alarm, given the genealogy of racism, which has immediately seized upon such reputed differences and assigned them immediate rankings in terms of superiority and inferiority. Sometimes Outlaw writes as if he is pretty sure there are these biological properties, other times not.

The profundity of this question is about being prepared to acknowledge, tolerate, and even celebrate such differences, rather than impugn them. Outlaw's point is that no one can afford to entirely dispense with the concept of race because of these subtle biological possibilities. From my point of view, this is an implication of skepticism.

The moral move would be to reconvene such potential biological differences, were they to be obtained, into matters of acknowledgment, toleration, expression, celebration.

According to Outlaw, race is different from ethnicity, not only because of its potentially biological aspects. It is also a social construction, different from ethnicity in a number of ways, which are, for better or worse, indelible in the contemporary world. However much an African American may wish to convert racial definitions into ethnic ones, thinking of his blackness as an ethnicity (as "African American") rather than as a race (as "black"), at some point, is stopped by social language and social practices. This is not simply because you can't as a black man get a cab after dark in New York—nor can you avoid the hostile stares of the other patrons in an Oklahoma diner nor, if you are an African American street kid, not stick out like a sore thumb in a fancy New York bistro. In those circumstances, you are a black man. Outlaw has more, however, in mind than this. His view is that in complex, systemic ways, your historical and social construction is different from that of a postracial ethnicity like Jews, or a nonracial ethnicity like white Anglo-Saxon Protestant males. Therefore, he argues, as a black person, you had better learn to live with race, and more than that, to learn to celebrate it in ways that are not identical with the ways postracial or nonracial groups (so constructed) celebrate their ethnicity. The argument is, I think, holistic. The broad spectrum of your definition is different, and indelible.

It is hard to say what this broad spectrum of differences is, but it will surely have to do with the relation between your ethnicity and the construction of your body (of your grosser features of skin and bone). You might be able to "pass," as Jews were able during European modernity or "colored people" during apartheid. But even then the stain of your passing will haunt you. This is the theme of Philip Roth's brilliant novel, *The Human Stain*, in which Coleman Silk lives a life passing as white. So white is he that he is kicked out of his university for having made, it is said, disparaging remarks about two of his African American students. What goes around comes around. Jews in America can say, "We were once treated as a race, but now we are an ethnicity." I don't think black people can. They can try though. And they do. And they should.

Now whether race is indelible in a given social world will depend on many things. The intractability of race as a social "reality" has to do with whether it is even *imaginable* that the language of race can be unraveled and replaced by another (e.g., ethnicity). Different people might answer this question differently. What one person can imagine is not what another can imagine. I find it dubious, but who can finally say until people try. And, moreover, perhaps some can and some can't. Intractability is less than certain. The best I would venture is, it is reasonable to assume it.

It might be thought that one way of dispensing with race is to simply redefine it as one kind of ethnicity. But then, everything depends on what is unique about this particular kind of ethnicity, and one makes no conceptual progress because the nagging issue of the indelibility/intractability of race remains within this new, hybrid category of ethnicity.

The question of what is at stake in replacing a racialized concept by another can be profitably compared with the example of "homosexuality." I rely here on the work of Arnold Davidson. Homosexuality is, like the *modern* concept of race, an invention of the nineteenth century.[9] As an invention, it melds a natural fact (the desire to have sexual relations with persons of the same sex) to a social theory that nineteenth-century psychiatry made up about norms for psychological health and disease. In the past, the "love that has no name" has had many names, many constructs through which it has been shaped and expressed, understood and disdained. It has been the object of violence before psychiatry came on the scene. What is new in the nineteenth century is the specific construction of the natural in terms of medicalized forms of practice, turning desire, sex, and love into a condition that is socially marginalized by virtue of its medical status as disease, and since it is this natural/social construct that is called homosexuality, homosexuality comes into existence only in that century.

In the 1960s the first thing that happens within gay culture is the changing of the name: homosexuality becomes gay, and as such, a medical concept is replaced by a concept of affirmation—science by a gay science, if you will. This, especially in male culture, where gay becomes the term of art (in the culture of women, it is more complicated, and something I cannot go into here other than to note that the history of same-sex stereotyping, and its overcoming, has consistently been formulated in the first instance as a male history). This change in words happens slowly but firmly, in the first instance by those within the culture, speaking in resistance to dominant ideology, then later by other segments of the speech community. But there is little doubt on the part of gay people that the concept first of all is replaceable, and second of all that it ought to be replaced. Part of the horror of AIDS in the United States is that, in being identified as a "gay disease," it threatens to bring back the image of gay culture as disease. The propensity to label AIDS a gay disease thus carries with it the return of the "homosexual" ideology, the medicalized concept/stigma.

There is little lack of consensus about whether the word "homosexual" should be reinstated in the language gay and lesbian people use or others use in speaking of them. With its inherently castigating medical baggage, the concept is not wanted. Gay and lesbian people do not wish to recognize themselves in its light, nor to be so recognized by others. It is a word that carries a victimizing power in its very anatomy, its very semantics. By contrast, it is not merely that the African American community cannot dispense entirely with the concept of race. It is also that they are in disagreement about whether they want to do this. For some, race is precisely the concept they wish to convert into "black is beautiful," the redolent intensity of skin-to-skin, the special luxuriance of the body in relationship to the self. Some of these people use race as a way of refusing integration into society at large: they are fundamentalist and imprison themselves in a rigid concept. Others are clearly not. They are about converting indelibility into expressivity. Lucius Outlaw is one of these people.

The Reconstruction of Race in South Africa

These points are highly relevant to South Africa, because in South Africa there has not been the kind of movement toward deracializing identities, and on a related note, toward converting them into ethnicities. The reality of race (how indelible it is) can only be established dialectically—when people push the envelope to determine how far they can go. But the general movement in South Africa has been toward reracialization, not deracialization. Racism against "colored" and "Indian" groups by black African groups illustrates the matter. But also the aesthetics of reracialization, which can be found in the African renaissance, where cultural return (to the great African traditions) is associated with racialism and the history of black nationalism.

This double association between blackness understood as cultural identity ("I am an African") and political power understood as black majority rule is what is crucially different from the American case. When DuBois wanted to find his roots, he invented Africa for African Americans. But Thabo Mbeki is not part of a diasporic minority; he is part of a "black majority" living in sub-Saharan Africa, which has been prevented access to citizenship and power by the history of colonialism and now asserts both. Blackness becomes the signifier through which political power is assumed, just as it becomes the signifier through which a majority reclaims their traditions. Hence reracialization in Africa is a response to different forces than is deracialization in America. In America, political power is predicated on deracialization (black conformity). A black man will be president of the United States only if he looks and acts like Colin Powell.

Reracialization is to a degree a distinctively South African phenomenon within Africa. Where the colonial whites have left, black against black power is played out through ethnicity, and it is well known that the black African state has been threatened by ethnic conflicts, which, in the case of Rwanda, led to genocide. Where the colonial group remains, as in South Africa or Zimbabwe, reracialization is an operation of political power and cultural identity asserted against what is seen as "white cultural hegemony." It does not happen uniquely against whites. Uganda threw out the Indian population for a related reason.

It can hardly, therefore, be expected, given the exigencies of political power in South Africa, that the ideal of a nonracial society would be held up by new black African leaders. Moreover, black communalization dictates return to a form of solidarity that is racialized where white people are around. Ubuntu, the ideal that individuals are individuals only in and through the whole village, is about blackness when it is reasserted in a multiracial society (where everyone around is black, then it is about the specific ethnicity of the village). Significantly, it was, in the first instance, white and Indian judges who attempted to free ubuntu as a signifier from this tribal connection and use it as a constitutional principle of justice. Ismail Mohammed, chief justice of South Africa during the mid- to late 1990s, was the one who deracinated ubuntu as "respecting the humanity of the other." Originally it was easier for non-black Africans to free the concept from the form of life in which it was set, since they were not part of that form of life.

In South Africa it is white and Indian people who are now the minority, and many whites find the thought of reracialization revolting. Plenty of them remain racist. All of them fear the implications for political power. For some, reracialization returns them to their guilty past, harking back to the system of racial estates codified by law as the apartheid state. Moreover, in the world of realpolitik, with a new black majority, racialism pinpoints their unequal ownership of resources (more than 90 percent of the country owned by less than 10 percent of people, mostly white) and their minority status. (Mbeki calls this the problem of "two nations.") So they have political and economic reasons to deny racialism, just as black African politicians appealing mostly to black constituencies remain wedded to concepts of race.

Significantly, in KwaZulu-Natal, the central black-identity formation is not black African but Zulu. And this is because Zulu nationalism is in conflict with the dominant political dispensation, the African National Congress, and remains, moreover, communalist.

Indians remain internally divided (between Hindu and Muslim), worried about black power (which has marginalized them), sometimes racist, subdued, and not, as a rule, racially assertive. They are and have been a politically weak and highly internalized minority. Ironically, part of what explains the Muslim fanaticism at the 2001 World Congress against Racism in Durban is the fact that South African Muslims (some South African Muslims and not others, since they are not at all homogeneous) rally against Zionism as a way of asserting what is otherwise a "racial identity" incapable of assertion in this racialized country.

This is not true of Cape colored Muslims, who "converted" to the Islamic faith only around 1900 and for whom, from the first, it was a proclamation of racial/religious identity for a dispossessed group.

What then happens, in the light of all of this stridency about race, when a boy resists being stereotyped by his ethnic/racial identity? When a boy in my town was asked what it was like to be a Zulu at Glenwood High School, he responded, "At school, I am not a Zulu, I am a Glenwood boy." He added emphatically: "When I am home I am a Zulu boy, but here I am a Glenwood boy." What should one make of this? The boy clearly does not like being identified as Zulu or black or African (are these the same?) at his school. Is he embarrassed or just tired, fed up with a blanket stereotype that gives him no room to maneuver in his way of thinking of himself? Or is he in flight from himself, trying to "pass"? Is he ashamed of being constantly pointed to as a Zulu at a largely white/Indian school? Or is it that at school he is "just a boy," playing with others, reading and writing like others, and that it is only when the crushing lodestone of race is yet again, for the hundredth time, brought down upon him through the asking of the question, "What is it like to be a Zulu at this school?" (as if it must be like *something*) that he reacts? All of these things, perhaps? At home, does he become Zulu, meaning black? Zulu, meaning language-speaking? Zulu, meaning cultural? Does he distinguish these things? Does this keep him down, embarrass him? Or is it just what he is at home, like when I don my yarmulke and go to the temple and pray on a Friday night?

Whatever is true of the role of racialism in postapartheid South African society, it can no longer function as the central defining concept of modern children who inhabit a global and local world in which identities are in flux. There is an analogy in the linguistic theory of code switching, according to which to understand language as a marker of identity, one must understand how postcolonial beings consistently switch from one language to another, or move between languages in ways that render them surprising and idiomatic. Code switches are always matters of power, and can be signs of ongoing domination, but the point is that how new people—call them young people in a young society—come to move between being African, being Zulu, being Glenwood boys, being South Africans, being modern subjects, and cannot be predicted or controlled. People must work these things out for themselves. Respect consists of respect for the fact that individuals may well disagree, even profoundly, in how they go about choosing to redefine themselves as X's, Y's, Z's, as tags that they apply to themselves, as registrations of how others conceive of them, and relative to actual group practices that constitute their lives.

Race is a lodestone, always referred to, seldom discussed, always proclaimed, seldom negotiated. Reracialization is in danger of recapitulating the apartheid state simply because it is happening along racially stratified lines, with little or no *conversation* between racial groups about race. In short, race is excluded from the conversation of democracy, the public debate about transition. This is, unfortunately, to be expected, given the politics behind reracialization, which are about using race for political hegemony, and also political hegemony along racially divided lines. And yet civil society, the workplace—these are meant to be places where hybridization and conversation ameliorate the politics of race (political and cultural), where people become more like each other, where race becomes less central a category, where identities become more alike and their differences more manageable. The classroom should be one of many spaces where race is reflected upon, and yet universities, schools, and newspapers are afraid or uninterested in pushing the conceptual envelope of race. They do not serve as sites for its negotiation, only for its proclamation, avoidance, or stridency. So this Glenwood boy has no place where his liberty to try (and possibly succeed) to reconvene his race and ethnicity can be acknowledged and cultivated. In short, he has no one to help him. He is all alone.

The lesson from African-American life is that an identity politics that thematizes and encourages revaluations of race and ethnicity is crucial if citizens are to exercise their liberty in more than lonely isolation. It is for this boy to try to work these things out for himself, to work out where he fits between Glenwood, his home, and, later, his place of work. He will not be free to obliterate the indelibility of race, but he will be at liberty to reconvene it. Whether this leads in the future toward nonracialism or multiracialism will be the task of the society to work out, given its political, social, and constitutional agendas. One will expect no consensus about such matters; one will look forward to no consensus about such matters. One just hopes the debate will really begin to take place.

5

The Genealogy of Modern South African Architecture

Modernism at the Margins

Public and private. North and south. We begin in the north, in public, at the center, to understand the periphery, the public, the private, the south.

If the cultures of modernism are to be divided into margin and center, it is because the modern art and architecture that arose in the cosmopolitan centers of Europe and America arose in the context of robust art worlds, and the art and architecture at the margins did not. In the first instance, the form of life that gave rise to the European modernisms and avant-gardes was urban. Critics, journalists, novelists, and private citizens conversing over endless coffees and bottles of Pernod spread the news and fomented public opinion. The bourgeoisie grazed, sampled, and consumed. The institutions of production (the painter's studio, the architect's office, the craftsperson's atelier) produced, the institutions of exhibition (the museum, the gallery, the Salon des Refusés) exhibited. All were part of a larger pattern of spectacle, speed, commodification, urbanization, nationalism, and industrial capitalization that constituted Parisian, and global, modernity. For better and worse, Paris was traversed too by a system of gazes: museumgoers gazing with a sense of ownership at objects taken from the colonies, the bourgeoisie watching itself and sampling the goods for sale in the newly created department stores on the newly created boulevards, men turning an appraising eye on the city's many prostitutes. These placed art at the cusp of pleasure, ownership, and commodification.

Modernism in art and architecture arises and dwells at the center of this urban world. The critical paintings of Edouard Manet could have arisen only because a web of museums, exhibitions, critics, bourgeois interests, buying, and selling was in place in Paris, "capital of the nineteenth century."[1] It is worth repeating these points because they sharpen the question of modernism at the South African margins: What is it like to produce architecture, cities, "modern spaces" at the margins of those cosmopolitan worlds, outside the geographical circuits of Paris, Moscow, Berlin, Milan, London, and New York, and far from modernity's lively circulation of cultural phenomena? How does modernism get itself invented where urbanization is fragmentary; where patterns of intellectual, cultural, economic, and political dependency remain colonial; where institutions, criticism, nationalist ideologies, and the fetish of cultural commodities exist haphazardly, if at all; where the circle of artists is small; where populations are split between subaltern and elite; where economies are rudimentary; and where life is stultified by the colonial yoke and the repression of indigenous traditions? Since a great deal of modernist history has happened under such conditions, from China and India to South Africa and Brazil, the question is hardly marginal to global self-understanding. And yet for the most part the emergence and experience of modernism in architecture and art in the various corners of the world have yet to be explored and presented.

The achievement of modernism at the margins takes place in the shadow of an ongoing dependency on the colonial center or its neocolonial successor, and for something new to be achieved, this dependency must be endured, accommodated, and at best worked through and converted into an opportunity. Lacking a robust art world of its own, the marginal location must depend on that of the center. Moreover, modernism at the margins tends to arise in situations of colonial or neocolonial dependency, where the marginal culture has been cut off from its own vital past and abjectly follows the master in all things. In the first instance, then, modernism at the margins is usually imitative of new creations radiating out from the center. Marginal artists or architects must depend on metropolitan models, which are never quite their own, never quite capable of bringing their culture, society, aspirations, and context to expression, never quite able to enter the fabric of the world of culture, which is also theirs. The blanket claim that modernism at the margins is inherently imitative turns a complex social condition into a defining state, a difficult creative starting point into an essential lack or inferiority. In any event, the originality and interest of the art and culture of modernity produced at the margins (that is, in most of the world), even in a "settler society" such as South Africa, simply belie the claim. This art has sometimes returned to captivate the center, but it is often excluded from the vigorous circulation it deserves. It is in the interest of the center to perform this act of exclusion, since it keeps the center from being "decentered"—a condition that finally happens anyway, but less overwhelmingly than is often thought.

The case of South Africa is especially interesting, since one way of understanding its Eurocentrism is that it is precisely the desire to continue this state of dependency, to rest assured of one's identity by sustaining oneself as an adjunct of European culture. Conceived of not as dependency but as a badge of identity (European rather than "native" or indigenous), Eurocentrism in South Africa expresses the settler's desire to claim cultural difference from the native and hegemony over him. It is the refusal of the project of remaking one's culture in a way that reflects essentially new conditions of existence that are neither European nor "native" but something as yet to be defined. It is the refusal of the sublime possibility of becoming a new subject, as yet unpresentable to oneself or one's tribe. In these circumstances, and in response to these pressures, Europe becomes a tribe; the colonial is the European become tribal. One can see this in the way colonials band together in groups, and in the way their architecture fiercely attaches itself to European models and refuses assimilation with the locality.

South Africa's history of settlers is a history of many generations, with a variety of settler types (Dutch, later Afrikaner, English, etcetera). Not a single of these is as stereotypical as a theory of colonial Eurocentrism might like, and countertendencies of all kinds will always be found. Irma Stern, the great South African artist of the 1920s and 1930s, was active in the German avant-garde and exhibited with *Die Brücke* until the outbreak of World War I sent her rushing home. For her, home was a provincial prison, with few galleries, little interest in new forms of representation, and little space for a creative woman to "be herself." Increasingly estranged and reclusive, she disappeared into her exoticizations of "the native." No doubt Stern is Eurocentric enough, as one might expect of a first-generation settler of German-Jewish extraction who emerged as a painter among the European avant-gardes.[2] She felt instinctively attuned to the German expressionist desire to find utopia in the vibrant and unbridled colors of the "primitive," and was a direct descendant of the exoticizing line that runs from Gauguin to Max Pechstein, her mentor.

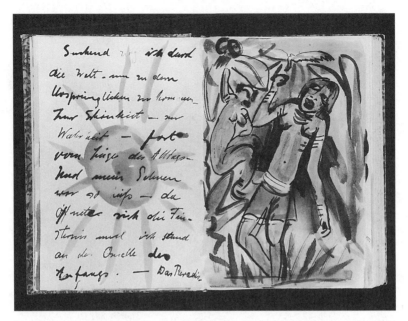

Irma Stern, *Watercolor,* from *Paradise: The Journal and Letters of Irma Stern* (1917–1933), watercolor. Irma Stern Museum, Cape Town. Reproduction by permission of the trustees of the Irma Stern Trust.

However, Stern had also grown up on African soil among African people, and her work goes far beyond exoticism in its poignant attachment to and identification with its idealized subjects. She portrays these "natives" as locals, with a degree of genuine subjectivity, foregrounding them where the viewer must engage with them directly (whereas Pechstein, say, would consign his figures to the landscape in the background). A drama between exoticization (about being distant) and locality (about being close) is played out in her work, a drama central to her identity as artist and woman. Stern felt the burden of living at the margins, caught between cultures, between being settled and unsettled, and though this hardly made her life as a creative artist any easier, it made her and her work more genuine, less tribal, and less contented.

The splitting off of European allegiance from African intuition and likeness—a split no doubt worthy of deconstruction, since it serves to sustain "logocentric" oppositions along racial lines—is one that Stern seeks to pass beyond only in a highly ambivalent way, and it produces her personal and artistic drama.

Irma Stern's work is important because it shows by contrast how *little*

Irma Stern, *Seated Arab Youth,* 1945, gouache. Irma Stern Museum. Reproduction by permission of the trustees of the Irma Stern Trust.

early South African modernism, created as it was by white settlers and their descendants, was motivated to recover African tradition, a form of life that was finally not its own. And her work also shows how the early gestures of reaching out to Africa were deeply implicated in exoticism, however much they rose above it. Not that all settlers saw South Africa in the same terms. The work of J. H. Pierneef, a gifted Afrikaans artist working at about the same time as Stern, reveals a feeling of bondedness with the landscape, rural farms, and towns of the Cape and Karoo, which can only be the result of generations of settler inhabitance. Indicative of a community (the Afrikaans community) "no longer European, not yet African" (in the well-known words of the author J. M. Coetzee), Pierneef's works hardly exoticize. Instead, their trees, rivers, rough green grass, soft clouds, and *koppies* (hills) are quiet, unchanging, and something between stately and a little dull. The combination of dignity and banality in these landscapes points to the fact that the landscape is his own, an Afrikaans landscape, claimed in the name of a tribe that has achieved at-homeness. It is not for nothing that Pierneef is the painter of Afrikaans nationalism and cultural revivalism, that he is painting for a Boer community whose disenfranchisement by the English (during the Anglo-Boer war) had the effect of producing a nationalism whose claim on the nation was articulated through landscape. "We were here first and the signs of this are in our settledness: this is our land, not yours," the Boer would say, thus grafting his identity onto the land with a fierce implacability. No doubt this claim

Jacob Hendrik Pierneef, *Twee Jongegesellen,* date uncertain, graphic work. Programme in Afrikaans and Nederlands, University of Natal, South Africa. Reproduction by permission of Marita J. Pierneef (Bailey), sole copyright owner of all his works.

remains somewhat dormant in the quiet work of Pierneef. His pictures sound the faintest flow of rivers rather than the loud cry of the politicians. However, one should not be misled: his are works in which, beyond the quiet, resides a will that will not budge.

The pictures then refer landscape to his own half-European, half-African tribe, and to the English, who are perhaps more excluded from, than included in, their grace. What they do not refer landscape to is the African, the San, the inhabitant whose body bore the sun and clouds of these patches of earth long before any of Pierneef's clan strained their limbs in its cultivation. One finds in these pictures not the slightest trace of an Africa that is other to the settler of German and Dutch descent; neither African people nor their cultures deign to appear. Indeed, no people at all appear; it is only the feel of a land that is one's own, while always retaining its touch of emptiness and foreignness, that matters. Hence, the extreme difference between settler types like Stern and Pierneef confirms the rule: either the native appears through the lens of an exoticizing otherness or the native does not appear at all. Either land and native exist as a utopian otherness to the settler or they are disowned by the settler.

With the following exception in Pierneef's case: when he turns to portraying a colored man called Markus, his representation is humanistic. He lends the "colored" man (probably Afrikaans-speaking) a tired, contemplative subjectivity and paints him close up, as part of the same emotional world in which the painter dwells. The influence of Rembrandt and Dutch figure painting is clear. Pierneef is selective about which "native populations" he portrays, choosing those hybridized peoples whose lives were inextricably part of Afrikaans settlerdom, even if lived at the back of the house or outside (as in the American South). He avoids black Africans. But there is real dignity in Markus, proving that nothing in settler life is ever completely "settled."

For later artists it would be different. The art made in resistance to apartheid would have little about it that was exotic. Later still, in the wake of the demise of apartheid, artists would experience a heady moment of freedom, in which the yearning for contact with other cultures and styles might be fulfilled, in which identity might be a matter of experimentation. African painters would appropriate abstract expressionism, recasting it with the patterns of Ndebele wall paintings, Zulu pots, or the landscape of the bush; young sculptors whose parents were immigrants from Europe but who grew up in this world of snakes, red earth, and the sublime violence of nature would find West African forms natural, thus confirming the thought that they too were African.

Jacob Hendrik Pierneef, *Rufus (Markus)*, 1910, oil on board. National Cultural History Museum, Pretoria, South Africa. Reproduction by permission of Marita J. Pierneef (Bailey), sole copyright owner of all his works.

Wagnerian Internationalism

In South African architecture, this cultural and stylistic intermingling has largely yet to take place. Indeed, modern architecture here hardly went through the phase of *exoticized* exploration with all of its problems, although it would surely have been enriched by the plethora of magnificent premodern styles that presented themselves, from Ndebele houses and Zulu kraals (hut communities) to Cape Dutch homesteads and Karoo houses. There are exceptions (see below), yet South African cityscapes show a diversity of building styles: Durban's Indian market, with its Indo-Victorian pleasantries and crowds and somewhat dilapidated bustle, gives way along the main streets of the city to an admixture of Victorian and art deco styles and 1950s department stores, which culminate in turn in a clearly colonial Victorian city square, with a cathedral, city hall, and post office. If this city, like all other South African cities, lacks public spaces, it is because these were a threat to colonial notions of divide and rule, and even more so to apartheid laws of separation. But the city remains a paean, in its crowded and dirty way, to the hybridization that was explicitly ruled out. We shall return to this point in due course, for it shows that, in spite of everything, South African cities are varied and complex in ways that speak of people commingling in the whirl of modernity. The Indian market, and those excellent imitations of metropolitan buildings with which it clashes, and the clash itself, are part of the history of modernity in architecture in this corner of the world.

It should be noted immediately that the production of architecture at the margins, however central to South African modernism, is different from that of painting, writing, or sculpting in crucial ways, and that these differences derive from the nature of the media in question. First, modern architecture is defined by international models and exists within the ambit of Euro-American diffusion in a very specific sense. The various architects who have been grouped together under the rubric of "the International Style," and who sometimes grouped themselves together in this way, would have found this kind of "Eurocentric diffusion" perfectly acceptable and harmless, since it rejected the very concept of imitation. How could a style that strove to be universal be imitated? By definition it could simply be expanded into new areas of application. Insofar as the great architectural modernisms were truly international movements, each considered by its subscribers—whether at the center or the margins—as "the only progressive course," such architects did not regard the lack of modernist reinvention in the local domain as a loss: their work was of a different order of avant-garde reality, more like a science than an art, and therefore less concerned with issues of diversity and locality. Architects at the margins did not think of themselves as marginal, but as part of a truly universal movement. These modernisms—Eurocentric too insofar as they arose in relation to specific problems that were not exactly those of the margins—were also part of an internationally expanding capitalism that was essentially homogenizing (in spite of the movement's Marxist pretensions). Such modernisms had their sophistications fine-tuned by certain "third-world architects" (Oscar Niemeyer and Lúcio Costa of Brazil, Charles Correa of India, Kunio Mayekawa and Kenzo Tange of Japan, Hassan Fathy of Egypt), and this collection of styles was finally decentered, like the flow of international capital generally. But it was only with the birth of postmodernism in architecture that locality and variety came to the fore again. And only recently has it become important to remake models from the center in diverse ways at the periphery, now better conceived of as a host of decentered multiplicities.

The one-size-fits-all approach of the international styles (Le Corbusier's, Kahn's, Mies van der Rohe's, etcetera) was the perfect complement to the settler's desire to produce cities reflective of his own Eurocentric separateness from locality, native, and cultural diversity, as if to say, "Because my city looks like Chicago, New York, or Berlin, because it conforms to international canons of rationality, progress, and civilization, it reflects me in domination of others rather than a me who, like Stern or even Pierneef, blends in, unsure exactly of who I am." The group of styles around Corbu, Mies, and Kahn conveyed to the settler not only a genuine need for urban development, but also a way of performing Eurocentrism in the colony.

This is also a genuine problem for architecture as a medium: to engender global connection while also seeking diversity. Architecture is in many respects a technology, and there has always been less scope for variety and invention in technologically driven art forms than in those that are more autonomous from their international currencies. Moreover, where the desire to resist imitating the center has arisen, the tasks of recovering "traditional modes of dwelling" for a modernizing society and significantly remaking international models in the light of local geographies and cityscapes have also been beset by a host of stylistic and economic concerns. In many of the other arts, there is room for individuals and groups to experiment, to make mistakes, to chance upon solutions. Architects do not have this space, except in abstraction on the drawing board: the city is not a blank canvas or a page, and this imposes both a conservatism and a radicalism on their work, making the slow process through which international models are absorbed and reshaped more difficult.

The remaking of modernist models by postmodern architecture in the light of a deeper spirit of place and people has been the exception rather than the rule. Japan might be regarded as the preeminent exception, but note why: Japanese modular construction was a central influence on modern architecture in the first place (Frank Lloyd Wright, Mies), as central as the African mask in the origins of cubist and expressionist painting

(Picasso, Kirchner). And in Japanese culture, nationalism is deeply invested in shared styles of representation, so there has been cultural capital to be gained from building in a "Japanese spirit" and, until recently at least, the financial capital to do it with. Japan has produced an architecture capable of inflecting international styles of steel and curtain wall with refined geometrical abstraction, a minimalist, efficient spirituality consonant both with contemporary Japanese society and with premodern design. Here the eternal return has a vivifying effect, as the Japanese house with its simple modularity, open plan, efficient use of space, and natural setting is reshaped by the global modern-design influences it first stimulated. Architects in other parts of the world, lacking this special relationship, may not find it quite so easy to invest global models with the traces of a reanimated self. Some traditions are simply harder to blend with what the modern world offers than others, even where there is the will and the money to make the attempt. As often as not, postmodernism has become a series of neoclassical pleasantries, nostalgic cleansings of past styles for those wishing for the comfort of a nice condo with the resonance of a Cape Cod cottage or a Cape Dutch wine farm, or the sleek "facadism" of the corporate world. This international language of building has as little to do with place as modernism did.

The architectural modernisms that have gone under the rubric of "the International Style" were not simply the shared ideology of a group of architects; they became the currency of builders, and this is critical for modern construction at the margins. As much as the style suited the unctuous few who wished to make buildings of the expensive sleekness appropriate to big capital, so its principles—applied in the crudest possible way with the cheapest possible material—suited the unscrupulous many who wished to find cheap solutions to rapid urban construction. It is a harsh irony that a style that arose in the name of avant-garde Marxist radical social planning and construction through new design should have ended up delivering exactly what was required for profitable mass construction, the bleak and corroded products of which now stretch endlessly from São Paulo to Mexico City to Detroit to Warsaw to Rome to Johannesburg to Durban to Shanghai. In South Africa, as in other marginal societies, the cities have frequently been ruled by builders rather than architects. One may see more than enough evidence of this in Durban, in the cheap, tasteless, and ill-kept 1950s curtain wall that bursts out around the Indian market, in the gaps between the Victoriana and the dirty-brown replicas of petit bourgeois English originals (preserved in the Birminghams of the builders' memories, one supposes). Other South African cities, even glorious Cape Town, fare no better. Nor do Rome, Caracas, Newark. In this respect, South Africa is not distinctive: it is set apart, rather, by its almost total lack of appreciation for local landscape.

Before we pursue this point, another irony of the circulation of international modernisms is worth noting: the utopian schemes of the architects and planners at the center were actually put into practice at the margins. Although these visionaries aimed to raze the cities and towns of the metropolitan centers themselves, the powerful would not indulge them. Le Corbusier never rebuilt Paris; instead, Niemeyer and Costa built Brasilia. Mies was given a chance to build the Illinois Institute of Technology south of the Chicago city center; Wright more or less filled a relatively open suburb of Chicago known for its many oak trees with his little masterpieces; but in general, when cities destroyed in World War II were being rebuilt, or when American suburbs were being citified with big buildings, the tune was called by the corporate builder, who wanted to build quickly, conservatively, and for maximum profit. Only in the colonies, with their open veld and relatively undeveloped cities, could the modern architect realize his dream of the city constructed from scratch. The third world rather than the first became the site of utopian design: Brasilia, Chandigarh, and Dhaka, not Paris, Rome, and New York.[3] Similarly, modernism could infest the "second world," with its war-ravaged cities and technocratic five-year plans: from Moscow to Budapest, lives would be lived in freezing conformity in massive, unornamented apartment blocks, warmed only by excesses of vodka.

A book could be written about the Wagnerian impulse to fill the "empty" spaces of the third world with modernist masterpieces and the utopian modernist city. For the gesture was perhaps the final gasp in colonialism's long history. In this gesture, power seems to find its clean slate, but only because it fails to notice—or refuses to notice—what it has cleared away in its grand modernist sweep. We can approach this through a central idea of Michel Foucault's, namely, that the medium of power is resistance. Foucault meant by this more than the obvious: that where power dominates, it will produce resistance. Such is certainly the case: the histories of fascism, totalitarianism, and apartheid have amply confirmed it, and Foucault's own interest in counterpractices, through which subjectivities articulate themselves against the grain of power, depends on it. Foucault's idea is more a physics of power, for it is about the medium through which power "moves." "Do not ask what power is, ask instead how it is practiced," Foucault advised us again and again. And in thinking about power as that which continually takes the next step, moving from terrain to terrain, consolidating, repeating, and intensifying itself, one must inherently think about the medium (context) through which it advances, into which it must blend, according to which it must continually articulate its forms in different ways. Were power to move through Newton's vacuum, it would not be power at all, since the concept of force would not yet apply to it. Only when one billiard ball hits another—even if "in a vacuum"—does a concept of power arise (as a product of mass times acceleration, etcetera). Power and resistance are correlative concepts; each has meaning only in relation to the other. It is obvious that Corbu's *Plan Voisin* lacks the power to overcome the resistance of its medium. No one (except another architect) would have taken the destruction of Paris seriously as an option, and the plan derives its charm and force from its complete incapacity. But where the world is believed to be empty, then power is assumed to move with the implacability of gravity and the speed of light. So it was presumed of the third world. Lands of childhood, places of endless sleep: Dhaka, Ahmadabad, Chandigarh, and Brasilia are the sites of modernity without resistance, of avant-garde rationality without limitation. Or so it seemed, but only because that which was there was reduced to the status of primitivist or anachronistic.

When Chandigarh was being built by Corbu and his associates, at a certain point the process was held up because certain villagers refused to move. Stating that they would only consider leaving their homes if Nehru, then the Indian prime minister, would talk to them, he dispatched himself to their site with exceptional alacrity and stood ready to listen to what they had to say. They asked him the following question: "If we do not move, will you kill us?" Nehru was deeply liberal, but he thought about the question for a while and answered, "Yes." "We just wanted to hear you say it," they said, after which they moved and the project went on to completion. It is worth noting that, after its completion, local populations began to use it in their own ways, thus subverting its claim to mold them in accord with the strictness of its modernist ideals. Between population and buildings a mutual dialectic emerged, according to which each exerted its will over the other and each became essentially different through the force of the other. This dialectic is one of power and its medium of expression. One finds it at work in the history of Brasilia,[4] and earlier, in the architecture of the South African missionaries and its use by local Twana[5] populations.

We will find this dialectic between power and resistance, control and dissemination, central to the analysis of the South African city. We note here that, for the various reasons that have been discussed, Eurocentric postures different from those that affect the other arts obtain in the creation of architecture at the margins. We have touched on two of these: first, cheap versions of the international modernisms—which originate in the European and American avant-gardes in response to conditions specific to their art worlds—spring up throughout the world; and second, the margins become a laboratory of utopian practices. A third form of Eurocentrism originates in the third world itself and is endemic to settler societies. In South Africa, it combines with the other two varieties to configure the entire landscape of building. This Eurocentrism is the satisfaction and complacency that come with remaining a dependent satellite of the metropolitan center. The Eurocentric modernist claims ownership over the colony by retaining the sense, or illusion, of ownership of the means of cultural production. By remaining a producer of what he thinks of as European modernism, he remains European rather than indigenous in his own eyes. Alienated from the South African landscape, unwilling to become one with people he views as wholly other in character and as no more than the material for his work force, attached to an identity formed in another country across the seas, the Eurocentric modernist views the South African colony without any sustained aspiration to set it free in the field of culture by inventing new cultural forms to give its difference expression and resolve the splits in a self. The Eurocentric modernist has few such splits, or at any rate prefers to preserve them (splitting off his love of the veld, say, or fluency in Zulu from his capacity as a modernist creator). This is why Eurocentrism tends to be a more powerful force in settler societies such as South Africa than in those where modernization is achieved by indigenous peoples. For it is the settler who defines himself (as often as not) as a transplant whose real cultural home lies elsewhere.

Central to the history of modern construction in South Africa is a split between public and private building. Some South African bourgeois homes are marvelously comfortable with their own hybrid identities. In Johannesburg, Herbert Baker built the grand homes of the randlords out of the beautiful, whitish-brown stone of the Highveld, and with an airy, Victorian grandeur worthy of mining magnates and craggy hills, effortlessly harmonizing dwelling and landscape (even if pylons, enormous mine dumps, gritty industrial spaces, and bleak corrugated-iron shantytowns tell another story of brutal and rapacious capitalism). Baker arrived in South Africa fresh from a grand tour of the classical sites, and his Palladian and English-country instincts taught him to blend site with stone, park, and garden into one harmonious whole (unfortunately, his Mediterranean impetus was confined to the building of private spaces). The houses of the Durban Berea, on the other hand, blend French Caribbean balustrades with English stone construction in idiosyncratic formulations that are nothing short of romantic. The Natal midlands home, sporting a traditional thatched roof overhanging French doors to provide an open, airy space covered from sun and rain and trellised with roses, is a colonial gem. These houses represent precisely the settler ambivalence about landscape. On the one hand, they are attempts, sometimes highly successful, at harmonizing house to climate, to landscape, to garden—to fitting in. On the other hand, they clearly bring the authority of the European settler to the new land and assert it in the new land: "I shall dwell in my old house, but also reach out and make it something new." It is this duality that allows the settler an experimental relation to the new land in the privacy of his home, while also indicating that the presence of the European badge of honor remains. The settler drama of nostalgia (the desire to live in a piece of the old country) and "taking up a new and better life in the colonies" is played out through this ambivalence, which is quite a bit like Stern's.

Public space is another matter, and there even this freedom to experiment and blend in disappears. White South Africans apparently had little taste for the creation of hybrid public spaces; public life was regulated, even before the rule of apartheid, by a severe Eurocentrism in design and mission. Although there is sunlight and warmth in many South African cities nearly all year round, precious little is made of it in urban public space. Only rarely did the builder or planner of public space recast European models and blend them with existing architectural and spatial forms; instead, it was designed to divide and rule, to incorporate the privileged into "European" culture and exclude all others. And "European" often meant northern Europe and Britain rather than the Mediterranean. Thus public space was park rather than piazza and domesticated landscape in the city rather than open meeting or dwelling space in streets and squares along the lines of, say, Italy or Spain. Baker's "Edwardian villa" remained a private indulgence.

The refusal to open space to an urban colloquy—both through forms that reach out to "African" (traditional styles, local climate, and culture) and through open, public spaces in cities for all—would have tangled the rules of division. It is as simple as that, for those rules are expressed and *composed*, in part through the way space is articulated.

Open Plans and Closed Worlds

The history of *public* building in Johannesburg is largely a history of reception: internationalism received from the position of the "internationalist at the margins," whose internationalism is a form of Eurocentrism. It is also a history of cannibalization: the discovery of gold in the late nineteenth century produced a tidal wave of immigrants willing to work hard and ready to strike it rich, and the city grew with astonishing rapidity. This rough-and-tumble excitement, the violent expansion of the resources of production, the formation of a city whose desires were as raw as its resources, required the immediate importation of style—style in which the captains of industry could celebrate their triumphal conquests of man and mineral, style in which the hordes of immigrants could inhabit the growing city, style in which capital could confirm its glory. Hence the Edwardian mansions, the colonnaded and domed banking houses, the skyscrapers from New York and Chicago. If Johannesburg arose in the marginal playing fields of capitalism, it also arose with the wild energy of a hyperactive infant.

Johannesburg wanted to be like New York, Chicago, London—and these were, after all, not so terrible to emulate, given at least the majesty of their modern forms of architecture. In a burst of rapid expansion from nothing to something, Johannesburg had to model itself on what was, take counsel from what was, import the style of what was. Nothing comes from nothing. Johannesburg in the first flush of its infancy clearly

Johannesburg's 1936 Building Boom. Loveday Street, Looking South, 1936. Africana Museum, Johannesburg. Reprinted from Clive M. Chipkin, *Johannesburg Style: Architecture and Society 1880s–1960s* (Cape Town: David Philip Publishers, 1993). Reproduction by permission of Africana Museum.

lacked the kind of robust art world, the cosmopolitan framework of life, which allowed *modernism* to dwell at the cusp of modernity. However, this was not something the infant temporarily lacks, but will develop as it matures: at the margins of modernity, surrounded by complex currents of Eurocentrism and dependency, the state of attachment to the cosmopolitan center is more or less permanent. This attachment, which prevented Johannesburg from ever becoming "the Second Greatest City after Paris" (as the artist William Kentridge ironically denotes it), had complex reasons, some of which have already been discussed. What is important to note is that the Eurocentrism that rested content with a dependency on modernist models from the center, in the belief that these would make Johannesburg a little piece of Europe rather than an extension of Africa, combined with the specifically architectural attachment to one of the international modernisms or another, to confine architectural experiments in localization and local identification largely to *private* space. The public/private divide became paramount, and remains so to this day.

I have said that the making of a city like Johannesburg combines two streams into one gesture: the settler desire to make a city that reflects Eurocentric origins and proclaims settler dominance ("the city shall look like I want to look and thus be mine") and internationalism, which argued in its modernist way that "one size fits all," be it Corbu's, Mies's, or, later, Kahn's. Moreover, a city that wants to make itself in a day, namely Johannesburg, needs to cannibalize what is happening everywhere so as to rise up like the wind. So, in a period of twenty to thirty years, Johannesburg goes up to the sky and down into the earth in a double movement, each supporting the other. The mines go thousands of feet into the earth and the buildings soar to the sky. At the outset, whatever variations Johannesburg architects gave to the models imported from Europe and America were fairly minimal. The history begins early, for the first high-rise buildings had arrived in the city by 1902. In his book *Johannesburg Style*, Clive Chipkin points out that the American high-rise appeared in Johannesburg even before it did in London. "This reveals, too, a new cultural factor, a growing New York–Johannesburg axis."[6] There soon developed a similar communication between Chicago and Johannesburg—"the one as originator, the other as recipient"—although with this difference: "While the Chicago buildings are light and airy structures, Johannesburg's Edwardian architecture is massive and weighty—a celebratory financial style that is related to the City, or, where blocked inset columns occur, to the contemporary reconstruction of Regent Street in London."[7] It is not as if there is no variation whatsoever on imported models: Johannesburg is, after all, a city with its own form of get-rich-quick materialism, its own brand of instant urbanism, its own mix of people, its own stone and geography, and its own architects and builders, and it would be odd to find a complete absence of local inflection. But very quickly the city understood itself to share deep likenesses with New York and Chicago, as well as London and the cities of the European north. And its desire was to create itself in the image of these cities.

The "Transvaal Group" of architects, formed in the early 1930s, was named as such by Le Corbusier himself, and revolved around an important disciple of his, Rex Martienssen. Martienssen had spent significant amounts of time studying Le Corbusier's buildings (and those of other European modernists, especially the German expressionist Erich Mendelsohn). The Transvaal Group constructed modernist houses in the wealthy Johannesburg suburb of Houghton and blocks of modernist flats and high-rises in the city. The influence of the master may be seen in Martienssen's House Stern of 1934 (Martienssen, Fassler, and Cooke, 1934). It is clearly modeled on Le Corbusier's famous Villa Stein at Garches in France. Chipkin, who highlights the lines of influence in features such as the external staircase with its powerful diagonal, the paved first-floor terrace "floating as an idea," and curved walls, puts it unequivocally: "Le Corbusier is everywhere."[8]

In the design of his own house in the Johannesburg suburb of Greenside, Martienssen reveals his personal love of the Italian Renaissance, especially through his subtle way of configuring abstract forms in glass and brick, with small Renaissance-Mannerist windows, highly asymmetrically placed,

House Stern (Martienssen, Fassler, and Cooke, 1934). Photograph by George Abbott. Published in *The South African Architectural Record* 22, no. 3 (March 1937).

punctuating a serenely proportioned facadelike front that announces its solidity even as it promises access to the space within. Moreover, the house commands the site in the manner of a palazzo, rather than being open to it in the manner of a "glass box": this is achieved by raising the structure slightly on what is otherwise a fairly flat and open site, and by running a low white wall across the front of it, with a set of stairs that must be climbed in the approach from "below." However, Martienssen's love of southern architectural styles is confined—as Baker's was before him—to the realm of private design.

As editor, writer, teacher, and builder, Martienssen became the center of modernist dissemination. Fully internationalized, he and his associates conceived of themselves as part of a worldwide aesthetic and cultural revolution, of which Johannesburg was simply a local "city-site." In this view, shared by the likes of Niemeyer and Costa, questions of locality were simply misplaced. "There are no problems of form, only problems of building," Mies had famously remarked, meaning that context posed no questions for the general theory of architectural form, but merely for its application in a particular place. Of course, Mies's principles of the steel and glass box with its open plan were not the same as Le Corbusier's, announced in *Vers une Architecture* (which Martienssen had read before going to Paris in 1933). So form in fact remained an issue for the modernists, as their contending allegiances demonstrate. However, Mies's open plan, with its "golden rectangle" capable of infinite variation in modular subdivision, and Le Corbusier's "free plan," or *"plan libre,"* which separated design from load-bearing structure, thus allowing freedom in the shape and skin of the building, were close enough in kind to allow for a mentality, or "style."

Martienssen and his group produced their own manifesto in 1933, which included these words: "The contemporary spirit is abroad . . . we should regard ourselves as drawing near to a remote future rather than receding from a historic past—indeed all living art is the history of the future."[9] The two rather different meanings of the word "abroad" are interesting here, as they suggest that the contemporary spirit is both "present everywhere," "in circulation" all around them, and "overseas," "in a foreign country." This captures the marginal position of these architects perfectly: they are abreast of the international trends, and yet they are also grasping at what is distant from them, so that their city might catch up with the contemporary, with the center, and truly live. Thus, while their manifesto, declaring its intention to erase the past and harness the teeming, utopian energies of the future, is avant-gardism at its most authentic,[10] they have

(I repeat) no Paris to scandalize, no Paris to raze. They find themselves in what is still little more than a mining town, surrounded by the recently constructed Edwardian and art deco buildings of the earlier generation. So this urban radicalism, existing in a still empty and unformed marginal space, must announce itself as arising both from here and from elsewhere; the full thrust of its radical attack is directed at a world that lies at a distance, in Europe, even if that world is also continuous in some ways with the immediate one, South Africa.

However, there is also a certain irony in the transposition of Corbu's ideals to a city regulated by colonial norms and principles (apartheid is not yet in place when these architects pen their thoughts). For if nothing else, the Corbu utopia is meant to be one of equality through rationally planned uniformity in design, and the resistance of the city of Johannesburg to any principle of equality was obviously endemic to its categorical divisions between white/European and black/Native. Equality, as in the original U.S. Constitution, was delegated only to those of the requisite type, rather than to all. It is for this reason that the Corbu utopia belongs in the undeveloped spaces of Brasilia and Chandigarh, which is to say, to the spaces of young postcolonial nations formally (if not substantively) dedicated to principles of citizenship based in equality for all. South Africa would take up this formal dispensation of rights only after apartheid's collapse, some many years later, and at a time when the Corbu ideal (of equality through rationally designed uniformity) was widely discredited. As it ultimately also was in Brasilia, where finally, the modernist city, in the words of James Holston, became subverted by the local forms of street life that disrupted its pristine spaces, and by the (again ironic) inequality in the apportionment of housing and workplace there (the rich and professional classes occupying the center, the poor and working class having to travel longer distances, being consigned to the city's periphery, etcetera).[11]

From first to last, every modernist style imaginable found representation in Johannesburg, from Victoriana to art deco. This openness to influence sometimes produced those delicious ironies that lend the study of history its peculiar pleasures. Chipkin, for instance, describes the "temporary fascination" of some businessmen and architects of the 1920s with the "Fascist house style," a blend of modernized classicism and futurism that reached Johannesburg as an "irradiation from Mussolini's Rome . . . either directly or indirectly via centres like New York."[12] Many of those who had fallen under the spell of this rhetoric later fought against the Fascists during World War II.

The Architecture of Apartheid

After World War II, South Africa made its own movement in the direction of the right, with the 1948 election (by means of gerrymandering) of the National Party to power, which immediately began to construct the apartheid state. The building of apartheid sought to articulate and extend the power of the state, with its apportionment of citizenship and space on the basis of racist essentialism, by recruiting the modernist principles of open planning, transparency of space, rationalization of architectural functions (circulation, work, leisure, etcetera) and using them to express a systemic panopticism. In the bare, modernist blocks of concrete that are the buildings of apartheid resides a "power that does not have to account for itself," in the words of Andries Gouws.[13] In the enormous size and scope of these buildings, in their rigid spatial formulae, resides the institution of bureaucratic control, the inflexibility of system, the refusal of openness. Gone from this architecture is the fluidity of the Miesian house, the Corbu machine, or the fantasy on Eurocentric copulation with whatever building happens to happen, be it Italian fascist or deco French. Gone is the connection to a modernism of excitement and elegance. Instead the bare brutalism of architectural force, the bare fact of inner metaphysical control, the massification of Corbu concrete, the bare inhabitance of prisonlike rooms—these are the features that begin to be highlighted. Thus is the University of South Africa (UNISA) made, the largest distance university in Africa, designed almost single-handedly by Brian Sandrock. It is nearly the size of the Pentagon, and has something of the massively intimidating effect of that paragon of power. Endlessly interconnected corridors dwarf the human; the faculties lining the corridors appear like so many cells. Asserting itself horizontally over the freeway from Johannesburg and Pretoria, it is literally in your face as you drive toward it and under it, as if to say, "Space is mine, you pass if you obey." Built in a horizontal format, the building graces itself with a single, monumentlike vertical thrust, which transmutes modernism into monument, the monument of a poetry drained of poetry and replaced by concrete. Finally, it monumentalizes itself with a Wagnerian or Aztec "fin" at one end, an elevated series of levels that take on, from a distance, the function of turning the building into a modernist sculptural monument—a monument to itself, its power, its capacity to install itself with maximum brutality on its site, its size, scope, and identity. Universities tend to be composed of multiple buildings, connected through tree-lined walkways and open parks; the question to ask is why this one chooses to express itself as a single, multistructural block of buildings connected by a horizontal spine—in the manner of airports, prisons, government buildings, army headquarters. The answer surely has to do with the gesture of power, security, and enclosure that is internal to the insecure nature of the assertive apartheid state.

The Rand Afrikaans University (RAU, now called the Rand African University), now a thriving, nonracial metropolitan campus but built originally as a bulwark of Afrikaner culture, exhibits the principles of apartheid construction to a T. The university was designed by Willie Meyer in association with Jan van Wijk. Built one year after UNISA, it is far more elegant in shape. A series of "blocks" surrounds a vast amphitheater. Students are meant to assemble here but they seldom do, for one feels dwarfed by the encircling structure and watched from every window. Perhaps the amphitheater with its Roman references encouraged a sense of embattled but secure identity among the white, Afrikaans-speaking students who daily traversed it in earlier years. The construction is intricate, indeed formally excellent, with a vast downward spiral of buildings reaching completion in the dramatic stage of the amphitheater. The floors of the buildings are of wholly unornamented concrete. One's location is defined in terms reminiscent of a prison: D Ring, Level 4, and so on. Each faculty branching off from the ring attains a measure of "privacy," but the larger effect is to make the faculties themselves disappear into insignificance: it is the great ring that matters, not its individual elements. This is grandiose architecture, and it is an irony that the architect was a pupil of Louis Kahn. Here, Kahn has been imported to the periphery, to legitimate Afrikaner nationalist identity. His meditative, elemental spaces have been rendered panoptic and larger than life.

Consider the way RAU monumentalizes itself. On the whole, the modernist public architecture of apartheid, unlike that of Italian Fascism or the German Reich, leaves little room for mythological referencing. Drained from the architecture of apartheid are even those wonderful and humane architectural legacies of the Afrikaans' settler past: the Cape Dutch house, the Karoo dwelling, the Baroque Eastern Cape Town—at least, in public architecture. For in private, the state functionaries who commissioned UNISA and RAU might have wanted to build themselves a little place (or a big place) of precisely this kind. However, in public, such buildings evaporate in an essentially modern system of power that solicits, and indeed requires, expression through the modernist principles of architecture, laid bare as panoptic in form and massified in scope. Public mythology becomes, in the buildings of apartheid, self-monumentalization in concrete—with one single, obsessively repeated exception: the Great Trek, as if all of history is reduced to this single point of reference. The RAU campus is "gifted" this reference, which is crucial for Afrikaner nationalism. The circular arrangement of the buildings and the tightly enclosed interior space are not simply panoptic; they also reproduce the image of the laager. The Voortrekkers, the Afrikaner pioneers who first colonized the interior of the country in the 1800s, would draw their ox wagons into a protective circle as a defense against attack. The impenetrable laager came to represent an implacable resistance against all outsiders, as well as a contained gathering place for the volk, for the people, and the RAU amphitheater surely carries these meanings. One might have expected the grand buildings of apartheid to resonate with the *architectural* glories of Afrikaner history. After all, the Cape Dutch homestead, with its whitewashed walls and French balustrades, is a masterpiece of simple elegance, while the little Karoo house, with its tin roof shading the front step against the desert heat, has an apt and delicate beauty of its own. But such references are almost entirely absent. When nationalism demanded a return to mythic origins, it was almost invariably to the Great Trek and the laager. By obsessively mythologizing the Trek as the founding event of the nation, the means through which the land was truly occupied and conquered, the nationalists claimed ownership of South Africa and asserted their entitlement to rule. The black South Africans who were there before them were reduced both to a vanquished enemy and to a mere aspect of the landscape itself, like the flora and fauna. These two contradictory images deprived the "native" of a founding role in the identity of the nation.

The use of this laager form is critical to everything that RAU is. On the one hand, it is meant to be a building that directly opposes the "liberalism" of the University of Witwatersrand, a refuge for Afrikaans/Nationalist Party identity politics against the "heathen liberal hordes," if you will. Hence the laager. Surrounded by its modernist ox wagons in poured concrete, this laager is what allowed the Voortrekkers to fight and beat the Zulu, and it is now what will draw symbolic and "moral" strength from that experience and allow the Afrikaner young who attend this university to formulate themselves into the next generation of powerful, tribalized youth.

The laager was meant to be the place at RAU where university functions, theater (as in the ancient Greek temple), and speechifying would take place. It is seldom used, for as one sits in it, one feels as if every window in the spiraling building that surrounds it is looking right down at one. This sense of being the object of a thousand panoptic gazes is fundamental to the place of surveillance and control in the construction of this

Rand Afrikaans University (now called the Rand African University), Johannesburg.
Photograph by Lucia Saks; reprinted with permission.

communalized site. You shall make up the tribe, but we are also watching
you. The laager at RAU is now mostly empty space.

Douw Van Zyl of the Faculty of Architecture of the University of Natal
has noted that Willie Meyer, the architect, conceived of this building as a
formally elegant spiral with multiple "fingers," which would allow for fluid
circulation and individual intimacy within each finger. Furthermore, what
is taken by me to be a laager was quite possibly in the architect's mind
merely a Roman amphitheater, taken over from his studies in the United
States and made "bigger and better" in the "small, peripheral" country of
South Africa, as if to outdo the center at its own game of size and shape.
This reading of the building is indeed convincing, which to my mind
proves how dominant *context* is in constructing meaning for a building. It
is my view that, given the way RAU was specifically part of the political
agenda of the apartheid state, the larger-than-life character of the spiraling
fingers and amphitheater simply was, in the minds of the architect's clients
(the university and, behind it, the state), the fortress/laager I describe. It is
certainly the way apartheid history construed this building. The moral is
that what makes a building an apartheid building may be a combination of
its monumental (larger than life) features and the context that at the time
dominates its meaning. Neither may be, by itself, sufficient to determine
architectural meaning.[14]

A building about which there can be no doubt of its meaning, however, is one that employs the same kind of mythological referencing: the Voortrekker Monument near Pretoria (in fact, quite close to UNISA), which was built at the inception of the apartheid state (1948). The monument is *the* major commemoration of the Trek in South Africa. It was designed by Gerard Moerdyk, who drew his inspiration from Bruno Schmitz's Völkerschlacht Memorial in Leipzig.[15] Both the enclosing wall with its ox-wagon reliefs and the circular interior echo the form of the laager. From the upper floor, with its "history paintings," the visitor looks down upon the cenotaph, where an eternal flame is burning (for the time being, at least). In the domain of public building, the spareness of modern architectural style tends to preclude massive ornamentation and referentiality; but in the realm of monuments, the level of creative play with symbols, signs, references, and styles can be intensified, and with it the level of kitsch. The result in this case is a graphic illustration of one of the operations of modernism at the margins. The monument takes art deco forms and renders them as ornament, hardening their fluid lines, imposing a religious severity and overstated indomitability. Moreover, it takes the multiple gothic, orientalizing references of its German prototype and reduces them to a spare, religious front (the architect had designed a number of Dutch Reformed churches with similarly arched, brick portals). The kitsch resides in the tension between the deco elements and the memorializing purpose: the building looks like a deco radio tower made to do duty as brick church or war bunker.

It is significant that the monument upon which Moerdyk draws is the Völkerschlacht Memorial in Leipzig. "Völkerschlacht" means "carnage of the people," or better, "carnage of the *volk*," and there is a special work of signification that arises from the "dialogue" between these two monuments. The Leipzig monument was built at the beginning of the twentieth century, just at the time when the Boer war was lost, the Afrikaner people were decimated, their power wrested by the English, they themselves in concentration camps. In the unconscious of the Voortrekker monument, it is this moment of Afrikaner loss that is being memorialized in Leipzig and being converted, at the moment of the formation of the apartheid state, into a signifier of group identity and state power revolving around the cenotaph of memory. And so the one monument speaks the terrible past of a people to the other, which replaces that past with a return to a deeper moral and political victory won by those people: the Great Trek itself. In this conversation between monuments, defeat is turned to victory, as the one monument replaces the other, but in a way that always carries the

Voortrekker Monument (Gerard Moerdyk, 1948), Opening Ceremony, 1949, outside Pretoria. National Archives of South Africa (photograph TAB 36514). Reproduction by permission of the National Archives of South Africa.

memory of the earlier one. This is precisely the way in which the National Party wished to imagine South African history: from Afrikaner victory (the Great Trek of the nineteenth century) to Afrikaner defeat (the Boer war) and again, back to the earlier victory that reemerges in the formation of the apartheid state, a state predicated on the surge of Afrikaner identity politics. And so issues of memorialization and loss become transposed into issues of retribalization, return, and victory. It is therefore natural that this monument is built at the very moment that the National Party wins the elections and the apartheid state comes into being, as a sign of immediate symbolization and victory.

The Voortrekker monument is probably also a way of voicing the pro-Nazi sympathies of many who founded the apartheid state, for it identifies Afrikaner suffering with German nationalism.

Group and Area

We have seen that apartheid sought to prevent the intermingling that is a mark of the modern. Apartheid may itself be described as an *architecture* of social planning: in the first instance the architecture of apartheid is not the buildings and monuments, it is apartheid itself. Verwoerd was considered "the architect of apartheid." Apartheid was an architecture, since it regulated space along principles of identity, citizenship, and circulation. Yet the intermingling persisted. Sometimes the incipient rhythms of modernity were so powerful that the only way of disrupting them was to obliterate an entire city quarter. Hence the importance of the Group Areas Act, without which apartheid would have been unsustainable as an "architecture" of space.

This was the fate of the Johannesburg suburb of Sophiatown. It was also the fate of District Six in Cape Town and Cato Manor in Durban. Each city had its para-city destroyed and its populations removed.

By the 1930s Sophiatown, a para-city at the periphery of a city at the margins of modernity, had already outgrown its identity as a shantytown filled with violence and poverty (which it surely was) to become the slowly emerging center of a new form of life produced by the urbanized black people who called it home. American influences—Harlem music, Hollywood film—went into a lively, hybridized cultural life of shebeens, jazz, dancing. The painter Gerard Sekoto found his genius in these winding streets by attending to the brilliant refractions of color and hard shadows that the dry, transparent light produced on corrugated iron and crumbling plaster. Paris, where he made his home soon after the institution of apartheid, would finally cripple his talent: without this place, this light, this color, he was finished.

In the 1950s, Sophiatown became the seedbed for a new generation of African intellectuals and artists, flaneurs whose gazes, when directed to the white world of the city (from which black people were excluded by law), could not help but become politicized. Moreover, the cultural forums of the Sophiatown era—most notably the equally famous *Drum* magazine, which provided a livelihood for some of these writers and photographers—were themselves places where the constructed and divided "races" of apartheid mingled and melded.

It is no coincidence that the Defiance Campaign of 1952, the first mass mobilization against unjust laws in the country's history, gestated in areas like Sophiatown. It was only because of the new identities, forms of flaneurship, and contiguities (spatial, intellectual, recreational) that the para-cities engendered that resistance could emerge out of a racially mixed conglomeration of people from all walks of life—politicians, professionals, intellectuals, workers. James Holston and Arjun Appadurai have argued in an eloquent essay that cities are perhaps the central sites where pressure is placed on the dispensation of formal rights (to vote, to move

Gerard Sekoto (1913–1993), *Street Scene,* 1945, oil on board. Permanent collection of South African National Gallery, Cape Town. Reproduction by permission of the South African National Gallery.

freely, to receive procedural justice) and substantive rights (to freedom of work, economic justice, health and welfare, equal education, cultural expression and identification, and the like) by new, dispossessed, or marginal populations. Since this apportionment of formal and substantive rights is in effect the apportionment of citizenship, cities are the central site (often, if not always) where citizenship is passionately and tumultuously questioned and finds itself inexorably changing.[16] To break up the forms of resistance—and more than that, the new identities being created in Sophiatown—it was essential that the para-city itself be destroyed. The history of anti-Semitism in Europe had already shown that even when forced into ghettos, Jews would seep back into the textures of the city as a whole over time, through assimilation, hybridization, intermarriage, economic embroilment, and shared forms of life that must of necessity arise in contiguous urban environments. A tour of the Prague ghetto clearly shows the movement of Jewish ownership, of Jewish capital and life, out of the ghetto and into the rest of the city in the early twentieth century. This urban embroilment brought pressure for change to bear on the system of rights, unequally apportioned to Christian and Jew, change that was brutally curtailed in 1939. Similarly, Sophiatown (later Cato Manor and District Six) had to be destroyed. What the apartheid state required was that a *physical gap* be opened up between para-city and city proper, so that the latter might retain its pure integrity—this, because it is a natural concomitant of industrialization that groups mix in space, idea, and identity. Forced removals, by rending the very urban fabric through which these new identities and, importantly, *solidarities* could be woven, deprived a generation of its language. An entire spectrum of African identities at the margins of the margins, a uniquely cosmopolitan set of identities and their now unimaginable potentials, were killed off. The forced removals began in 1955, and by 1960 Sophiatown was rubble.

When resistance finally reemerged in the mid-1970s, steeped in the brutalities of apartheid and the impoverished rhetoric of the Eastern bloc, in anger and exile, it spoke a more violent and intolerant language whose echoes are still heard today.

The Group Areas Act knew exactly what it was doing. Its point was not simply to intimidate and separate populations, to categorize, dissect, and destroy. Its point was to prevent: to prevent those natural concomitants of urban modernity that produce new kinds of people with new interests and new capacities from flourishing—and to retain colonial power formations based on apartness, which were apt in rural African cultures but required state terror for their implementation in a modern, urban society like South Africa.

Partly following work by Mahmood Mamdani,[17] it can be said that apartheid South Africa is about re-creating decentralized power arrangements in which African "native" populations remain "in their own areas" while European cities are the sites of civil and political rights and powers. The attempt was first to control African native populations through the system of the "dompas," which required natives to gain permissions from the authorities to work in cities, travel through provinces, and move. This system of bureaucratic control refused, for example, a black African worker the right to remain in Johannesburg between ten at night and four in the morning. When the system of the "dompas" proved unmanageable, then the Group Areas Act, already on the books and half-enforced, became the dramatic instrument of forced separation and, through it, control.

To state what everybody knows, *even* in the confrontational years of the late seventies, public space evolved that rejected the strictures of apartheid: in the Newtown area of Johannesburg, in the old fruit and vegetable market and the surrounding buildings, a dynamic zone of nonracial culture developed. At the hub of it was the Market Theatre itself, where some of the most renowned anti-apartheid theater was developed and performed, and there were also galleries, restaurants, bars, music venues, art schools, flea markets. The area has a chaotic informality that is distinctively South African. Nearby, the modernist skyscrapers of downtown Johannesburg, towers of unadorned concrete and reflective glass, remind us that we are on a peculiar frontier where the first world meets the third.

So we return to the theme of a city whose urbanism, whose juxtapositions of form and personality, whose inflections, interminglings, and gaps bespeak a complex, convoluted modernity that neither colonial nor apartheid rules could prevent or undo. Johannesburg (like Durban and Cape Town), defined by strict rules of public construction that sought to prevent the natural intermingling that is part and parcel of urbanized modernity everywhere, remains vibrant with difference. Despite the poverty, despite the crime, it is the kind of city Baudelaire extolled, one whose contingencies, fragmentations, paths of intermingling, and shifting processes of life cannot be theorized from any single angle, but instead require the work of witnessing, enjoyment, and fascination, which is that of the modern painter.

Johannesburg should always have cultivated the modernist work of free-floating fascination and critique. But can we imagine Baudelaire's "painter of modern life" here? Can we imagine a Manet of the Highveld? This mythical genius would have had to reinvent himself, finding a new position, working his Parisianisms through in order to give representation to a different kind of city, one of unadulterated capitalism and desperate poverty, a city of lively Sophiatowns and barren squatter camps, a city both excited by the opportunity it offers and bored by its remoteness from the center. This reinvention would also have displaced him, since South Africa's grave history would not easily have accepted the light touch of the flaneur. And if this genius were to arise today? Perhaps he would find the lack of a robust, cosmopolitan art world in South Africa less of a problem than the global trade in installations and those art events that have become standard biennales, flowing in the well-worn channels from center to margin, with its postmodern imagespeak that drains locality as surely as any international modernism ever did.

It was only as a pair—law on the one hand and space on the other—that the apartheid state could produce power. Law by itself—that is, laws prescribing racial segregation—are already laws about space (who can do what where and with whom in virtue of their construction as racial types). But space undercuts the rule of law insofar as modern space is about intermingling (urbanization, circulation, movement of people in uncontainable ways). And so the rule of space must be asserted with increasing violence to buttress the rule of law, just as the rule of law (the police, the acts of terror) must be asserted with increasing violence to buttress the rule of space. Hence, the first wave of resistance to apartheid is crushed by both: on the one hand, the erasure of the para-cities (Sophiatown in Johannesburg, Cato Manor in Durban, District Six in Cape Town); on the other, the arrest of the leaders (Mandela, Sisulu, etcetera), the Rivonia trial, and their confinement at Robbin Island, which earlier served as a leper colony and was a perfect site of Foucauldian isolation.

Now insofar as law functioned only in conjunction with space (the buildings of apartheid, the planning of the townships at sufficient distance from the cities to prevent intermingling, the refusal of transportation systems, the placement of Bantu universities in the middle of nowhere, namely in the Bantustans), it was crucial that modern architecture and city planning were already in effect for the apartheid state to emerge and take shape. Consider two plans: the one, a block of flats from 1939, with its classic Corbusian placement of space inside the compound and its rational, "transparent" arrangement of buildings on the site; the other, the site plan for a native township.

Three-Dimensional View of Flat Blocks, 1939, Johannesburg. Photograph from P. H. Connell, C. Irvine-Smith, K. Jonas, R. Kantorowich, and F. Wepener, *Native Housing: A Collective Thesis*, Witwatersrand University Press, 1939. Reproduction by permission of Witwatersrand University Press.

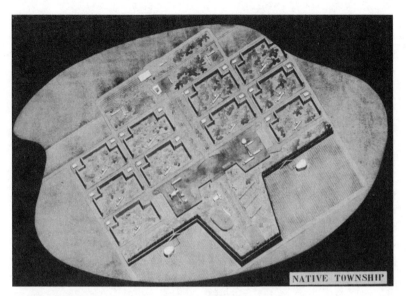

Site Plan of Native Township, 1939. Photograph from P. H. Connell, C. Irvine-Smith, K. Jonas, R. Kantorowich, and F. Wepener, *Native Housing: A Collective Thesis,* Witwatersrand University Press, 1939. Reproduction by permission of Witwatersrand University Press.

Their remarkable similarity should bring the point home. Modern architecture is a condition of the possibility of township planning, which, parenthetically, began before the institution of the apartheid state in 1948, and, indeed, well before 1939 with the development of housing on the mines. It is only because an epistemic regime of building was in place, with its values of transparency, rationality, and division of space in accord with function, that the specifically panoptic, monumental, and containment functions of apartheid building and planning could arise. Ditto for the building of Stalinist Russia and other "savory" sites of modern architecture. These inflections of larger epistemic patterns, as Foucault would put it, are part of the history of modern architecture, part of its history of articulation and dissemination. I want to say this clearly: apartheid is part of the history of modern architecture in roughly the same way that the dropping of the bomb on Hiroshima is part of the history of physics. The history of modern architecture does not "cause" apartheid (which would be ridiculous). Nor are all modernist buildings equally panoptic or confining. City planning is not always, in Corbusian terms, as destructive to the movement and freedom of human lives as the townships were. And yet modern architecture is never free of the traces of these principles of pan-opticism and confinement, never entirely so. Even Mies's houses for the rich always face the problem of people looking in (a basic problem of steel and glass), as Corbu's face the problem of confinement within machine-like walls, even where he so magnificently achieves open gardens within a building form (as in his houses at Ahmedabad). It is this that brands the variety of styles of modernism (Miesian, Corbusian, etcetera) that have in the past gone under the name of "the International Style" and that in reality constitute a variety of styles with overlapping epistemic principles (Foucauldian). And were it not for the broad epistemic principles of trans-parency, panopticism, and modularity, which are rules for the production of elements in modern life as different as the post office, the town plan, and the freeway, apartheid as a system of state planning would not be pos-sible. In this apartheid is one of various extreme inflections of the broad epistemic regime through which modern power is articulated.

Freedom in South African Modernism

Not all buildings made during the apartheid years are rightly called "the architecture of the apartheid regime." That regime pursued an exacting expression of political structure, concerning itself with who comprised the South African nation and how it would live with the rules of identity and citizenship. At the same time, a lot of modern buildings were built in the forty-year period of apartheid that do not share this desire to construct and symbolize the system. At the same time that the buildings of apart-heid were being built, an offshoot of the Transvaal Group took modern-ism into a new phase in South Africa through a critique of Corbu. This group of Johannesburg architects included Norman Hanson and Gordon McIntosh, both associated with Martienssen earlier on, as well as John Fassler and Roy Kantorowich (Martienssen himself died prematurely in 1942). This new "group" sought to extend and refine international models of European origin by softening Le Corbusier's philosophy of construc-tion. Although they always denied that they were part of a "movement," Julian Cooke has argued that they shared a deep concern with a set of ideas developed in Europe from the 1930s onward, which he summarizes as "a new classicism, vernacular traditionalism, and a revised and softened functionalism,"[18] and that they took the European buildings generated by these ideas as their models. The group associated with Hanson and Kantorowich, taking their cue from recent tendencies in internationalism, included local materials and ornamentation in their designs to reduce the severity of pristine modernism. If "nationalism" meant anything to them, it was simply the idea of favoring the local environment as a source of materials and ornaments. Their buildings were of apartheid in the sense of having been built within the economy that kept its politics going. They were of apartheid in the sense of conforming by law to its rules of use. However, they were, in fact, about a kind of architectural indifference to political system, an indifference with which, it must be said, Corbu and Mies would probably have felt comfortable. Instead, their point was to slowly introduce response to locality into the severe forms of modernism.

Under the influence of Brazilian modernism, which traveled into Mozambique and from there into Johannesburg, these architects began to think about what it meant to build in the intense heat and the harsh landscape of the south. Looking to Niemeyer's use of sun-filtration paneling, which Corbu had already thought about when designing houses in India, and looking also to the bright ornamental tilings and facade work of the Brazilians and Mozambicans, these architects began to open the modernist building to local function and local decoration while also preserving its underlying structures.

Cooke describes the group's interest in shifts in European architecture, such as the revival of "National Romanticism" in Sweden and the adoption by South Africans of similar strategies to make architecture "warmer and more approachable": "The minimal range of materials of heroic modernism, detailed to almost nothing, was replaced by a larger palette: facebrick, terrazzo, mosaic, travertine, random rubble stonework, timber, wrought iron—a far cry from painted steel windows and glass." They also returned to decoration, which the Transvaal Group had despised, and "[a]bstract forms were softened with texture, wide eaves, gently pitched roofs and pergolas."[19]

In a well-known essay,[20] Kenneth Frampton identified this kind of movement within modernism as "critical regionalism" and argued that it was a way of reasserting cultural identity against (if also within) the confines of total internationalism. Features of critical regionalism include, according to Frampton, an enhanced tactility and an enhanced interest in the site (locality) the building will occupy. It is interesting, then, that the South Africans made this assertion largely through the act of *importing* already regionalized forms from Brazil and Mozambique, rather than immediately turning to Africa and rethinking their modernisms in its "light." Moreover, South African architects did their importing largely in private, rather than public, spaces. Again, we come up against the limitations on spatial construction given within South Africa.

However, both tendencies (to import localism and to do it in private) also had their exceptions. In the late 1950s and early 1960s, the architect Norman Eaton went furthest toward imbuing his buildings, including his *public* buildings, with a feeling for African life and design. Eaton traveled extensively throughout Africa and incorporated design features based on Zanzibar buildings, North African texture patterns, and Ndebele facades. Exoticizing Africa, in the manner of Irma Stern, as a vast oneness, and also in love with its light, open space, red earth, and design patterns, Eaton blended these elements with his "Mediterraneanism" to incorporate marvelous wall murals, striking chevron-brick and tiled-floor designs, and "Africanized" circular forms in the concrete "parks" around his buildings. Eaton's designs are exceptional in their attempt to hybridize modernist and local styles. And this exceptionality returns us to the main argument: modernism here is sufficiently purist and constricted to prevent a more pervasive hybridization.

In private Norman Eaton attempted more thoroughgoing reconfigurations of form in the light of local geography, landscape, materials, and historical legacies. His Greenwood House (1949–1951, stoneworker's quarters) in the Highveld is built from mushrooming towers, in Highveld stone, and capped with Zulu thatching from the Kraal form. Fragmented and decentered, the dwelling seems like a zany mythic ruin, a piece of the landscape that had been discovered by some proponent of the African renaissance who went out searching for the great Zimbabwe ruins and took a wrong turn. The building, combining elements of the English cottage, the medieval castle, and the African Kraal, is a creative attempt to truly overcome the principles of modernism. It is nontransparent in form, more aesthetic than functional in idea, and above all, it obliterates the distinction between structure and ornament crucial to all modernism. Wildly exotic, combining a museological gaze on the African ruin and the panoply of facadist styles in Africa, it places, finally, modern architecture in the domain of the settler painter, the one who combines love, proximity, fascination, and the museological gaze into a single, less than coherent canvas while also refusing the settler's refusal to become part of things. It has, by contrast, gone native in its Africanization of space.

Architecture and the Public Sphere

Thus viewed, the building of public space in the age of South African modernism, with its division between public and private space, appears as a system regulated by principles of modernist internationalism and its sty-

Kopje-stone workers' quarters, Greenwood House (Norman Eaton, 1949–1951), Pretoria. Photograph by Clive M. Chipkin. Reprinted from Clive M. Chipkin, *Johannesburg Style: Architecture and Society 1880s–1960s* (Cape Town: David Philip Publishers, 1993). Reproduction by permission of Clive M. Chipkin.

listic control on the one hand and administration, colonial control, essentialization, and exclusion on the other. These are twin hegemonies. Again, no city is reducible to these forms of control, as any history of Durban or Johannesburg would show. In postmodern, late-capitalist times, new forms of public space are developing in the highly imitative, postmodern malls of South African cities. The Pavilion, located outside Durban just off the freeway, is a veritable monument to global capitalism. In nearly the largest mall in Africa, the vast interior spaces of modern department stores meet the Crystal Palace and Brighton Beach. The glaring fake-Victorian structure, whose glassy green and golden domes can be seen, like Chartres Cathedral, from a distance of fifty miles, recalls English colonial style with a nostalgia worthy of KwaZulu-Natal's Anglophile tendencies and celebrates late capitalist consumption with a brashness worthy of Los Angeles or the Home Shopping Channel. The mall is an homage to ongoing Anglophilia, but of the Anglo-Indian/Empire variety—that is, of the golden age of the "Jewel in the Crown." It is worth pointing out that this has great popular appeal for the middle- and upper-middle-class Indian communities of Durban in particular, who revel in its over-the-top orientalism as only a diasporic group perhaps could.

The mall pours with crowds at all times, for it is safe (something rare in this crime-ridden country) and unique (something even rarer in a shrinking world). In addition to the history of global capitalism, according to which the mall gets invented, the entire history of South African space, constructed on the principle of "divide and rule," must enter into the genealogy of the South African mall, which, through a vast irony, becomes one of the few genuinely *public* spaces in an underpopulated country and a rare melting pot for races who continue to live highly separate lives. Television, if we concede that it is "public space," might be another arena where the "rainbow nation" of the new South Africa begins to exist. The new malls, like the new clubs, bars, gyms, and shops, commingle a new interracial middle class predicated on shared yuppiedom and shared pleasure in consumption, a rainbow class formed in the image of late capitalist liberalism. The members of this new class are not (yet) as absorbed in consumerism as their American counterparts, just as the spaces they occupy are not (yet) as corrupted by the excesses of late capitalism, and it remains to be seen what relationships their new proximity will produce.

Were one not to rest content with a new South Africa built to order as an adjunct to global postmodernism, one would have to return to the themes of return and intermingling: a return to those marvelous premodern architectural forms that grace South African space and that have yet to be absorbed into the creation of new forms of *public* building and design and an intermingling of them in forms different from what any of them have been to date. That is: return as intermingling.

In South Africa the new nation now rewrites its entire past for a new colloquy. The Zulu kraal, the Cape Dutch and Karoo house, the Victorian building on the Durban embankment, the cave, the Ndebele mural—these are now potentially the cultural legacy of the entire nation, which is finally ready to accept them as its own and entitled by law and spirit to do so. The nation will not become a nation until its citizens come to imagine this diverse and fragmented architectural past as potentially belonging to everybody and available for their appropriation, while at the same time understanding well that each bit of history was made by some specific group as part of its own visage, and is thus in some fundamental way their unique cultural property. This twin recognition of the visage of the other as the other's, and as potentially also one's own, is crucial to the ethics of citizenship, of belonging.

It was a central theme of Hegel's that a nation, the sign of reconciliation, requires the dissolution of the master-slave dialectic and a new form of recognition. No longer does the master see himself as owning the labor of the slave, who remains unrecognized by him, reducing him to a speck of dust on the horizon. Nor does the slave see himself abjectly as mere material for the master's field of glory. In the struggle for recognition, each finally comes—for the first time—to see himself through the eyes of the other: the master as slave to the slave because he is nothing but a house cat, dependent on the work and skill of the slave; the slave as master to the master, because he is able to begin to imagine himself as working for himself, for the recovery of his deadened culture. At this point, we may say, reading beyond Hegel, each becomes like the other and both become different. The field of symbols is then similarly reapportioned so that the slave's past again becomes *his*. The master's past is no longer merely for him—a mirror for his distinctive, essentializing, tribalist recognition, which produces power over the other—it is now for everybody. At this moment, the problematic of modernity at the margins is returned to and happens again. For the question of how to recast this past so that it might live again in the new dispensation of recognition cannot be resolved by reference to the past alone. Since each party is now different and their lives are different, old forms of recognition, themselves tainted by the history of separateness, must be preserved, but also new forms must be reinvented from them, which might begin to articulate the new dispensation.

These are the stakes of citizenship. Citizenship is not simply a value defined by constitutional law, but also a value achieved through the articulation of new styles of recognition between citizens, who thereby participate in defining themselves. There is no single image adequate to the ways in which the new national colloquy might come to recognize itself. That of a Rainbow Nation, composed of distinct yet separate bands of color, is one image; a tapestry in which each band, through a mysterious process of staining, slowly bleeds into the next, producing a variegated and untraceable collusion of patterns with its own particular iridescence and leaving no color in the end fully distinct, is another. My point is that if architecture is to discover again its great thematic capacity for the symbolization of life, if it is to do this by participating in the invention of new forms of recognition, it must return to the project of working through the center, of working through its history of Eurocentric dependency, in the name of the difference of the periphery—a project it never has adequately taken on in the history of South African life. It must become, at this postmodern juncture in late capitalism, modern again: *modern at the periphery*. Granted the overcoming of the two hegemonies that have ruled South African public building—internationalism and neocolonialism—it is now possible for South Africa to expand the purview of its originality and to *become original* by returning to its sites of past originality and to the originality in its peoples. To rest content with the postmodern preference for the copy and the postmodern pleasure of referential game-playing, to rest content with these forms of global play and television that appear on every hotel TV screen where CNN can be watched, would be to repeat once again an act of imitation that has never faded from the South African scene.

Let me not be naive. One would never presume to state some claim such as, "All future South African architecture must return to its vernaculars, remake and intermingle them," as if that were the only route to originality. Return to past vernaculars can descend into a romanticism about myths of origin; one must monitor the African Renaissance for this. It can turn into the most rank version of postmodern pastiche, as in the Rosebank office park with its sleek Cape Dutch facade that says, "I am a Cape Dutch facade," as in the Karoo tin roof that states, "I am a charming Karoo house with a green tin roof in a safe townhouse complex," as if they were signs from some Las Vegas casino or nostalgia items from some catalog of dress, furniture, or cuisine. Such referentiality is not "almost all right,"[21] for it commercializes the past and further represses diversity by homogenizing it, turning diversity into a series of packaging items from the South African designer catalog and South Africa into an appendage of global-information capitalism, specifically of American signage and sentimentalism. No doubt South Africa is that, no doubt it will remain that. But how totally, how completely must it be subsumed by this system of power? With what cooperation and co-optation, with what lack of resistance? Insofar as South African architecture wishes to be more at the moment of transition to democracy, insofar as South African architecture wishes to be *original*, it cannot reduce itself to this system of production. Indeed, since the vernacular includes the history of internationalism (which, in spite of tendencies toward an antivernacularist stance, produced the exact prototypes for a vernacular and has indeed become the global vernacular), of South African modernism specifically, including its Pretorian guard, to retreat into the premodern architectural past can represent a failure of memory, a failure of confrontation, a failure of working through. It would be impossible for architecture to take the next step except through a deep invocation of many aspects of modernism, which remain and must remain in its work today.

Return need not be return to a specific set of vernaculars; it can simply be return to aspects of the lived environment, to the forms of life that people inhabit, in the name of innovation. Indeed, true innovation can never be a mere jumbling of vernaculars, a mere return to what was. Return and dissemination ("That which does not return," Derrida) go hand in hand, like control and hybridity (Bhabha). There is a crucial place for the kind of invention, moreover, that refuses return. The case of America illustrates all of these. America began as a series of vernacularizations on the one hand and imitations on the other. In the late eighteenth century, Thomas Jefferson in his design for the University of Virginia incorporated copies of key European architectural masterpieces, which he believed every student requiring *Bildung*, or cultivation—and certainly every student wanting to design the then new and open America—would perforce have to study. To him it was clear that America—empty of all but the "native," whose dwellings would hardly have been thought capable of serving the new settlers well, and lacking cities and traditions other than those imported from Europe—could progress to a "culture" of its own only through copying examples and using them as models. And since most Americans of his generation would never see Europe, he would bring Europe to them as best he could. It took many years before American architecture began to do more than bow before the altar of these copies and transcended its position as a "copier of copies" (the degraded position that Plato believed was common to all art, but which we now associate with specifically *dependent* art). However, even at the moment when Jefferson was designing his university, there were already originals (in every sense of the word) that had been made in America and bore the stamp of its unique future: Shaker furniture, plainspoken clapboard houses, perhaps even Jefferson's own Monticello. America began to give the world models for the new, built in accordance with its own sense of ideality and integrity, its sense of its people, their dwelling, and destiny (the Chicago skyscraper, the Chrysler Building, the houses and factories of Frank Lloyd Wright), once its place in the flow of international capital had been secured in the late nineteenth century, capital always being a condition of building, on account of financing but also on account of the way new forms of production require new spaces. But there is more: nineteenth-century America looked inward and began to conceive of itself as a new land requiring a new form of self-articulation. This project of *thinking* the identity of America into existence by acknowledging an America already (incipiently) there, of course, required architecture. While originating in the American transcendentalists (Emerson, Thoreau, the Alcotts), while carried forward into Whitman, the inheritance of this project carried on into architecture, which holds in its palm the exigencies of space but also the daily material, cast in the concrete of reality, through which symbolic recognitions of self, group, nation, present, past, and future may take place. American architecture gave the city of Johannesburg new forms of building in which, to a degree, the middle-class and mostly white inhabitants of that city could recognize themselves, although not in the same way as Americans might, since the buildings of Johannesburg, we have seen, not only modernized, they also colonialized, cordoned off, excluded. (The same building in a different context has a different "meaning"—not totally, but enough: this is a basic principle of "meaning" in architecture.)

Later, when the landscape of America became understood by the likes of Andy Warhol as one of signage, the question of the American vernacular became less one of a surging desire to occupy land and sky with the Gothic icons of religious capitalism (as Henry James disparagingly called the Woolworth Building in New York, upon returning to America after many years in Europe). Warhol was a populist as was Robert Venturi, and both found in this unruly landscape of signage a feel for ordinary people and the pleasures of lives lived in television and plastic. Only an American could declare Las Vegas "almost all right," as Venturi famously did. The French would call it divinely scandalous and invent poststructuralism to describe it, the English would call it horrid (while enjoying the fun and sun). But almost all right? Is this the "almost" of an "almost perfect score" or the "almost" of "Shelley, clinging to the mast of his ship in the stormy, Italian harbor, almost made it to shore but drowned," to the horror of modernism and the pleasure of America? There is much to consider when an "almost" enters the scene, and Venturi has always exhibited a certain ambivalence about how big a gap is opened by the "almost"—that is, about how adequate is the vernacular of Las Vegas and Leavittown with its tool kits of modernist construction supplanted by catalogs of kitsch.

What Venturi discovered without quite realizing it was that modern architecture had produced a new American vernacular: suburbia. A vernacular is a localization by dialect or language from an international form of communication—as the romance languages sprang from Latin, and American suburbia sprang from modern architecture. Suburbia, composed of do-it-yourself, put-together modular constructions of this split-level design or that, this Louis Quinze table, this Chippendale highboy, this Mies van der Rohe chair, this Corbu lounge, this late medieval tapestry turned dining-room curtain, this Bauhaus lamp, this art nouveau ash tray, this 1950s bubble chair, this Waterford crystal glass. Suburbia—the ranch house, post office, notions shop, restaurant—recast in pure, unadulterated plastic and all from your local department store, directly imported from Peoria, Illinois. The stylistics of suburbia (those of "inclusion and allusion") Venturi understood to be a mass-produced, broadly American vernacular for those who had made it through the Great Depression and the terrible war, who had survived the McCarthy trials, who lived with the possibility of nuclear war, for persons who could watch the new medium of television in the privacy of their own newly minted split-level ranch homes. Newly minted because what Venturi really discovered was that this culture of the mass-produced sign, whether late Chippendale or early Bauhaus, was, as I said, the legacy of modern architecture: suburbia, the legacy of a culture of modular constructions whose mass-producible parts were conceptualized prior to all building contexts and capable of endless combination and recombination in endlessly varying American homes—like mine and yours, if you were an American then. Suburbia was modern architecture turned Americanese, speaking with an American accent. It was a tool kit for production, in which the liberty to do it yourself in your own way combined with the great American desire to blend in. And so everyone in suburbia became different from the next person by choosing differently from the same catalog of architectural parts. Liberty was, for the new middle class, a matter of choice of products or consumable items that would define individual idiom while also securing group identity. It was the comfort of having what everyone else had, the same thing again and again, but with the freedom of individual choice (I choose ham and cheese rather than . . .).

Venturi discovered a trend in suburbia, following Warhol's discovery of the landscape of signage. This trend already, in Venturi's exhibition, *Learning from Leavittown*, included as product types the true American vernaculars, or provincialisms: the Cape Cod house, the New England clapboard, the Evanston Victorian, the Southern Belle, etcetera. Architectural capital was inclusive of the history of styles. Jameson would later call this transformation of style into tool kit, or "capital," the cultural logic of late capitalism, or postmodernism.[22]

It becomes art when the comfort of Warhol eating his soup and sandwich in the (then) coffee shop at the Waldorf-Astoria Hotel as a true American boy imbibing mother's milk becomes turned into individual idiom by "the factory," which is at once mass-produced in look and fato a mano, thus "almost" the same as the original. Similarly, Venturi's own buildings defer to local vernaculars, whether the East Hampton weatherboard, the Pennsylvania Dutch, or the seaside cottage, while also casting these and other, juxtaposed forms into proclamations of advertising, if you will, or complex codes of signage. Thus the advertisement is humanized, or the human advertised, or both—have it your own way. At the basis of his work is always strongly clarified architectural function and superb stylizations of neoclassic types, and, more than that, redolent of the Italian *maniera*. His houses and public buildings speak a double language of signage (proclaiming their elements in harmony and juxtaposition) and of formalism. (This double game was how Jencks defined postmodernism years ago.)[23]

Many postmodern architects are closet neoclassicists in one way or another, and experts at self-advertising through idiomatic use of codes of signage. They too commute style into self-proclaiming advertisement, while turning advertisement into high style. You could do worse, even if these buildings, as often as not, carry the brand identifications of architect as fashion designer: "the Michael Graves," the "Robert A. M. Stern." These vernaculars remain, but it is the new one that matters for us here. Because it has the capacity to recycle the old in the guise of product value, image as repeatable sign, currency, a facade whose product value, whose exchange value, is understood independent of context, as a merely repeatable item. And so, by a mechanics of global currency and dependency, South Africa gets the endlessly repeatable Cape Dutch facade, while insufficient numbers of South African architects explore the playful aestheticization of it in forms of Africanized *maniera*, or even the throwing off of regional vernaculars and the thinking of what architecture that makes new contact with African space, light, forms, and materials might be.

This global condition of architectural play is thus everywhere noted in South Africa. Once again, it speaks of a commerce of global dependency.

To state that South African projects of return and intermingling, of return and invention, are destined by the brute facts of global capitalism not to happen—except in the form of global postmodern office product—is to consign architecture to an inevitable continuation of its history of Eurocentric global dependency, a dependency that now takes place in the form of architectural CNN. There is no *aesthetic* reason why originality cannot happen in the *public* space of South Africa since it is already happening—somewhat, not enough—in private, *and has always happened in private.* Take a look at the designs for game parks in this country, with their Africanized modernist spaces, and think again about what public space is and what it should become. They are amazingly creative. There is nothing a few dollars cannot do to stimulate a creative architect who can work in a bubble. The harder part is to work in public spaces, which are already composed in the ways they are already composed, where there is a diversity of people, and, very important, where the signals buildings give off are part of the conversation of democracy and transition.

Public architecture is part of the public sphere. The failure of invention is a failure of civil society.

In a symposium I organized at the University of Natal during a seminar offered in the School of Architecture, I invited various architects to speak about Africanization in the new South Africa—in, that is, a legacy in which everything from the past is now part of the contemporary heritage of builders and designers. The responses were illuminating. One, Andrew Makins, who along with his partners in OMM Designs is designing the new Constitutional Court in Johannesburg, spoke about the importance of using materials and forms of construction that South Africans could themselves produce, thus generating economic work within the country. His work is worthy in humane invention and bridge-building of the pre-amble to the constitution itself (a fact Albie Sachs, former ANC activist and now constitutional judge, noted when, as part of the panel of judges, he argued for OMM's getting the commission). Makins also spoke of the need to listen to light, landscape, and form and the way people circulate in rural Africa, and to make the new in the light of the best of what one can hear. Others spoke of the importance of consultation with local communities when building for them. Naturally, they are not experts and cannot speak to every issue of clerestory paneling or modularity and materials, but they offer a great deal about what they want and need, and what they believe will feel most comfortable. What is built should, to the best of the architects' abilities, be the result of this dialogue. The architects Sarkin and Jain, students from the Harvard School of Architecture and, in Jain's case, a former student of the great Indian architect Doshi, spoke about using images that are ordinary and immediately recognizable, and that therefore allow users maximum capacity for their own interpretive creativity. Ambrose Adabajo, a Nigerian and Viennese-trained architect, spoke of the exemplary city of Mombasa in Kenya (where Adabajo has worked and where his wife is from). There, a hybrid architecture—Muslim, sea-faring, modernist, soaked in local Kenyan styles—has developed with its own inner coherence and idiomatic richness. This is, he argues, because people have lived together. His claim is that an African renaissance can happen only when people begin to live again together, apart from the Group Areas Act and what it has wrought, so that spaces naturally emerge from their reinhabitance of what was. In short, the African renaissance awaits casting as people begin to dwell together, in new ways, and their forms of life enter into new conversations, new rhythms. All spoke of the importance of training a diversity of architects: black Africans, females of all kinds, etcetera. None, it is fascinating to note, had anything at all to say about the past and its reuse. All were about invention of something that has not yet happened, and that has nothing to do with return-to-past styles.

This is not about the homogeneous assertion of regionalism or vernacularism, but hybridity, diversity, working from fragments of the past, all or none of which may be chosen to count. South African cities (with the partial exception of Cape Town) never had integrated regionalisms. They had colonial rules, forms of global dependency, and a mixture of regional and indigenous styles, pasted together in varying ways. Chipkin called Johannesburg a dustbin for every modernist style you can imagine (this, plus Herbert Baker); Durban is an illustration of the Natal settler house sitting near the hybridized Indian market, the colonial center, the classic concrete high-rise, and an esplanade of "regionalist" late modernism interspersed with buildings of ornate colonial grandeur. It is a boisterous, half-crazed colloquy, which, like the South African population, does not want final homogeneity (were that even possible) but growth and vitality.

Let us hope that the economy holds out so that there is enough work for architects and city planners to inaugurate what is required of the revolution in space, the return to space, the innovation in space, that a new country demands. As Kant said, "ought" implies "can." Inauguration requires room for the neonatal infant to breathe and enough cash to allow the steel rods to get placed in the ground, thus securing a new foundation.

In returning to the diversity of forms, and to the landscape, light, and cultures that must perforce inflect all of these positions, in producing new forms that are not yet part of the landscape, a reorientation in the terms of ownership occurs. What is mine and what is yours? What is ours together? What is an inheritance, a heritage, and what is its importance? Who is the inventor and who the listener? These questions, clear and indeterminate, also do not want answers, but instead the reinvention of their terms for recognition. They require the conversation that is building (the building of conversation). The ethics of citizenship demands no less from the architect, or from any other citizen.

6

Postmodernists of the South

People of the South

Dali Tambo, son of Oliver of past African National Congress fame and
host for the dazzling and inventive television show *People of the South,*
appears in the lightness of a complete African wardrobe, his long green
garment flowing to the ground as effusively as his gestures. His guests for
the day include the effervescent and biting Peter Dirk-Uys, appearing in
the form of the Uys alter ego, part anima, part animus Evita Bezeudenheit.
Also onstage in this spectacle of the south, part traditional in its African
style of participatory enjoyment, part postmodern in its capacity to stand
identities on their heads in the "simulacrized" world of the televisual, is
Walter Sisulu, who as a political prisoner spent many years on Robbin
Island. In the course of this social intercourse, Evita, in the best tradition
of folksy, kitschy Boere paternalism (or is it maternalism?), says to Sisulu
something along the lines of, "Ach, if we had known you were so nice, we
would have let you out ages ago," giving him a pat on the knee at the same
time. He laughs, and how can he not? It is a moment of genuine screwball.
Now we may relax in this screwball, since it does not take a genius to realize that after nearly a century of colonial gravitas, South Africa can use
all the lightness it can get, lightness signifying an open space, a clearing

ground, in which old identities and forms of communication may be shed and new ones tried on.

This proof of identity—proof not in the Cartesian sense of its assurance as an eternal item, but instead in the Latin/Italian sense of *probare,* to try something on, as in a new suit of clothes or a new African wardrobe— suggests that even South Africa, perched at the edge of human history in its formerly archaic separateness, is part of the global continuum. In what part and to what degree, we may ask, expecting that no clear answer could possibly be arrived at by any epistemological means other than those of general comparison and ready-to-hand (ready-to-wear) impression. Enough, we may answer, so that questions of postmodern critique might have genuine application here. This essay explores the question of that application. It begins in the north and gradually wends its way southward.

It is a general fact of postmodern cultures that their great futures mostly now reside in their pasts. Contemporary criticism is making a field day out of past visions of such futures and the havoc they have wreaked on the face of the world. This interrogation of past visions of progress, expansion, and claims to make the world safe for Western modernity; this suspicion of past visions of utopia, according to which there was never to be a criticism of the future but instead a future so filled with augur that the new man (be he a creation of the avant-garde revolutionaries or of the blood mythologers) would be capable of inhabiting it; this distrust of the enthusiasm harnessed in modern societies through such visions of the future; this critique of that tense called "the future perfect" and the violence it unleashed through its claim to perfection is in the first instance associated with the names of Marx, Nietzsche, Weber, Adorno, and Heidegger, and later with Derrida, Lyotard, and Foucault.

The condition of a future perfect now in the past and a future imperfect now in the future certainly obtains in South Africa, whose great and idealized trek into that special tense (and site of tension) called "the-future-biblical-past" is, we all know, over, even if other colonial (in)vestments, such as Anglophiliac forms of industrial colonialism and bloated postnationalist bureaucracies, remain in full gear (in spite of GEAR—the Growth, Employment, and Redistribution plan set forth by the minister of trade and industry). South Africa, whose former policies of state terror were brought into being by means of a master plan (that is, a plan of mastery), about which Joseph Conrad would undoubtedly have said that it took "all Europe to contribute to its making," undoubtedly calls for concepts of panoptic power, logocentrism, and ideological totality to unravel it. I state this immediately because such interventions in the discursive formation of the past and its traces in the present are not my concern here. When Dali Tambo, again merrily clad in his rainbow garments, interviews Ronnie Casrils, former commando from the struggle and at the time minister of defense, by sitting on a tank, he plays the game of placing the tank *sous rature*, as if a tank in the new South Africa is now the occasion for the spectacle of play rather than of modernist state terror. This detachment of the tank from its web of all-too-vivid meaning and (past) use depends on its appearance in the context of a new kind of image, a context whose play at imagining life differently by imaging it is as postmodern as one can get. The tank is still there, but what is tried on is a new image of it.

No longer in Kansas but in Oz, no longer in Pretoria but in the land of new national styles tried on over the nation's own airwaves, "we" have finally made it to the new South Africa. It cannot finally be divorced from the tank on which Tambo sits (a tank that has been around for a long time), but its game is to gain purchase on that tank in the whirl of a new form of visuality. It is *this* South Africa onto which I wish to try the postmodernist garment.

South Africa's emergence is that of a liberal democracy whose terms for national life, community, and policy are being forged just at the moment when the country finds itself immersed in global circuits of media, spectacle, and information. What does it mean for a "developing nation" like South Africa to formulate its plans in the midst of the global? I speak of those neoliberal forms, televisualities, and bursting hyperspaces that a South Africa hungry for global life and world legitimation uncritically absorbs (ironically repeating old forms of colonial dependency in a new garb). The question, having been posed, is impossible to answer, since it is really too early to tell how (under)development will play itself out in global conditions here. Some would say that the South African moment of nation-building has come too late, just as the nation as a modern institution is buckling under the weight of multinationals and the infinitesimal lightness of hyperspaces, and that a T-shirt for South Africa should be made that reads, "I arrived at the (national) party just as it had broken up and everyone had gone off to their (transnational) sleep." This is obviously too simple, since the nation is not collapsing (nor even the National Party), and nation-building is taking place here, but in ways informed by current global conditions (postmodern and late capitalist).

It is partly over the airwaves that national slogans that acknowledge difference and that build solidarity happen, slogans like the South African

Broadcast Corporation's "One Nation/One Station" and "Semunye: We are one." Nation-building is happening just at the time when the South African white middle classes are becoming increasingly globalized and decentered (one child in Australia, one in England, etcetera). The effects of these intrusions of the postmodern are matched by others, which makes South Africa an important place to try on the postmodern garment. For example, one has to wonder if the ambiguity in the African renaissance between its image of a liberal and diverse South Africa, with ample room for Africans of different persuasions, and its reversion to the image of a black-centered pan-Africanist African identity is not precisely a debate between the modern South Africa of nation-building and the postmodern South Africa of postapartheid multiculturalism. Nations build themselves on the basis of power politics and the language of majorities, and it is only natural that a South Africa reeling from Eurocentric colonialism and apartheid would revert to power politics stressing national unity in terms of black majorities. This is the history of most every modern nation: that it arises through the struggle for recognition as a contested terrain where citizenship is defined in hegemonic terms. It would make South Africa modern. And yet, the postapartheid, postmodern emphasis on diversity proves not only that South Africa has inherited the best of the Enlightenment (its abstract language of equality for all, no matter who you are and what you are wearing), but that its nation-building is coming at a time when national hegemonies are no longer acceptable as strategies. Hence the need for the pan-Africanist element in the African renaissance to remain *unspoken* (see earlier essay).

South Africa is an important test case for thinking about postmodernism, situated as it is between the claims of development, nation-building, and the global commerce of information, including information that appears in the form of television. Since much postmodern writing, including the poststructuralist writing that has had a crucial role in articulating it, tends (one would hardly have expected otherwise) to downplay the importance of structures that arose in *modernity* and remain in place "today," South Africa, as a place in which modernity requires building (in the form of efficient infrastructure, national consciousness, and development) as well as overcoming (through genealogy, globalism, and the Dali Tambo show), will serve as a site in which to probe the efficacy of certain postmodern discourses. We cannot understand the new South Africa without postmodern theory, nor will we find that such theory fits entirely comfortably in South Africa. The dialectic is to rewrite the theory in a way that gives South Africa its due and brings the theory out of its cocoon.

The Things One Means by the Postmodern

There tend to be three different ways in which the "post" has been construed in the family of interrelated discourses that make up the history and range of what is called "postmodernism." This is as one should expect, since there is no single picture adequate to convey, nor set of examples adequate to exemplify, everything that is (or ought to be) conveyed by the term "modernity."

Each of the three main lines of postmodern attack addresses a distinct region of what is called modernity, and claims that it is now in a "post" phase. Each has implications for subjectivity. The first strand takes the "post" to mean that social structures central to the history of modernity are, in some sense, "over." Such structures are usually taken to be society, the nation and nationalism, the family, the difference-free polity as theorized by the Enlightenment (Hegel's "I that is we"), and/or the various forms of absolute spirit in their roles as figures for the state. Postmodernism inhabits a world that is transnational, fragmented in family structure and social forms, in which art is "over," religion an artifact of spiritual shopping or "encounter" groups in hot tubs, and philosophy is either a branch of artificial intelligence or a dinosaur masquerading in the artifice of intelligent truth. Such a world may or may not obtain in various ways in northern climes— also in Japan, India, Hong Kong, São Paolo, and other postcolonial sites of attraction. It also sits (but uncomfortably) at the South African borders. While the South African (middle class) family is globally splayed (one child in America, one parent in the Cape, etcetera), the South African nation is in the process of construction, and is so in a transnational corporate world. While religion as a form of the state's self-recognition more or less went out with the Great Trek, freedom of religion is a crucial component of current liberal identity politics, and the Christian sentiment of forgiveness still toots its horn in the Truth and Reconciliation Commission hearings in the high-pitched voice of Archbishop Desmond Tutu. While new forms of art are arising that rely on, express, and celebrate the diversity of South African traditions, the claim that art is capable of expressing "the national aspiration" is at best half-believed.

The second postmodern line of attack is on those narratives that have impelled the history of modernity—narratives of the future perfected and the Great Trek toward it. "All Europe contributed to the making of Kurtz," Joseph Conrad writes, and it is true. When Kurtz finally gets exposed in the missionary position with his pants down, up close and personal, truth has become a lie. Nietzsche had already stated this about truth some fifteen years before Joseph Conrad's trip up to the *Heart of Darkness*, and had stated it in inverse form—Nietzsche's work being about the philosophico-Judeo-Christian history of Western self-disempowerment, while Conrad's was about the West's mad history of power over the "outside." Freud will soon thereafter take religion to task (as Marx had yet already done the job on it), and so will the language game of interrogation commence, no doubt in the interest of overcoming and justice. What follows, it might be thought, is Dali Tambo on a tank—Dali, whose Januslike gesture looks forward to and celebrates the force of the new South Africa while also peering back at the tanked-up old South Africa. However, and this is crucial, the image of Dali on a tank does not critique; it *visualizes*. Narrative is stood on its head by being commuted into spectacle, not through the language game of interrogation. Image overrides object and sign and speaks volumes.

Visualization brings one to the third way in which postmodernism has been understood: namely, as the culture and effects of late capitalism. As capitalism has shifted from mechanical forms of production (of polished diamonds, mass-produced automobiles) to information-based forms of production (speculation in stock and currency markets, speculation in and through information systems, overcapitalization on images), broad changes in the texture of life, work, the body, and subjectivity have taken place, and these are identified as postmodern. Among those changes is the "society of the spectacle," in which sign becomes image, and image is inflated into the logo-speak of signage (that is, Dali on the tank). Everything from the world of Microsoft to the endlessly self-produced body of Madonna, from the Internet to the world of advertising, high-concept production, and commodification of the total subject, is part of the ramification of this world. Its most radical flaneur, Jean Baudrillard, will claim that the combined onslaught of CNN, radio, advertisements, and the culture of the spectacle has caused reality to drop out of the picture and be replaced by its models, models delivered by Larry "the King" Live and Oprah "the Victim" Winfrey, by election polls, by televisual wars that "do not take place" except over the airwaves, by global violence detached from its place and rearranged in the form of image bites, and by a public sphere that, in America, is played out by the likes of psychiatrists dispensing remedies over the radio and talk-show hosts dispensing analytical wisdom. It is a world of issues replaced by media events, and ideas turned into products. Hence . . . the city of Angels, that postmodern antidote to the city of Paris, which was so beloved by the likes of Jean-François Lyotard and others with their country houses in the simulacrum.

Where South Africa fits in this picture is complex and varied. In many respects it does not fit at all, since it is about weak states unable to deliver basic needs to a population still racially stratified with huge gaps between rich and poor, the failure of economic development, rampant disease, and deep rifts between urban and rural life. Many South African citizens do not have electricity or running water. Many have little idea of what citizenship is, other than voting for a single party in which they have diminished faith. The South African constitution is a marvel of negotiation, but it is unclear how the South African poor conceive of it, or if they do, what they think its force is and whether they would not put it aside in a second were basic goods to be delivered by an authoritarian regime such as Cuba or China. This is hardly the stuff of postmodernism. Or Dali Tambo, even if his father (Oliver Tambo) were very much of that world of suffering and struggle. Dali, like Thabo Mbeki, is a second-generation superstar who lived abroad for many years. Dali has an English accent of Edwardian elegance and the suaveness of a floating, diasporic signifier.

Take a walk down La Cienega Boulevard in West Hollywood, California, hoping you are not waylaid into an excess of designer discount shopping. As you approach the Beverly Center, that *Centre Pompidou* of shopping just around the corner from the "European cafe" where the great Hollywood director Billy Wilder sips his afternoon coffee and nibbles at his cake, the last vestige of a Europe that nearly "represented" him (as a Jew) to death, you will be greeted by huge billboards plastered on the curved sides of that mammoth structure. These massive billboards picture the former great Olympiad of gymnastics, Nadia Comaneci, posing half-nude in Jockey underwear before the devouring gaze of millions. Or an eighteen-year-old model of the Brad Pitt variety aromatically posed above a piece of logospeak that tells us that, "The world is getting closer: smell better." On the other side of the mall and across the street from it is another piece of signage with immaculately aerobicized dancers, contorted into a relationship of unsustainable perfection, advertising the precision of the new Swiss watch, Parsifal. Albert Speer himself would have been proud had he seen the body disciplined into this level of gleaming, machine-line perfection (if only for the amount of time it took to shoot the camera). This replacement of the future perfect by the perfect Parsifal-image, advertising a piece of jewelry that not one in a hundred of those who gape at the sign can afford, announces the triumph not of the will but of the will to consume.

Thus even a single city block of "flaneuring" in the postmodern West can generate enough material for a book on the topic of the cultural critique *à la mode postmoderniste*.

Now *spatziere!* Take another walk. Amble your way down a street in Rosebank, Gauteng, hoping you are not waylaid into an excess of designer nondiscount shopping while your automobile is hijacked. You will see shopping malls, but opening onto a kind of street-selling that is unique to place. You will visit cinemas playing the latest double-action fare or the latest Parisian love triangle. Parsifal watches will be bought and sold (also stolen), the materials for global capitalism and postmodern consumerism firmly implanted. But you will also notice an absence of signage as you look up toward the transparent blue of the Highveld sky with its luminous clouds and resonance of southern eternity. And you will notice that houses are open English gardens hidden behind laagers, so that to penetrate into the fragrant gardens and lovely English lawns of these great bourgeois brick-and-stone houses of white privilege and pleasure, you must first get yourself over the razor wire and past the huge dogs and complex alarm systems, then to actually get inside one, you must transgress a system of gated doors, internal bars that separate parts of the house like the inner sancta of temples from other parts, and more alarms—a system so complex that were a fire to break out one wonders whether anyone could possibly succeed in escaping from the inside. Even this American import world of shopping malls has a different use in South Africa, since it becomes a haven in a crime-ridden and insecure world, and perhaps a new space in which formerly divided parties to the new democracy may commingle as a new yuppie/late-capitalist national class. And even in this corner of the nation, the world is far less commodified than its Los Angeleno counterpart (which is, in turn, far more commodified than more regional American climes, where actors do not take to crudely sunning themselves in private, before the eyes of millions, with the "nubile girlfriends" of their daughters).

There are other walks to be had in South Africa, where the flat landscape of consumerism will quickly evaporate before the fact of overwhelming and desperate social need. Walks in Crossroads, where the deluge of Cape rain recently forced inhabitants out of their cobbled, windowless shacks, built of rotting timbers and corrugated iron, covered in plastic and set in sand and mud. When these people returned, they found that all their possessions had been stolen by others.

We shall peer in their direction soon enough. They number in millions of persons, millions in a country of fifty million.

Together, these walks are a graphic illustration of uneven development—of the failure of economic growth to trickle down, of the differential system in a society where huge amounts of wealth are concentrated in one city

(Johannesburg) and in business, where foreign investment is not happening, given regional and local insecurity (crime, poverty, disease), where global capital flows are largely uncontrolled by a state that cannot facilitate the kind of late capitalism that, at the end of history, depends on and produces a middle class. South Africa is indeed two nations, one postmodern, the other lacking access to the structures even of modernity (the state, information systems and the public sphere, the economy, the expression of identity through public cultural forms and institutions, the law). Therefore, South Africa's postmodernism has to be in certain respects different from that of the advanced capitalist countries, unless it entirely takes place in a bubble. Rosebank is in many ways a bubble, even if the people are dour (emigration always on their minds, the tough brutality of the city weighing on them, the crudeness of a city of mines and money, preyed on by crime, living behind razor wire in fear of the gun), and even if there is also evidence of a new black middle class, however small and self-contained. But Dali's show is not a bubble, if only because it too is related to the nation-building exercise and the trying on of new identities, which Dali wears with such aplomb. His is a pleasure taken in the outrageous, and that is a different kind of outrageousness, and a different kind of spectacle, than a European counterpart might indulge, say, in London or Berlin. For what is being flaunted and flouted are different, and the extreme gap between the two South African nations—rich and poor—is part of the outrageousness, as well as part of what it obliterates, perhaps rightly, perhaps wrongly.

Lyotard, Politics, and Knowledge Production

The way modernity and postmodernity are being built up together in South Africa demands, I will argue, the writing of Jean-François Lyotard to get it straight, even if that writing is also problematic. So it is to Lyotard I turn. His work and story are well known, and I will try to be brief.

Under the combined pressures of late capitalism and a century of the most horrendous violence, the grand narratives by which modernity has lived its life have broken down. Late capitalism, with its capitalization on information and visual bits (advertisements, logos), pressures knowledge to reduce and quantify itself into immediately usable bits and to agendize itself in the form of slogans, advertisements, and avant-garde shock values. Knowledge is pressurized to produce fast outcomes and clear quanta. All knowledge that fails to respond to this pressure of quantification is dispensed with by modern capitalism as unfit for use. Finally, the very fabric of "society," as well as its concept, has fragmented. There is no longer a social world in anything like what was envisioned by modern theory; instead, what is evidenced is a corporatized family of social practices ("language games") and a diverse colloquy of people to perform them. This web of practice and people computes to no overall "social form" but is, essentially, "fragmentary."

Granted the pressure on both art and knowledge to "measure up" and deliver itself in the form of "outputs," with which late capitalism may make its hay, the tendency is (we may improvise in the spirit of Lyotard's work) to turn all aspects of knowledge production in the "highly developed societies of the globe" into forms of production forced to legitimate themselves in terms of their fast, quantifiable "outcomes" and their use in clearly demarcatable systems of production, such as advertising, contracting, corporate buyouts, national expansions, and new world orders. This must entail that neither the arts nor the academy are spared. Education, research, and art-making all become "output oriented," formulating themselves into products to be fetishized by the marketplace. Academic writing becomes a matter of the reduction of philosophical thought to the rapid deployment of theoretical agendas and pragmatized schemes.

On the other side of Lyotard's postmodern picture are the capacities for justice that arise out of the condition of knowledge, if knowledge production is willing and able to resist the encroachments of the output-oriented commodity form. Postmodern knowledge, insofar as it is capable of resisting the pressure of capitalist quantification into outcomes and bits, is now freed, Lyotard believes, from the shackles of grand narratives to invent new schemes for the interpretation of the subject. One may contextually rewrite the huge repertoire of past knowledge practices in new and imaginative ways. Legitimation, being contextual, is free to discover the complexity of the subject in all of its particularity. What legitimates new forms of knowledge is their avant-garde character, their capacity to pass beyond the limitations of the existing rules by which disciplinary knowledge has been constructed, so as to imagine and create alternative ways of posing the question of this subject in its particularity, be the subject a person, group, nation, language, history, or place. This refusal to subsume the autonomy of the subject under a totalizing conceptual net places a full stop on the knower's immaculate claim to cleanse the otherness of the other under a tide of conceptual projection. So, for the knower to give the otherness of the other its due is therefore for him or her to pass beyond the container of existent rules and to face the epistemic experience of no longer knowing how to represent the other, speak to the other, read the other's interests, negotiate terms of mutual recognition between self and other.

It is a general mark of poststructuralist writing, a mark of what was fresh and new in that writing, that it has in all kinds of ways pointed to the fact that domination is a matter of representation. There is no human domination in modernity without systems of representation to carry the load and systems of representation to contain their own complex weight, which may dominate even those who consider them most liberating. Needless to say, domination has in the history of thought been approached along other fault lines (institutional, economic, class-based, technological, etcetera), which render representation an adjunct of these (representation as superstructure). Even when treated as central to the fault of domination, representation has in the past, it is the poststructuralist desire to show, been analytically straitjacketed by a series of *grandes recits* (Enlightenment humanism again, Marxism), which tell us more about those framing the explanations than they do about the representations in question. A great deal of poststructuralism wishes to correct these faults; however, like all styles of framing, it also causes other factors to recede into the background, and this too requires correction.

The same point can be made about the related poststructuralist approach to justice (Lyotard's, Derrida's), which presents justice as the working through of the relevant problems of representation. For Derrida, justice is the only concept that is not deconstructible. But justice is never thought apart from its specific representations, and where there is law, norm, institution of meaning, and text, there deconstruction resides, in the name of justice. In Derrida one also finds a kind of classical skeptical position: to be just is to learn the art of inhabiting representation in all of its diversity, uncertainty, and ambivalence. It is to know that every rule, every way of framing the world, every position taken requires revision, reframing, or deconstruction. While Jean-François Lyotard conceives of justice as a multiplicity of language games, none reducible to the other (economic, social, ideological, communicative), his own foregrounding of justice as a working through of the representation of otherness (we shall return to this below) tends to subdue, if not marginalize, the framing of this multiplicity of games and their relations.

Speaking very generally, excessively so for purposes of this discussion, there tends to be a deficit that can be found in various poststructuralist approaches. Any southern venture would have to keep these liabilities in mind.

Widely shared by poststructuralist writers (and therefore widely inherent in thinking about postmodernism) is an epistemology (and related conception of value) that is unable to give all that is right in modernity its due. Until the problematic character of this epistemic tendency is properly unearthed, postmodern theory (with its poststructuralist foundations) cannot make an adequate southern venture.

The fault derives from the poststructuralist critique of those totalizing, grand narratives that have indeed played a role in the articulation of modernity's forms of domination. It is relatedly proclaimed as a response to the quantifying pressures of late capitalism (Lyotard). It has two parts:

(1) Poststructuralist writings widely tend to equate epistemic or conceptual determinacy with domination, so much so that before one knows it, conceptual determinacy is considered *in essence* to be a form of domination. Conversely,

(2) Epistemic or conceptual indeterminacy of the right form is adulated to be that which *in essence* resists the rule of determinacies and restores the human.

I turn to these following a brief consideration of what determinacy or determinate thinking means.

Determinate thinking takes a family of forms, each of which is glossed as a "totality." Determinacy as Hegel announces it and as poststructuralism interrogates it is a composite concept. It is partly about the disciplining of the objects of knowledge under increasingly rigid conceptual and referential schemes. As Frege, the master of determinate sense, puts it, "A concept without hard edges is not a concept at all." There can be no flexibility or looseness in matters of sense and reference. Of course, Wittgenstein replied by remarking that the command "Stand roughly here" is exactly what is needed in certain contexts, and in such contexts is completely clear, while its counterpart, "Stand exactly here," may in those contexts be completely *unclear,* that is, baffling to everyone who hears it. The right level of determinacy is relative to the appropriate context. Still, the modern norm of concepts with "hard edges" and of names with the precision of numbers is associated with the prestige of science and the rule of technology in modern times, and indeed with modern, bureaucratic forms of thinking.

Equally important is that determinate thinking aims to subsume all aspects of reality under a single system of conceptual relations, defined by a single scheme or "superconcept." The thinking of determinacy claims that human languages, societies, groups, histories, or identities can be surveyed and explained by reference to this single "superrelation." It is not for nothing that Wittgenstein, in formulating his critique of essentialist philosophy, makes it clear that for him the replacement of the thought that concepts come with essences must mean that they are held together not by any single "superconcept" but instead by many different "strands of similarity." For Wittgenstein, the assumption that the world conforms to a superconcept is a violence perpetrated on ordinary thought.

The poststructuralist critique of determinacy is not simply about the history of philosophy; it is about the way human societies have imposed order, authority, categorical forms upon nature, other humans, and themselves. It is a critique of those forms of domination, those ideologies, which depend upon determinate ways of representing the world.

While Hegel associated deterministic thinking (the production of conceptual totalities) with historical progress and the social good, poststructuralism, in reversing the terms of the wager, has tended to uncritically identify determinate thinking with totalitarian repression. In doing so, it has been as unable to come to terms with the many ordinary and productive ways that various forms of conceptual determinacy have been and may be central to our language games, as Descartes and Hegel were perhaps unable to acknowledge the ways in which *indeterminacy* has been productive in them. It is once again to the pages of Wittgenstein that one must turn if one wishes to find a more adequate discussion of the various uses that clarity, precision, synopticism, and rational planning—determinacies all—can have in our language games and social practices. "Stand roughly here" may be just right in some contexts,[1] but in others it is the precise order "Stand exactly here" that is required (as when the marriage ceremony can come off only if the bride and groom stand *exactly* next to each other and not merely in the same space, or when in a shooting gallery persons not exactly in the right space may be accidentally shot). Again, from the fact that there is no indeterminacy when I answer my friend's telephone call with the remark, "Daniel Herwitz here," it hardly follows that I have participated in an essentialist and repressive construction of my own identity. Determinacy is itself a context-relative notion, and it is this fact that the poststructuralist critique tends to remain silent about, obsessed as it is with the inheritance of specific epistemic regimes in which certain configurations of determinacy played their horrendous roles.

It will be retorted that every poststructuralist writer knows these things. How could they not? Nevertheless, poststructuralist norms tend to subdue them and it is important to be reminded of them. Now, their omission may seem trivial and easily corrected, but it is not, for the failure to acknowledge the context-sensitive nature of determinacy has vastly limited the poststructuralist picture of what modernity is. I shall return to this.

Second and related, poststructuralism maintains the Hegelian dichotomy by adulating *indeterminacy* as uncritically as Hegel cast it down into the inchoate terrain of the premodern. Poststructuralists tend to adulate almost beyond measure—that is, exactly beyond measure—the political force of opacity as that semantic condition that has the power to resist the repressive force of determinations. In a magnificent aestheticization of history and of contemporary culture, almost every poststructuralist writer fixes on some special sociocultural site or practice whose opacity the writer in question sets forth as having a power to resist the rule of determinacy. Thus, just as determinate thinking is claimed to have enormous repressive power, indeterminate thinking is given equivalent power, and given it through the sublime. For Foucault, whatever resistance there is to modern disciplinary regimes comes in somewhat ambivalent but highly Nietzschean gestures (culminating in his own explosive and ultimately Pyrrhic rompings in the world of the San Francisco bathhouse). In Derrida's analysis of law, law always requires deconstruction, and deconstruction, in celebrating skeptical uncertainty, frees the imagination and opens up the human.[2] In Kristeva's analysis of women, "woman" becomes herself by reversion to the pre-oedipal state of "semiosis" in resistance to the determinate law of the oedipal father.[3] In Homi Bhabha's analysis of colonialism, the hybridity of the colonized subject resists the equally determinate law of the colonial father. Finally, in Jean-François Lyotard's analysis of postmodernism, authentic art and knowledge practices are exactly those that resist the encroachments of totalitarian thinking on the one hand and modern capitalistic quantification procedures on the other. They do so by speaking in a wholly indeterminate voice.

This revelling in opacity is evidently an aestheticization of politics by other means, no longer the aesthetics of totalities but instead the *politicization of aesthetics*, as if by finding or inventing a special cultural site in which unclarity can reign, one can gather the power to speak against the rule of repressive determinacy in the name of human emancipation. While modernity overcapitalizes in the aestheticization of politics, in postmodernity it is the politicization of the aesthetic that is the object of overindulgence, even excessive capitalization, by the academic and art worlds. This is part of what impels the postmodern desire to produce representations with the requisite indeterminacy, as if this production will automatically invest them with political power, or to theorize representations in such a way that everyone can believe them to contain the requisite indeterminacy when they do not. The critique of representations, from this perspective, is nothing short of a way of politicizing them by theoretical means.

Southern Planning and Southern Ventures

In South Africa, one can hardly ignore the brute force of social reality, for unemployment is currently at around 30 percent (depending on who is doing the measuring), housing is grossly inadequate, and one of every three persons in KwaZulu-Natal is HIV-positive, with one in four being the national average. If in South Africa representation attempts to subvert reality, it is perhaps through such items as the so-called African renaissance, which is, I have elsewhere said, a renaissance mostly about words, a discourse in which talk of rebirth replaces the need to confront the failure of rebirth in reality, a discourse through whose means despair is commuted to enthusiasm. No doubt an exaggeration in the political force of representations, the language of the African renaissance is a postmodern phenomenon of the south, a way of inflating words with the illusion of political force. Later, I will suggest that Dali's show can be viewed along somewhat similar lines.

Insofar as South Africa dedicates itself to developmental projects, it is a place where postmodernism would appear to sit uncomfortably. Development requires social rationalization, productivity, and greater efficiency. It requires the rooting out of corruption, the streamlining of bureaucracies, and the raising of levels of human capital through the inculcation of trainable skills and greater professionalization. These goals are, in various respects, incompatible with the poststructuralist critique of modernity, for that critique brings to light the defects in each and every one of them. But more than that, the poststructuralist critique begins from the position of taking for granted everything that is right with modernity and then lambasting modernity for its determinacies. Insofar as poststructuralist writings contain the norms I have attributed to them, insofar as they identify everything that falls under the motley category of "determinacy" with domination, they are incapable of acknowledging the importance of various kinds of determinacy for a society that works and prospers—which would include the importance of a rational state bureaucracy, of social planning, of a society's capacity to train a new work force, and the like. Without modern state apparatuses and clear plans we would have mass societies in chaos. When one ventures out from England and France to, say, Zimbabwe or Nigeria, with their inefficiency and corruption, the value of social rationality looks quite different. I repeat: one way of diagnosing a failing of the "posts" is to determine that they take for granted all that is right with modernity, since all that is right is already in place, and proceed as if the element of social rationality inherent in modernity is dispensable when it is not. Their logocentric epistemologies (determinacy = domination) fail to allow for the appreciation of varying degrees of determinacy in social development.

Since the standpoint of development must thematize social planning, rationality, and training as goals, it is hardly compatible with the poststructuralist critique. Anthony Appiah, writing in 1986, argued that postmodern vocabularies by and large bypass Africa, because Africa remains neocolonial and underdeveloped, even if exploitable by global, postmodern markets. Since many African states have not gone through a period of national modernization that has "worked," they are not in this crucial sense postmodern (post to their modernization). Postmodernism and underdevelopment are, in key respects, competing conditions: the conversion of genuine social problems into mediaspeak and its glossy images is always partly at odds with local development. And insofar as even these African states are increasingly liable to global circuits of postmodernism, circuits of media and information, and products, they remain in ongoing states of dependency. Indeed, there is little reason to speak of globalization in terms of center and periphery apart from the question of dependency: dependency on circuits of commodity forms and types that are not of one's own making, which one has no alternative to, and which, perhaps, if dependency theory is right, keep one from pursuing one's own developmental paths. Perhaps this is obvious. Development and postmodernism, considered as a global system (there are other ways to consider it), are always partially at odds. Perhaps a strength of the Dali Tambo show is that it is a way of converting global televisual dependency (on the fare of talk shows, CNN, and the like) into one's own, into something more. Dependency, thus, in the usual way, shades into creative translation or remaking.

Now, from the perspective of epistemology, development is always partially at odds with indeterminacy because it requires measurement. No doubt there is no ultimate, metaphysical distinction between facts and values, since what we choose to measure and how we take our measurements (about higher gross national product, better housing, lower unemployment, better health, and the other goods that development is meant to bring) is a matter of evaluation. Still, without numbers, all talk of better housing would become somewhat meaningless, or even incoherent, from the developmental point of view, which shows that development is in part a matter of numeracy.

All of us know that the need for rational planning in a developing nation like South Africa is obvious, that the language games of justice here must in part be those of transformation in the fields of education, jobs, housing, water, electricity, and access to information and markets. Transformation may have a utopian ring, but in essence it means construction, rational planning, and determination, as well as liberalization and openness in thought. It is noteworthy that Lyotard stresses the multiplicity of language games associated with justice, but has little to say about the role of social institutions in the formation of justice. Yet institutional change is crucial for a developing nation, and institutional reform always takes planning, since institutions are by nature composed of high levels of recalcitrant structure. One reason the African National Congress, now the South African government, has delivered a disappointing performance (to date) in the fields of civil and political development is that the ANC is profoundly hampered by what it has inherited—namely a bloated and inefficient bureaucracy from the National Party as well as a culture of business that has historically been indifferent to the national good. So no one is praising bureaucracies.

The African National Congress—both in its first days after the election of 1994 as part of a "Government of National Unity" and later, when that coalition failed and the ANC assumed increasingly the status of a one-party state—has a number of concrete plans for rational social development. In the words of Rodney Davenport and Christopher Saunders,

> The state of the economy offered no hope of rapid growth, owning to the braking effects of earlier sanctions and a racially restrictive training system, which now thwarted the country's capacity to expand production of beneficiated goods for the now available world market. Growth was also undermined by the massive diversion of revenue to service high-interest loans raised in the sanctions era, a consequent rise in personal tax levels, and the hesitancy of foreign investors to risk entering a small-scale market protected by exchange controls and seemingly threatened by wage-hungry trade unions. But in spite of all this, the GNU [Government of National Unity], through its successive ministers of finance and economic development, announced their preference in 1996 for an open economy with a new Growth Employment and Redistribution policy (GEAR), which aimed to rebuild the economy by means of orthodox budgeting, tight control of inflation, and the creation of new jobs through the promotion of exports and the freeing of the money market.[4]

And so the Reconstruction and Development Programme (RDP), planned by the Mandela Government of National Unity to be a powerful program of delivery to the poor and downtrodden, was derailed by a more conservative, fiscal-oriented plan aiming, finally, at foreign investment.

I shall discuss this further in the following essay. What I want to say here is not merely the obvious point, that GEAR is an assimilation of supply-side economic thinking in its current neoliberal/Thatcherite twist. Nor is it merely the also obvious point that it is a plan that finally proves the weakness of the state vis-à-vis business, which is given laissez-faire capacity to do what it likes almost without constraint. Nor even do I want to make the political point that the government, caught between an old Marxist model of "seizing the capital" (which it knows it cannot do) and a neoliberal model of "business as usual" (which gives business the license it has always enjoyed to avoid national commitment except in a purely voluntary way), has not learned the art of providing incentives for capital investment by business in national development and *disincentives* for its failure. I want to say that this plan has been taken up by the South African state as part of a global network of imitation. Some will say there is no choice in taking it up, given the conditions for global investment that rule the South African economy; the only way to bring about an improved GNP (gross national product) in the country is through assimilation of global economic norms. I half-believe this, since there is much evidence for the fact of a global system in which investment agendas are set by stronger nations, leaving the weaker ones little scope for creativity. However, I also believe that neocolonialism, while aided and abetted by ongoing systems of economic dependency, is also obscurely in place in a Eurocentric country like South Africa and that this too informs planning. Even if the skin color of the ministers has changed, the templates remain largely the same.

To see how planning has been contingent upon neocolonial templates of conceptual dependency, where the south sits in wait for models from the north and fails to reflect upon itself until it gets these in place (in the manner of mirrors), consider the kind of planning where there would be more scope for creative variation in the country: planning about education. Nothing is more germane in this regard than the current academic plan contained in *The Education White Paper 3: A Programme for the Transformation of Higher Education* (July 1997), and I briefly sketch it to bring the point home. While Blade Nzimande of the Parliamentary Task Force on Education has attacked globalization as the "ideology of neoliberalism" from whose contamination South African educational transformation must cordon itself off, it is ironical that the terms for the transformation of the university contained in the white paper are precisely those of the new information circuits Nzimande wishes to resist. The white paper, the guiding educational document of the new dispensation regarding higher education, is about many excellent things. It stresses lifelong learning and the need for universities to facilitate that. It emphasizes the relevance of research models to the social good. It speaks to the new global university, which increasingly, like it or not, must learn to work cooperatively with the state, the corporate sector, and the wishes of multiple "stakeholders," as the lingo goes. However, as I mentioned in the introduction, the new South Africa continues to exhibit a neocolonial dependency upon commonwealth models, and these are very much in evidence in the output-oriented and quantification-oriented models that are imposed upon the university in its program development and research agendas. In the future, universities will be funded in virtue of their capacity to deliver "programs" that are immediately "relevant" to the construction of the educated person in South Africa. Such programs will be weighted toward the professions and the applied sciences. And the "human sciences" will be funded only insofar as the indefinable subtleties of the liberal arts associated with the words "reading," "interpretation," "reflection," and "values" are redefined as simple, usable bits ("measurable skills") that can be immediately assimilated by students and demonstrated to have "relevance" to current South African life—that is, to the improvement of new South African markets.

Read in one way, the white paper provides an excellent norm imposed on universities—that they should remake themselves so as to redefine how education might create a new and improved kind of thinker and actor who will be capable of entering the (unfortunately unregulated and untransformed) South African market in a cleverer, more reflective, and more civilized way. Read in another way, its transformation goals may end up disastrously regulating the system of education in accord with corporate, ultimately global pressures to make programs conform to market-oriented outcomes. The situation is unpredictable.

This picture of what may be at stake in South African tertiary education, however briefly stated, is enough to allow one to encapsulate the issue of determinacy with the right degree of nuance. For while on the one hand determinacy is what is required for transformation, it is also co-opted in an age of late capitalism by the distinctively modern forces of technocratic professionalism and the reduction of "educational immeasurables" to quantifiable outcomes. Thus, those of us at South African universities are in the position of having to play the game of designing neopragmatically oriented programs with the illusion of *measurable* (i.e., market-valuable) outcomes while resisting the terms of this game by building into those programs an avant-garde interdisciplinary complexity, a new set of ways to address the whirl of contemporary events, a sense of the revolutionary nascence of South African life, and the need to educate a Socratic student capable of reflection on South African nascence. If this is not Lyotard's postmodern condition, then nothing is.

It should now also be clear just how ambivalent and uncertain the textual meaning of the white paper is, and how opaque and contradictory the dissemination of its meaning has been. To put the point in the semantic mode, one does not know what counts as satisfying the truth conditions set forth in that document, nor even what its truth conditions exactly are. For an American like myself, accustomed to the clear legibility of state pronouncements, the manner in which South Africa produces current policy documents and speaks to their meaning is chaotic and disorganized. When the American state says it is going to do something, one usually knows quite clearly what it is the state is going to try to do. Whether the thing will be done or not is a matter of whether it is subverted by special-interest groups, media events, and/or the refusal of the middle classes to fund it. What is at stake in this situation is, according to Zygmunt Bauman, the very structure of the postmodern state.[5] Bauman argues that the state has become increasingly decentered in a late-modern fragmented world of corporate capital, nongovernmental organizations, professionals, functionaries, and the like, and yet it has also become more powerful in the sense that its efficiency is far more potent: its capacity to regulate, control, get things done. This combination of decenteredness and efficiency has produced a circumstance in which the state is delegitimated. No longer is it to be understood in terms of its role vis-à-vis constitutions, founding documents, moral truths, political ideals, and the like: rather, the state is a system of circulation and containment, of production and reproduction. I often feel this way about the United States (naturally, within bounds). Yet here in South Africa, the state is both highly legitimated (as a postapartheid new democracy) and highly inefficient: it pales before the neoliberal capitalism, which is about the only place where "business gets done" in South Africa, the exception being the transformation of universities from within—on a good day. In direct response to its weakness, its high degree of legitimation, and the combination of Thatcherian Stalinism, which its cadres follow as a postmodern, post-Marxist template, it produces an amazing amount of papers, rules for transformation, formulas for equalization, and the like in direct proportion to their dissipation within the texture of South African society. This was perhaps even true of the apartheid state, which was, in spite of its bureaucracy or perhaps because of it, in the Afrikaans word, *slapgat*, or "slapdash." Had it been of German origin, things would have been indescribably worse, however terrible they were. But the fact that even the underclass is nostalgic about the apartheid days, when "at least the police protected the streets and the trains ran on time," is worthy of Italy. At the same time the South African state is postmodern in Bauman's sense by existing in an increasingly fragmented, neoliberal world where a formerly intact group of cadres have now splintered into those who mine the mines and businesses of big capital and speak a totally deracinated neoliberal language, in spite of their trade-union origins; into those who in government still speak the language of an (increasingly racialized) transformation; into those who have taken up positions as professionals, and the like. These disparate sectors of the society no longer speak anything like the same language, except in certain neoliberal moments or moments of transformational nostalgia. Nor are there the systems of circulation between them that would allow for a powerful state.

Relevant to the topic of the white paper, not to mention the fact of chaos, is that both the meaning of "programs" (their vocational impact and directedness, the degree to which universities must remake their curricula to engender them) and the extent to which the whole point of the policy exercise is to allow for a clearing space (like that of the Dali Tambo show, in which new forms of education might be tried on like so many new garments in these new times) is all unclear. The extent to which the government will allow for this freedom of response from universities is equally obscure. Do they even know? Should they know? Read in a generous way, the white paper is vague enough about what a vocational outcome is to invite a dialectical response by universities, who are thereby requested to rethink the matter of transformation and "complete the meaning of the document" by recasting the idea of what is at stake in a vocation. The paper is asking, on this reading, for a series of responses from universities that it will then, in the course of a fruitful dialogue, consider and respond to. Read as a professionalizing, technocratic document of a crude kind (in line with a long South African colonial history of technocratic educational practices and South Africa's contemporary dependency on neoliberal norms), the white paper precisely turns the humanities into a Derridean supplement, which will provide new professional and applied scientific programs with the "little extras" they need while remaining in a marginal position—as if the sciences were "complete in themselves" but just needed a few flourishes (extra skills) from the humanities of a "core kind." A well-known dean of studies in South Africa once told me such a story. He went on to say that the sciences already teach the history and morality of science in their science courses and require only the humanities to help prepare students with business-oriented skills such as writing and "presentation." Reduced to a designer of good presentation, the humanities end up in the marginal camp, which Derrida claims writing was placed in throughout much of the north's philosophical history. Thus John Locke: metaphor is a nice feminine way of presenting a clear masculine truth claim, as in the dean of studies who believes the humanities are helpful handmaidens. No doubt a victim of an old-style, Anglophiliac, South African, one-subject education: the man hasn't studied any. There is certainly room for the transformation of *him*.

Insofar as it is read to construct margins and centers on neoliberal grounds, the text of the white paper requires deconstruction. And yet again, the white paper can be interpreted to give the humanities something of their rightful place, since they are, after all, one of the main areas to be identified as crucial for the new South Africa.

Finally, while written as a foundational policy document, the white paper could simply be one provisional stage in the development of policy, with a number of future documents or "emendations" following. One does not know. Hence, writing in the "now," the document's "constitutional" status is unclear—another complication for its meaning and dissemination. Every year one hears of a major transformational plan that either does emerge (only to disappear into oblivion) or is about to emerge, or is squashed before it sees the light of day. These keep the blood pressure from sinking too low, but accomplish little else—at least at the moment.

Evidently one must dialectically respond to the white paper through multiple readings and responses, some textual, others in terms of its relation to social practice (itself obscure enough). The *posts* are required for that. South African developmental policy therefore needs these *posts* to explain the nature of its policy and to articulate styles of critique and resistance to policy. One then hopes for the best.

And as for the Dali Tambo show itself? One might wonder if the show, with its African identities on parade, does not participate in the postmodern smoke screen. Images of new Africans speaking on cell phones and prancing about in makeup and headdresses create a middle-class black market before the fact of the arrival of that class by imagining it or staging it. But they also fill in the void where no middle class is really arising by staging it. Similarly, the show celebrates the capacity for all citizens to try on new identities in an African marketplace, while also providing the illusion that their recalcitrant, historically conditioned characters might just disappear in the glow of the camera. The show thus participates in the inflation of the representational sign beyond its justice, while also calling into being that very sign through the pleasure in its spectacle. It is neither good nor bad but both. One might similarly wonder if the ANC's strong-armed and highly visible harping on the transformation in such relatively weak institutions as universities and museums is not, in part, a way of producing a similar smoke screen—a display of change in highly visible areas, granted the ANC's weak capacity to effect transformation in the realms of industry, the opening of markets, housing, and the like. Considering that at least certain universities have already substantially transformed themselves (all could do better), and will/must continue to do so through affirmative action, the harping on these institutions cannot but point to a fetish of the areas where the government has control, a way of parading this control to the public to fill in a void from somewhere else. Thus does the university become a national spectacle in postmodern times.

Edward Said once quipped that he wanted there to be a Palestinian state so that he could begin to criticize it. I want new South Africans to try on the postmodern garment, right on the Dali Tambo show—and in universities—so that, in the thrill of cross-dressing, this garment may become part of the African wardrobe. Does it fit? Can it be tailored? That would be worthwhile, since postmodern theory would finally then emerge from its first world enclosure to explore a series of global situations elsewhere (in India, Japan, Hong Kong, Rio, Johannesburg, etcetera) as a "family" in Wittgenstein's sense. Such an expansion of the concept of the postmodern would in turn prompt a further rewriting of the concept of the postcolonial.

Dali has now switched to a one-on-one format, perhaps because he wanted to extend the "depth" of his interview situations to that of such searingly "intensive" programs as the *Larry King Live* show and, at a slightly less egregious level, BBC's *Hard Talk.* Or perhaps because his inauguration of the new South Africa, an inauguration that placed identities on parade by juxtaposing them, is not sustainable. For at a certain point the real work of mixing and matching must transfer from the television to the society. The honeymoon is over, and probably without having ever taken place, which means we are by now, more than five years into the new South Africa, at the end of the beginning.

7

Ongoing Struggle at the End of History

Fukuyama and the End of History

One person dead and one hundred and fifty thousand demonstrating at the G8 Summit in Genoa. Demonstrations against the injustice in globalization in Seattle, Davos, São Paolo. All this at the end of history. Africa in shambles, and all this at the end of history. President Thabo Mbeki gaining back some of the moral capital lost during the AIDS debacle by impressing the G8 nations with a plan to help Africa.

Thousands dead in the September 11 attacks on the World Trade Center, the Pentagon, and in Pittsburgh, at the end of history.

The end of history: Francis Fukuyama's *The End of History and the Last Man*[1] is among the most important works of the last decade of the twentieth century, the decade during which South Africa became a liberal democracy and vowed to enter into the spirit of a flourishing, global economy. Fukuyama's well-known view is that history has come to an end. To be more precise and more pedantic about this: Fukuyama's well-known view is that history has come to an end, or is about to come to an end, or is in the process of coming to an end in most if not all parts of the globe, or is in the process of coming to an end in significant parts of the globe but perhaps not most, or is in the process of coming to an end in some but not all other places on the globe while some of those parts of the globe that seem about to be coming to an end may well slide back toward the beginning into less adequate historical shapes, others remaining perhaps for some time to come mired in the historical mud but, one hopes, over time, rising to the occasion of liberal democracy and so coming to completion, that is, fruition (one hopes in the next fifty years but one doesn't know for sure). We are *in media res* toward the end of history, in the middle of the inauguration of the ending of history, the moment at which the institution of liberal democracy and "the free market system" is happening throughout the globe. Who can deny it? Who can prove it? It is the point of Fukuyama's book to state this fact, or about-to-be-fact, or intuition with significant empirical juice behind it. But far more than that, it is the point of Fukuyama's book to argue two things, both of which are half-empirical and half-metaphysical: first, that liberal democracy arises in tandem with the free-market system. This is because each facilitates, occasions, encourages, makes "inevitable," the rise of the other. The concept of "dialectical necessity" usually stands for this kind of interactionist tendency, once the tendency is diagnosed as historically inevitable with metaphysical implications. These are encapsulated in Fukuyama's claim—or almost-made claim—that liberal democracy (the two factors in combination) will prove ultimately satisfying to the human spirit and therefore represent the end point of history. This is an empirical thesis about human satisfaction, but also a metaphysical thesis about the essential conditions for it, and hence the relationship between human nature and history. This thesis Fukuyama adopts from Hegel, or almost adopts from Hegel, because he actually gets it from Alexandre Kojeve and, through Kojeve, Alan Bloom. The second thesis Fukuyama's book argues is that, metaphysically, liberal democracy is a historically emergent shape finally expressive of human essence, of what humanity requires for its flourishing. The shape allows for the human need for "recognition" by others, by state, society, political institutions, communities. And it allows for the human instinct for gain, since it facilitates capitalism, the buildup of goods and services. This shape is historically final; there can be no other, or be imagined to be no other, at the present time at least, since the shape contains no inner "contradictions."

It is clear that Fukuyama's book is about the end of history in the advanced capitalist countries of the world, those that control the process of globalization. Others, like South Africa and then other parts of Africa, will follow suit. Now, I do not believe Africa suffers from globalization. It suffers from a failure of globalization. The end of history will never happen for Africa until globalization happens in a just way within the continent of Africa. It was Thabo Mbeki's rhetoric to understand this. It has not happened. It has not happened because globalization is about production and consumption and Africa has not proved competitive in either domain. It lacks stability for production and it lacks a robust middle class for consumption. So, at least in the short term, it is left out. The rich get richer, the poor get poorer. This is not a recipe for the end of history just yet; it is a recipe for the end of history in the advanced countries where liberal democracy and economic flourishing have melded.

Fukuyama has many important things to say about how, for these countries, the advanced countries of the world, liberal democracy and economic flourishing are mutually interdependent and facilitating processes. An authoritarian regime might facilitate economic growth at an early moment in development when a country needs control, stability, and order. It might, as in the case of Cuba or China, hugely supply material rights such as housing, education, medical care, employment, pension, etcetera. Their satisfaction might, in the short term, contribute significantly to the growth of human capital. However, when an economy becomes as robust and complex as that of the former Soviet Union's, or currently China's, liberal democracy—that is, liberalization—is required to facilitate it. Free-market competition is necessary for growth at that point, along with a flexible economic system capable of responding to new and unpredictable economic forces and opportunities. Moreover, advanced technological and information capitalism requires an open civil society (which authoritarianism by definition represses) for the free flow of information and appropriate creativity in fields such as advertising and publicity. . . . Beyond a certain point, human capital, furthermore, can grow only if cultivated by a robust civil society of universities, the media, critique, etcetera. . . . Conversely, democracy requires in the long term a free-market economy for its sustainability: popular democracies where the means of production are owned by "the people" inevitably lead to chaos, or elites who tacitly exert authoritarian control. Macpherson,[2] writing before Fukuyama, had already argued that liberal democracy is the political system of choice for capitalism, and argued it convincingly. And many have argued the converse, that democracy as a form of governance is sustained only by a free-market economy. Hence the tendency, or process, by which, dialectically, the form of governance and the economy come to "entail" each other.

By "the end of history" is meant something more than that a tendency toward this mutual entailment is happening. What is meant is a *metaphysical* conclusion, a conclusion in the Hegelian sense of there being no further shape imaginable that could *better* satisfy humanity. And more than that (since Churchill had already stated that democracy is the worst form of governance, except for all the rest), what is meant is that this shape satisfies human aspirations, that it is an institutional structure and functioning system that allows for human happiness. This in itself is meant to be a philosophical conclusion reached in part by empirical means. Fukuyama earnestly believes, or almost believes, that the current state of liberal democracy has significantly enveloped the world since the late 1980s, when his famous article was written, and in the early 1990s, when his famous book was written. He therefore writes in a millennial spirit. He writes in the wake of the collapse of communism and the birth of Eastern European liberal democracies, in the wake of the exfoliation of new breakaway nation states with their own sovereignty and democracy, in the wake of the collapse of dictatorships and "authoritarian states" all over Latin America and their replacement by liberal democratic ones (with better GNPs and other statistics of the kind the International Monetary Fund and World Bank thrive on measuring). These events intimate, so to speak, a historical end point. With the help of (his) theory, they demonstrate, as it were, an end point. However, Fukuyama also, toward the end of his book, hedges, holds out, is reasonably, appropriately modest about whether liberal democracy is a metaphysical end point, or will be, or is about to be, in being a shape that is completely expressive of human flourishing and, hence, completely satisfying. One could believe that liberal democracy has a lot to offer. One could believe that liberal democracy is the current name of the game, the current historical parameter, given the collapse of all alternatives or their evident stagnation. One could, in believing those things, even come to the conclusion that there is no better form of government imaginable at the moment. Nevertheless, one could also think that a certain intellectual modesty is in order, a certain skepticism about the capacity of this or that instance of liberal democracy (in this or that part of the globe) to produce equality in the distribution of goods or in the apportionment of recognition, to engender economic flourishing for some or all, to solve the problem of a dispossessed minority or of a general feeling of cultural atrophy, to meld traditional styles of social life with new forms of global capitalism or local democracy, to produce over time new styles of being in the young (for whom current gaps between styles of doing things will then appear less threatening), to educate the young so that liberal capitalism might flourish. Would these be failures in instituting liberal democracy or failures in its structure?

Moreover, there is the enormous question, so easily posed a decade after this book appeared, about whether the states of the Middle East are tending toward liberal democracy, and, more than that, about whether liberal democracy should be assumed to be the best form of representation for the people who live in those states, even if it is, as Rorty would put it, the best system for "us," and even if I personally find the authoritarian structure of such states, and the presumption of terror built into radical disaffection within their populations, utterly unacceptable.

The End of History as a Philosophical Structure

What gives Fukuyama's book its philosophical structure is that it does not rest content with a modest and sanguine picture of the world as of 1990 (when he is writing)—in its better or worse instances—but instead boldly asserts, while modestly hedging the assertion, that liberal democracy is, for all intents and purposes, completely satisfying, or will soon be. The book is in one sense a meditation on what is philosophically at stake in this claim, while in another something quite close to a defense of the claim. Throughout, the claim changes—and there are, on my count, at least three formulations of it, implicit and explicit, which I shall turn to below.

The claim that liberal democracy is completely satisfying to human life is the claim that it satisfies our deepest aspirations. The idea is Hegelian. History is rational in that it is the process through which human beings come to discover what their deepest aspirations are, and to build a social world that is completely expressive of them. Only through history—through a process of construction and failure, only through what Hegel calls "the dialectic"—can humans come to simultaneously understand who they are and what they want, and to construct a world that gives representation to this knowledge. The end of history takes place when, finally, the institutions of modernity completely and transparently reflect the truth of human aspirations. This process redeems all of the subterfuge, chaos, death, violence, and pathos of history. It is a struggle that can be read, so the view goes, from the history of ideas but also of wars.

Fukuyama believes the pages of history and philosophy together have shown two aspirations that are essential to human life: the aspiration for freedom and autonomy and the aspiration for making one's mark on the world (what he calls the "tymotic urge"). A society is completely reflective of human aspiration when it gives recognition to these aspirations. Liberal democracy can do so because 1) it allows for freedom and autonomy, and 2) its economy allows for making your mark on things, for not keeping a good man or woman down.

Fukuyama the economist is, like others who have lived through the 1980s, writing in the wake of a vast movement in the direction of liberal democracy throughout the world. This includes the collapse of communism with its Velvet (i.e., Prague) and not so Velvet (i.e., Russian) revolutions, the struggle against fascist and authoritarian regimes in, certainly, the apartheid state, but also in Latin America, Asia, and Europe. For Fukuyama's Hegelianizing mind, the events of the 1980s have confirmed the centrality of two things: the human need for recognition as a free, autonomous, participatory citizen with democratic rights (this is what people struggled for), and the failure of planned/noncapitalist economies to grow beyond a certain point.

His Hegelianizing mind interprets history not simply as strong empirical proof of the importance of liberal democracy in an overwhelming number of instances, but as proof of what is essential to human aspirations. He offers no demonstration of why one should make the move from overwhelming empirical fact to metaphysical essentialism, nor even what is at stake in doing it. Recall that for Hegel, the move is made because the course of human history is the same course as that followed by the human mind when it develops into a knowing subjectivity: for Hegel, the shape of history and of genetic epistemology are one. This is why the dialectic is "necessary": it is not merely historically necessary, it is a condition of the possibility of knowledge per se. Whatever problems there may be with Hegel's grand picture, it does make clear why empirical truth should also be metaphysical truth. Fukuyama slides from empiricism to metaphysics by dint of mere pronouncement. (And in saying this, I am not denying that the aspirations he fixes on are crucial to human life: I am sure they are.)

The tymotic urge is more troubling to him. This is because at the end of history what is lost is precisely the capacity to make your mark on history, to start with nothing and achieve greatness, in accord with the Horatio Alger myth and the American-immigrant dream. Work becomes an all-consuming venture, with economic pressure for faster turnover of products and increasing competition making life rife with anxiety. And yet, one becomes bored with a world increasingly defined as a department store of endless products, which is how things appeared in America in the 1990s. So dot-com millionaires book $200,000 flights into space, simply to make their mark or to keep themselves from total boredom, and the system becomes more and more debilitating just at the moment of its greatest success.

Fukuyama never provides a successful explanation of this loss. It mitigates the idea that at the end of history there are no problems generated by the achievement of the end itself.

There is a certain opacity that follows about how Fukuyama imagines the end of history. I detect three formulations of it in his book, two of which are explicit, the third implicit. The first two can be found in the following paragraph:

> The problem of the end of history can be put in the following way: Are there any "contradictions" in our contemporary liberal democratic social order that would lead us to expect that the historical process will continue, and produce a new, higher order? We could recognize a "contradiction" if we saw a source of social discontent sufficiently radical to eventually cause the downfall of liberal democratic societies—the "system," in the language of the 1960s—as a whole. It is not sufficient to point to "problems" in contemporary liberal democracies, even if they are serious ones like budget deficits, inflation, crime, or drugs. A "problem" does not become a "contradiction" unless it is so serious that it not only cannot be solved within the system, but corrodes the legitimacy of the system itself such that the latter collapses under its own weight. For example, the steady impoverishment of the proletariat in capitalist societies was for Marx not just a "problem," but a "contradiction" because it would lead to a revolutionary situation that would bring down the entire structure of capitalist society and replace it with a different one. Conversely, we can argue that history has come to an end if the present form of social and political organization is completely satisfying to human beings in their most essential characteristics. (Fukuyama: 136)

The present form of social and political organization must be "completely satisfying in their most essential characteristics" for this to be (or about to be) the end of history. This is the first sense in which an end point of history is given a metaphysical definition.

Is the deflation of desire, the deflation of the capacity to make your mark on things, a failure of complete satisfaction of an essential human characteristic or not? Perhaps the most interesting aspect of Fukuyama's approach consists in its worry that even paradise may lack the attractiveness it appears to have and hence, from the human point of view, be less than completely satisfying. We may remember the moment when Voltaire's Candide and his faithful servant Cacambo find themselves in the best of all possible worlds, that world of the mythical Incas where the streets are lined with gold, the food is better even than that served in the best Parisian restaurants, and rational science perfectly coheres with religion. A benevolent dictatorship where at the same time all are free, this is a world without the human instinct for power, the all-too-human desire to be richer than one's neighbor. The place where bucolic lyric replaces human passion, for as Hume, that brilliant philosopher of the human, said, "Of all the human emotions, greed is the most universal, perpetual, and insatiable." Whether true or not, it is true enough by Voltaire's standards to make Candide and his friend eventually tire of life in perfection, since they found themselves incapable of indulging in these all too human passions. The point concerns the failure of the tymotic urge for self-interested gain in an ideal world, the failure of the satisfaction that comes from struggles overcome, difficulties surmounted, eternity won through brilliant invention, a mark made on the scarred face of history by the young lion or lamb of the times. A world where critique is not in the offing, nor change possible, may be a world that evacuates that social and individual enthusiasm which produces the historical sublime. It may be boring, a world of understimulation. Fukuyama correctly notes the problem, then goes on to make some astonishingly vacuous claims about the way in which group life and associations (that is, collective civil society) may serve to compensate. He is, rightly, a bit skeptical of what he says in this regard.

It is well known that the end of history can appear as a homogenization of all aspects of life into forms of information capital, from palimony agreements to the conversion of leisure time into a mere occasion for discount shopping. A great deal of postmodern writing has been about the terror of human homogenization and the reduction of life to consumption, which never ultimately proves satisfying. Even child-rearing becomes a matter of how many special experiences Yuppie consumers can afford to buy for their child while they are busy working ceaselessly to pay for their house. Family time takes place over the Internet and on the psychiatrist's couch. Are you ready for emigration, South Africans?

I repeat: are these failures of a system to deliver the structure for essential human satisfaction or not?

This brings us to a second way that "complete satisfaction" is construed by the book. Consider this quotation:

> It is not sufficient to point to "problems" in contemporary liberal democracies, even if they are serious ones like budget deficits, inflation, crime, or drugs. A "problem" does not become a "contradiction" unless it is so serious that it not only cannot be solved within the system, but corrodes the legitimacy of the system itself such that the latter collapses under its own weight. (Fukuyama: 136)

Here it is acknowledged that liberal democracies may contain grave difficulties, so long as they do not produce a "contradiction" that would lead to systemic collapse. This may allow for significant problems to remain at the end of history. However, Fukuyama now owes us an account of the distinction between systemic and nonsystemic contradictions in a way that is not totally ad hoc. Needless to say, the distinction between "systemic" versus "grave but nonsystemic" difficulties is hardly clear, and yet the criteria rests upon it. Contradictions within the system would be those that flow directly from its terms of composition, as opposed to by-products or side effects, or whatever. Liberalism in the full sense of liberal democracy, is, in combination with free-market economics, a *complex system*. Complexity theory is a family of related sciences and research programs, and there is no single understanding of a complex system to be had nowadays. However, what most of these research programs share is a sense that a mark of complex systems is multiple modeling. Various models may be provided, each with its pragmatic purposes. None takes ultimate precedence over the others. Witness debates between economists about how to understand structural dynamics of current economies, the many ways economies are interestingly modeled, and the point will be intuitively plausible. One should be skeptical about any ultimate capacity to formulate, that is, to model the difference between a systemic and a nonsystemic contradiction in liberal democracy, beyond particular pragmatic purposes, indeed, the very individuation of the system: political economy, especially given the interlinking of many such systems in the global world, may well be a matter for alternative modeling schemes.

Contradictions—what are they? Let us take them as internal instabilities that are generated by the system and cause it to react against itself. But every complex system is constantly reacting against itself, including every economy, which since Keynes has been considered internally unstable in its very mechanism. The question is, does the system contain the capacity to correct itself, change itself, solve its problems, cure itself? How do you decide that about liberal democracy considered as political economy, for now or for the future?

The vague idea is that if the system is stable with respect to the big things, the little things (such as its failure to allow for making your mark as life allows for this in states of huge transition or instability, such as the system's forcing more and more professionals into nonending workweeks) can be allowed. Complete satisfaction does not mean a world free of problems, but a world that "works." How well, therefore, must it work for us to allow that it is not internally contradictory and hence completely satisfying? One begins to feel that these metaphors ("internal contradiction," "complete satisfaction," "essential human aspiration") themselves form a system of concepts that is mutually supportive. Where each metaphor fails, one turns to the next one, all around in a circle. Hence the incoherence of any clear statement of what the end of history would be, given the ideal of "complete satisfaction."

It should be clear that a certain waffling about the relations between a society free of contradictions and a society capable of delivering complete satisfaction is going on throughout this dense, millennial book. In one sense, it is because the society is free of contradictions that it can deliver complete satisfaction. In another, complete satisfaction is somewhat mitigated by the "grave difficulties" a society may face, but history is still at an endpoint if the political economy is free of contradictions. This waffling leads to the third way the end of history might be construed. Here we have to dig back into the pages of Hegel.

There is a third way to take the end of history, which Fukuyama does not develop, but which derives instead from the work of Hegel itself: namely, that the end of history is happening now, with its associated problems. But these problems are not as we think they are. Instead, it is *we* who have to come to a better recognition of these problems. This change in our mode of recognition will show us that they are not grave, but instead, in the nature of things. It is the task of philosophy to demonstrate this. Hegel calls this task that of reconciliation. In reconciling us to our world (with its problems, now known differently), we will, in turn, be better social agents and history will, in fact, improve. Hence, the final stage of the end of history is this change in "human capital."

But reconciliation is also possible only because society is, in fact, rational. This is the key, as Michael Hardimon puts it. The function of reconciliation is therefore to

> [free] oneself of expectations that one has justifiably come to regard as unreasonable. People who seek consolation [as opposed to reconciliation] regard the non-satisfaction of their expectations as a genuine loss for which some kind of replacement or compensation is due. People who attain reconciliation come to see that the fact that their unreasonable expectations were not fulfilled does not constitute a real loss at all. . . .
>
> Reconciliation is not a matter of thinking that everything is wonderful. Hegel's celebrated rich and suggestive claim that reconciliation consists in recognizing "reason as the rose in the cross of the present" . . . illustrates this point.[3]

Reconciliation can therefore mean that the end of history contains problems, so long as it is still fundamentally good and so long as one can find a way of coming to terms with the limitations of the present. Reconciliation is a way of accepting the limits of what is as limits on the rational expression of humanity per se, and therefore as no real loss. Insofar as rationalization is not mere accommodation or based in some kind of mistaken judgment, insofar as it shows the world to be fully human and fully humanizing, it leads to what could be called philosophical satisfaction, a mature sense that one is at home in the social world. This philosophical satisfaction, which follows from rational justification, is complete, insofar as it is founded on the knowledge that is completely convincing, indeed philosophically demonstrable, that society is a true home, that is, a rational entity. Rational justification, meaning for Hegel philosophical justification, demonstrates the rationality of society. This objectively shows that history is completed and provides the means for agents to reconcile with it, for to say that society is rational is to say that it completely expresses human aspirations, provides essential recognition of human desires.

Everything therefore hangs on what would be at stake in proving society rational. My point is that this is a more open-ended claim than Fukuyama's, since it might be sufficient merely to show that the basic institutions of state, civil society, culture, citizenship, and functional economy are enough. Contradictions, partial dissatisfactions: these are the cross on which the rose sits. You learn to live with it, to reconcile yourself to it, to develop a better attitude toward things. Hegel's point is that the end of history depends upon your change in attitude and not simply the objective processes that are in place.

We do not know what a "rational system" is until criteria are given. The problem is that, again, persons may disagree about how to answer this question. Even if they agree about terms, they may disagree about whether those terms are satisfied by a given society—enough. At the time of Hegel's writing, the signs of a home were those of bourgeois nationalism: a home was a nation in which the bourgeoisie could live lives of autonomy and community. However, those terms were hardly terms for consensus, given that the postscript to Hegel included Marx, Nietzsche, and Freud, not to mention the revolutions of 1848, the moment of greatest colonial exploitation, the birth of modern racism, and then World War I.

A certain skepticism would seem to be in order about the prospects of a general rationalization of society along Hegelian lines—and therefore about the project of reconciliation.

The End of History as a Parameter

In a more modest voice, Fukuyama intimates (in spite of himself) liberal democracy as a parameter. In this voice he emphasizes process rather than result:

> If man is primarily an economic animal driven by his desire and reason, then the dialectical process of historical evolution should be reasonably similar for different human societies and cultures. That was the conclusion of "modernization theory." . . . Modernization theory looks much more persuasive in the 1990s than it did fifteen or twenty years earlier when it came under heavy attack in academic circles. Almost all countries that have succeeded in achieving a high level of economic development have in fact come to look increasingly similar to one another, rather than less. While there are a variety of routes that countries can take to get to the end of history, there are few versions of modernity other than the capitalist liberal democratic one that look like they are going concerns. (Fukuyama: 133)

These remarks should be read in conjunction with more recent remarks about the importance of human capital in *Trust: The Social Virtues and the Creation of Prosperity*.[4] There, Fukuyama characterizes the quality of economy and liberal democracy at the end of history in terms of the capacity for human beings, in this society or that, to recruit and cultivate enduring forms of associations. The practices or moral infrastructure of what is called civil society are in that book understood as fundamental for both economic growth and human satisfaction. The book, in short, has more genuine recognition of how complex a system liberal democracy is, and on a related note, of how deep its failures can be. Thus, even at the end of history, where structures of liberal democracy and economy are reasonably stable, a society could limp and suffer on account of its postracist lack of community, its incapacity to realign its economy and society generally in the light of the best of its specific traditions, or its inability to get human beings to cooperate successfully. The De Tocqueville of contemporary life, Fukuyama here wishes to point out but also to warn: as America in particular is in danger of losing its sense of public spiritedness, retreating into a dot-com maze of Web sites, paraphernalia, and megadollars, its economic as well as moral capacity may be at stake. Moreover, it is a point of *trust* that different societies (the United States, Japan, Malaysia, Italy) bring different forms of association or lack thereof. None of these societies, it would seem, is capable of fruitfully dealing with "all possible socioeconomic problems." Thus society A will, given its traditions, perhaps deal very well with problem X, while not very well with problem Y, and so forth. Whether Fukuyama realizes it or not, the implication is that since human capital is contextual, history is not over, because society A, with its particular form of human capital, may find itself at a moment of struggle to overcome problems at some time in the future, problems that will give rise to further historical change. There is no reason to envision an absolute end point, where the human capital of society A can solve all problems in a satisfactory way.

Finally, how stable is liberal democracy, even considered as "the parameter"? Fukuyama writes about the world as a discrete set of nation states, but it is a globally interdependent world. How stable is the global system, given its current predication on a Middle East comprised of authoritarian, corrupt states with little social delivery, massive popular disaffection, and immense oil power? How stable is a liberalism where a single set of attacks can nearly cripple the airline industry? And is, I repeat, democracy truly the only human parameter? I would wish it so; others might not.

Shifts and Conflicts within the Parameters

There can be no end to history because the parameters according to which history is understood to come to conclusion themselves *shift* with history. They modulate through changes in the conditions of production and consumption, through sociopolitical changes, through human struggle. Moreover, capital growth and liberal justice are hardly the same; there can be an active antagonism between them. The growth of markets has not adequately led to liberal justice in the global south: neither to liberal democracies, where rights are over time being instituted fairly and equally, nor to economic prosperity. To attract foreign investment, South Africa engaged in a self-monitoring process of structural adjustment: GEAR, or Growth, Employment, and Redistribution. It tightened its belt, reduced the size of its state apparatus, etcetera, doing everything the World Bank requires a country to do to receive a loan—even though it did not need a loan and was not applying for one. South Africa did this, under the ministrations of Alec Irwin, minister of trade and industry; however, the net effect was to produce a tightened, strained economy with little foreign investment on the scene. Former Stalinists did not understand that the mere readying of a country for competition is not a guarantee of success. Rather, everything hangs on whether South Africa is as attractive a place for foreign investment as "the competition." It seems, at present, not. By a historical irony, China is the currently attractive place, par excellence.

This is because China has done such a decent job in supplying workers with economic rights (housing, medical care, etcetera) that companies can pay workers next to nothing and have them survive. So Communism has readied the world for the next batch of cheap labor! South African companies are themselves looking to produce in China, and in the past few years South Africa has lost a million jobs. This in a country of fifty million people, one third of whom are out of work. So much for the justice in globalization.

GEAR is certainly what the business sector *within* South Africa wants, for it stresses the accretion of capital investment without constraint. And it is laissez-faire. The government, caught between an old Marxist model of "seizing the capital" (which it knows it cannot do) and a neoliberal model of "business as usual" (which gives business the license it has always enjoyed to avoid national commitment except in a purely voluntary way), has not learned the art of providing incentives for capital investment by business in national development and *disincentives* for its failure. This is a failure of political negotiation. However, it must be said that the real purpose of GEAR has been to take on structural adjustment unto oneself to be attractive to globalization, which has always been willing to give you a tip (send money for a housing community or build a university a building) but which will not or cannot take the risk of *investment*.

Producers will argue that they must look to the most competitive production sites (thus leaving Africa in the lurch), that they are not free to be just, because competition is so tough that they will be out of the game should they not act as ruthlessly as they do. So it is a system in which no one is free. Marx said this some time ago and there is a certain truth in it. In turn, South African companies are looking to sell in parts of the world other than Africa: to China and Latin America, where there are already substantial middle classes with consumer power. And so they leave their own countries in the lurch. Again they claim they are not free. To survive, one must search for expanding, viable markets. That is the law of the game. Perhaps. But if so, it shows that the vagaries of capital flows mean that there is no reason why, even at the end of history, there should not remain vast inequalities and injustices, widening rather than collapsing the gap between the haves and the have-nots, for production and consumption will remain selective and "discriminatory."

Recall one fact about America: every one of the rights instituted into law that protect citizens against the vagaries of capitalism has been achieved through struggle. At the beginning of the twentieth century, there was no right to an eight-hour workday, no minimum wage, no laws against child labor, no right to unionize, no right to workers' compensation, no right to a pension, no right to appeal if fired, no regulatory mechanism for ensuring safety in the workplace, no Securities and Exchange Commission to prevent monopolization and fraud, no welfare state. Each and every one of those rights was achieved in the first forty years of the twentieth century first through blood, and then through negotiation. These are rights and regulations that humanize capitalism in the name of human life. By now we *also* realize that those rights and regulations facilitate rather than restrict capitalism, or rather, facilitate it as much as they restrict it (for even at "the end of history," the system is not consistent; it is riddled with conflict). This is Fukuyama's point. (It is similarly known that a vibrant civil society, with higher education, courts of law, and a good system of social benefits such as health care also facilitate markets by accreting human capital.) My point is that such rights and regulations are fought for and won; they are part of the struggle for recognition too. Fukuyama restricts his vision of the struggle for recognition to struggles in the name of liberal democracy and liberal economy. Equally important are struggles to humanize these very features of modern life, to render them palatable.

Then who does one struggle against, to achieve access to globalization and justice within nations, given that globalization is a transnational affair? The terrorist attacks on the World Trade Center and the incipient "campaign" against terror have caused the World Bank to state that it expects U.S. investor interest in South Africa and the African continent to plummet as a result. Some in Africa have been speaking about the need to sign on to the campaign as a way of negotiating development aid in exchange, but in South Africa the African National Congress remains wedded to its former struggle allies (Libya) and its complex (if also disaggregated) Muslim constituencies, and has, so far, acted with absolute ambivalence. The meaning seems to be: less development aid, in the short term, at least.

Then how does one presume to negotiate for aid from a position of lack of wherewithal if one is unwilling to "play the game"? The answer is hardly obvious—no more obvious than the question of whom or what you "struggle against" in a context of globalization, nor by what means. And yet economic justice in the global "south" depends on the answers to these questions.

Notes

INTRODUCTION

1 See Ludwig Wittgenstein, *Philosophical Investigations*, trans. E. Anscombe (New York: Macmillan, 1968), p. v.
2 Ibid.

1. THE COAT OF MANY COLORS

1 See *Truth and Reconciliation Commission of South Africa Report*, vol. 1 (Cape Town: CTP Book Printers and Juta and Company, 1998), p. 107. Hereafter, all references to the five volumes of the report will follow the quotes with volume number and page numbers.
2 See Antjie Krog, *Country of My Skull* (London: Jonathan Cape, 1998), p. 29. Hereafter, all references to Krog will follow the quotes with author's name and page numbers.
3 See Dori Laub, "Bearing Witness," in *Testimony*, Shoshana Felman and Dori Laub (New York and London: Routledge, 1992), p. 58.
4 See Jean-François Lyotard, *Just Gaming*, trans. Wlad Godzich and Samuel Weber (Minneapolis: University of Minnesota Press, 1985).
5 Although transitional justice is distinctive, one ought not to make too much of its distinctiveness, for every society that lives as a democracy contains within itself an ongoing conversation of democracy, in which dissent is crucial. Hence, every society contains within itself the seeds of "transition" of some kind or another.
6 See Geoffrey Robertson, *Crimes against Humanity: The Struggle for Global Justice* (London: Penguin, 1999), p. 266.
7 See Deborah Posel, "The TRC Report: What Kind of History? What Kind of Truth?" delivered at University of Witwatersrand Conference on Truth and Reconciliation, 1998, p. 4–5.
8 See Colin Bundy, "The Beast of the Past: History and the TRC," delivered at University of Witwatersrand Conference on Truth and Reconciliation, 1998.

9 See Posel, p. 27.

10 Ibid., p. 3.

11 Ibid., p. 3.

12 In keeping with the spelling of this sergeant's name as it appears in the report, I have changed Krog's spelling to "Mothasi."

13 She presents five but there is no conceptual loss, I believe, in reducing them to three, because the other two consist of a fictional account and a very brief notice in the newspaper *The Sowetan*.

14 See Michael Hardimon, *Hegel's Social Philosophy: The Project of Reconciliation* (Cambridge and London: Cambridge University Press, 1994), p. 89.

15 Ibid., p. 95.

2. SOWETO'S *TAXI*, AMERICA'S *RIB*

1 See Donald Davidson, *Inquiries into Truth and Interpretation* (Oxford: Clarendon Press, 1984), p. 183–98.

2 See Richard Rorty, *Contingency, Irony, and Solidarity* (Cambridge: Cambridge University Press, 1989), p. 197.

3 See Friedrich Hegel, *Phenomenology of Spirit*, trans. A. V. Miller (Oxford: Oxford University Press, 1977). Hegel, believing the West to be the only culture capable of generating genuine history, will not think of the colonial slave as one whose misery is a result of the devaluing of his particular historical experiences, since, according to Hegel, there is nothing in the culture of the slave that is worthy of giving rise to history. It will take Hegel's legacy in the work of Frantz Fanon (1961) to write of the slave's experience as the result of such devaluing.

4 See Stanley Cavell, *Pursuits of Happiness: The Hollywood Comedy of Remarriage* (Cambridge and London: Harvard University Press, 1981).

5 Ibid., introduction, p. 1–45.

6 The interrelation of iteration, repetition, and difference is a key aspect of the work of Jacques Derrida, and is a way of understanding the philosophy implicit in the film. See Jacques Derrida, *Limited, Inc.*, trans. Samuel Weber and Jeffrey Mehlman (Evanston: Northwestern University Press, 1988).

7 Toyi-toyi was the dance of resistance displayed in black South Africa during apartheid. It remains so today.

3. AFRO-MEDICI

1 See Thabo Mbeki, "I Am an African," reprinted in *Africa: The Time Has Come* (Cape Town: Tafelberg, 1998), p. 34.

2 Ibid., p. 31.

3 Ibid., p. 32.

4 Johan Jacobs has pointed out that these acts of "mimicry" can be understood as the dependent position of a nonnative speaker of English on the idioms of the "great English writers" Mbeki has read.

5 Mbeki, 1, p. 34.

6 Ibid.

7 See William Makgoba, *Mokoko: The Makgoba Affair* (Johannesburg: Vivlia Publishers, 1997).

8 See Antjie Krog, *Country of My Skull* (London: Jonathan Cape, 1998), p. 111.

9 Mbeki, 1, p. 34.

10 This collection was published late in 1998 at the moment of Mbeki's about-to-be-presidency of the South African state (elections were held in June 1999).

11 See Frantz Fanon, "On National Culture," in *Colonial Discourse and Post-Colonial Theory*, ed. P. Williams and L. Chrisman (New York: Columbia University Press, 1994), p. 37.

12 See Thabo Mbeki, "The African Renaissance," SABC address, August 1998, in Mbeki, 1, p. 299.

13 See Thabo Mbeki, "At the Helm of South Africa's Renaissance," on the occasion of his inauguration as chancellor of University of Transkei, May 1995, in Mbeki, 1, p. 243.

14 See Nelson Mandela, *The Struggle Is My Life*, quoted in "The Laws of Reflection: Nelson Mandela in Admiration," Jacques Derrida, in *For Nelson Mandela*, ed. Jacques Derrida and Mustafa Tlili (New York: Seaver Books, 1985), p. 24.

15 For a discussion of this, see Christopher Miller, *Blank Darkness: Africanist Discourse in French* (Chicago and London: University of Chicago Press, 1985).

16 See Kwame Anthony Appiah, *In My Father's House* (Oxford and London: Oxford University Press, 1992), pp. 28–46.

17 See Leopold Sedar Senghor, *Optima* 16: 1 (1966).

18 See Thabo Mbeki, "The African Renaissance," in Mbeki, 1, p. 299.

19 Zygmunt Bauman has argued that the postmodern state, by which he means the advanced states of Europe and America, no longer is able to depend on legitimations. And yet it is in one crucial respect (at least) stronger than ever: it facilitates economy through efficiency. The converse would be that weak states require legitimations—and the concentration of power in authoritarian state forms on account of their deeper failures to make things happen. The postmodern state in Europe and America no longer requires legitimations; it facilitates capital. By contrast, states such as South Africa have a huge legitimation capital but little relative power to make things happen, hence the need to rely on legitimations as spectacles and ideologies concentrating state power where it is otherwise weak. Cf. Zygmunt Bauman, "The Fall of the Legislator," in *Postmodernism: A Reader*, Thomas Docherty (New York: Columbia University Press, 1993), pp. 128–40.

20 See Thabo Mbeki, "At the Helm of South Africa's Renaissance," in Mbeki, 1, p. 201.

21 Ibid.

22 See Thabo Mbeki, quoted from an interview with the *BBC World News*, January 1, 1999.

4. RACIAL AND NONRACIAL STATES AND ESTATES

1 See Gerhard Mare, "Race Thinking and Thinking about Race in South Africa," unpublished paper, University of Natal (Durban) History Seminar, April 2000. Italics are Mare's.

2 My reconstruction of remarks by a person who shall remain nameless.

3 See Charles Taylor, "The Politics of Recognition," in *Multiculturalism: Examining the Politics of Recognition*, ed. Amy Gutmann (New Jersey: Princeton University Press, 1994), pp. 25–73.

4 See *Natal Witness*, August 1998.

5 See Kwame Anthony Appiah, *In My Father's House: Africa in the Philosophy of Culture* (New York: Oxford University Press, 1992), p. 37.

6 Ibid.

7 See Lucius Outlaw, "On Race and Philosophy," in *Racism and Philosophy*, ed. Susan Babbitt and Sue Campbell (Ithaca and London: Cornell University Press, 1999).

8 See Stephen Jay Gould, "Humbled by the Genome's Mysteries," *New York Times*, February 19, 2001.

9 See, for example, Arnold Davidson, "Sex and the Emergence of Sexuality," *Critical Inquiry* 14: 1 (1987): 16–48.

5. THE GENEALOGY OF MODERN SOUTH AFRICAN ARCHITECTURE

1 For a reading of Manet's work against the transformations of Paris and the flow of capital in the nineteenth century, see T. J. Clark, *The Painting of Modern Life: Paris in the Art of Manet and His Followers* (New York: Knopf, 1984).

2 For a measured approach to Irma Stern's exoticizing gaze, see the introduction to *Paradise: The Journals and Letters of Irma Stern, 1917–1933*, ed. N. Dubow (Diep River: Chameleon Press, 1991).

3 For a fascinating discussion of the Brasilia project and its subversion by local populations, see James Holston, *The Modernist City: An Anthropological Critique of Brasilia* (Chicago and London: University of Chicago Press, 1989).

4 Ibid.

5 See J. Comaroff and J. Comaroff, *Of Revelation and Revolution: Christianity, Colonialism, and Consciousness in South Africa*, vol. 1 (Chicago and London: University of Chicago Press, 1991).

6 See Clive Chipkin, *Johannesburg Style: Architecture and Society 1880s–1960s* (Cape Town: David Philip, 1993), p. 44.

7 Ibid., p. 49.

8 Ibid., p. 168.

9 "Zerohour," quoted in ibid., p. 89.

10 For discussion of the mentality underpinning the avant-garde pronouncement and its ideas of starting from scratch in the name of a utopian future, see Marjorie Perloff, *The Futurist Movement: Avant-Garde, Avant-Guerre, and the Language of Rupture* (Chicago and London: University of Chicago Press, 1986), and Daniel Herwitz, *Making Theory/Constructing Art: On the Authority of the Avant-Garde* (Chicago and London: University of Chicago Press, 1993).

11 Holston, p. 4.

12 Chipkin, 7, p. 75.

13 From private conversation.

14 The possible gap between architect's intention and the context through which the building signifies, and, similarly, the partial indeterminacy of the building's structure to determine this meaning, give rise to a number of interpretive questions about meaning, identity, and historicity, which are crucial to the recovery of an architectural past in the present. These questions are similar to Aldo Rossi's controversial claims that the buildings of Italian fascism are not identical in aesthetics to the regime's intentions for them, and their general context of signification, and that such buildings are therefore recoverable as contemporary prototypes. This is a dicey business that I would approach with great trepidation. See Aldo Rossi, *The Architecture of the City* (Cambridge and London: MIT Press, 1988).

15 Chipkin, 7, p. 280.

16 See J. Holston and A. Appadurai, "Cities and Citizenship," *Public Culture* 8: 2 (1996).

17 See Mahmood Mamdani, *Citizen and Subject* (New Jersey: Princeton University Press, 1996). Mamdani argues that colonial African spaces were arranged in a decentralized fashion, allowing native populations the autonomy to remain traditional, but under the auspices of traditional leaders who were, in turn, controlled by the colonial powers. Space was divided, he argues, into cities (sites of civil and political rights and powers) and rural areas (sites of native life where apartness was cultivated under the illusion that cultural rights were being "gifted" to the natives). This "decentralized despotism," he claims, divided populations into citizens on the one hand and subjects on the other. Apartheid is the "re-gifting" to these populations of the "cultural rights" conditional on racialized apartness. However, let it be noted that when it is people who have already become different by living in cities that are "gifted" the return to traditional apartness, when that apartness is prescribed by law, when it is pushed in the faces of people who have been kicked off their lands (in 1913) and now work in cities, when it is for people who are placed in planned townships (the work of modernity) rather than landed areas, the power system has changed in fundamental ways. It is no longer the same colonial arrangement, no longer, Foucault would say, the same configuration of space in relation to power.

18 See Julian Cooke, "Shifts after the Thirties," in *Architecture SA* (July and August 1993): 24–25.

19 Ibid., pp. 26–27.

20 See Kenneth Frampton, *Modern Architecture: A Critical History*, revised edition (London: Thames and Hudson, 1992), pp. 314–27.

21 Cf. R. Venturi, D. Scott-Brown, and S. Isenour, *Learning from Las Vegas* (Cambridge: MIT Press, 1977).

22 See Fredric Jameson, *Postmodernism, or the Cultural Logic of Late Capitalism* (Durham and London: Duke University Press, 1991).

23 See Charles Jencks, *The Language of Post-Modern Architecture* (New York: Rizzoli, 1977).

6. POSTMODERNISTS OF THE SOUTH

1 See Ludwig Wittgenstein, *Philosophical Investigations*, trans. Elizabeth Anscombe (New York: Macmillan, 1968), no. 88.

2 See Jacques Derrida, "Force of Law: 'The Mystical Foundation of Authority,'" in *Deconstruction and the Possibility of Justice*, ed. Drucilla Cornell et al. (New York: Routledge, 1992), pp. 3–67.

3 See Julia Kristeva, "Revolution in Poetic Language," in *The Kristeva Reader*, ed. Toril Moi (New York: Columbia University Press, 1986), pp. 89–136.

4 See R. Davenport and C. Saunders, *South Africa: A Modern History* (Houndmills and London: Macmillan, 2000), p. 570.

5 See Zygmunt Bauman, "The Fall of the Legislator," in *Postmodernism: A Reader*, ed. Thomas Docherty (New York: Columbia University Press, 1993), pp. 128–40.

7. ONGOING STRUGGLE AT THE END OF HISTORY

1 See Francis Fukuyama, *The End of History and the Last Man* (London: Penguin Books, 1992). All quotations from this book will be noted in the text as Fukuyama: page number.

2 See C. B. Macpherson, The *Real World of Democracy* (Oxford and London: Oxford University Press, 1966).

3 See Michael Hardimon, *Hegel's Social Philosophy: The Project of Reconciliation* (Cambridge and London: Cambridge University Presss, 1944), p. 89.

4 See Francis Fukuyama, *Trust: The Social Virtues and the Creation of Prosperity* (New York: Free Press, 1995).

Index

Capitalism: cultural effects of, 178, 181; global, 163, 166, 181, 209; humanization of, based in conflict, 209–10; quantification under, 186; technical-information capitalism, 166, 181–82, 198

Cavell, Stanley: *Pursuits of Happiness*, 56, 57–58

Chandigarh, 140

Children: orphans of HIV/AIDS, 99–100

China: foreign investment in, 208–9

Chipkin, Clive: *Johannesburg Style*, 144, 147

Christianity. *See* Judeo-Christianity

Citizenship, 165; global, 80

City planning, 159–60

Civil society, xvi, xviii, xxiv, 109, 111; intellectuals' role in, xvi, 198; whether it is rational, 206–7

Class struggle, 209–10. *See also* Radicalism

Clinton, William (Bill), President, 94, 95, 98

Coalition for a Democratic South Africa (CODESA), xi–xii

CODESA. *See* Coalition for a Democratic South Africa (CODESA)

Code switching, 126

Coetzee, Dirk, 23

Coetzee, J. M.: *Disgrace*, 55–56

Cohen, Ted, xxiv

Colonialism, 81, 97, 156; architecture and, 139, 214–15n.17; colonial genealogy of South African architecture, 130; dependency and, 193; settler societies, 141; the Wagnerian impulse and, 135, 139, 148. *See also* Decolonization; Postcolonial states

Color difference. *See also* Racialism

Colored (mixed) minority in South Africa, 74, 123

Comedy/humor, 172–74

Commodification, 179, 182; signage and, 168, 169–70

Communalism, 95. *See also* African communalism

Communication, 48–51

Communism: in China securing a strong worker base, 210; collapse of communist governments, xi, 201; Marxist or Stalinist viewpoints, 82, 93

Complexity theory, 117, 204

Conflict: class struggle, 209–10; Hegelian dialectic, 55, 200, 201

Conrad, Joseph, 110, 174, 177–78

Constitution. *See* South African constitution

Constitutional rights, 20

Contextuality, 182, 185

Contradictions vs. problems: Fukuyama on, 202, 203, 205, 207–8

Cooke, Julian, 160, 161

Coovadia, Jerry, 98

Corbusier, Atelier Le (Corbu), 137, 140, 146, 147, 160, 161

Cosmopolitanism, 156, 158; para-cities under apartheid, 154–56, 158

Countries. *See* Advanced countries; Developing countries; National transitions

Courts. *See* Judiciary

Cukor, George, 57. *See also* *Adam's Rib*

Cultural politics, 77, 102–3; language and, 80–82, 84, 91–92, 102–3; racial identity politics, 126–27

Dal Josefat, 46

Davidson, Arnold, 122

Davidson, Donald, 48–50

Day of Reconciliation, 24

Decentralized power, 156, 214–15n.17

Decolonization, 53, 89. *See also* Colonialism

Defiance Campaign of 1952, 154

Democracy: built into South African constitution, xv–xvi; democratization process, 49. *See also* Liberal democracy

Deracialization or nonracialism, 104–5, 124

Derrida, Jacques, 82, 186, 212n.6

Desire: deflation of, 202. *See also* "Tymotic urge"

Determinate thinking: beneficial aspects of, 187–88; poststructuralist dislike of, 184–85. *See also* Quantification

the context of, 176, 177; transnationalism, 177

Global-local vernaculars, 166–67, 168, 170; and the African renaissance, 171–72

Global violence, 178

Gordon, Ruth: and Garson Kanin, 57. *See also Adam's Rib*

Gould, Stephen Jay, 116–18

Gouws, Andries, 148

Government of National Unity (GNU), 189

Grand narratives, 181, 182, 183, 184. *See also* Modernism

Great Trek, 41, 149–50, 152, 153

Greenwood House, 162, 163

Group Areas Act, 156

Growth, Employment, and Redistribution (GEAR), 189–90, 208, 209

Habermas, Jurgen, 37

Hanson, Norman, 160

Hardimon, Michael, 42

Healing truth. *See* Restorative truth

Health care, 100, 101. *See also* HIV/AIDS

Hegel, G. W. F., 42, 185, 197, 198–99; Hegelian dialectic, 55, 200, 201; Hegelian rationality, 200, 205, 206–7; Hegelian reconciliation, 42–45, 54–55, 164–65, 205–6; *Phenomenology of Spirit*, 52–54, 212n.3; reversal in, 52–54

Hepburn, Katherine. *See Adam's Rib*

Herder, Gottfried, 84

Hindu/Muslim divisions of Indian minority, 125

History. *See* "End of history" notion

HIV/AIDS: anti-retrovirals and drugs treating, xxvii, 98, 99, 101; cultural politics and state failures regarding, 95–100, 101, 102; Durbin HIV/AIDS conference, xxvi; infant-mother transmission, 98, 99; infection rate, xxvi–xxvii, 100–101; International AIDS Conference (2000), 95; orphans of, 99–100; research programs addressing, xviii, xix, 101; sexuality/gender relations and, 100; Treatment Action Campaign, xxvii; in the U.S. as a "gay disease," 123

Holliday, Judy. *See Adam's Rib*

Hollywood, California, 179

Holocaust, 7, 11; apartheid distinguished from or compared to, 31; as "the big lie" (far-right claims), 30–32

Homogenization, 203

Homosexuality, 122–23

Human capital, 207–8

Human complexity, 117

Human Genome Project, 116, 118

Human Immunodeficiency Virus. *See* HIV/AIDS

Human rights, 20

Human Rights Commission, 29

Human rights violations: during apartheid, 5–6, 8, 25–26; of pro-and anti-apartheid forces weighed, 25–26, 27–28; redress for victims, 106

Hybridity, 167, 172, 186; in forms of architecture, 141–44, 171; in use of local materials, 160–61

Identity politics, 108; racial, 126–27. *See also* Pan-African identity

Ignatieff, Michael, 30

Income stratification, 107–8, 124–25, 180–81

Indeterminacy: at odds with rational planning, 188–89; poststructuralist liking for, 184, 186

Indian minority in South Africa, 74, 123, 125

Indigenous people, 98, 101

Inequality, 107–8, 124–25, 180–81

Information capitalism, 166, 181–82, 198

Inkatha Party, xii

Innovation Fund, xvii–xix

Intellectuals, xvi, xx, 154. *See also* Universities

International AIDS Conference (2000), 95, 96

International Style, 135, 137, 138–39, 160

Investment, foreign, 190, 208–9

Irwin, Alec, 208

Islam: Muslim alliances of South Africa, 210. *See also* Middle East

Jacobs, Johan, 212n.4

Jews, 155. *See also* Anti-Semitism

Johannesburg: "Fascist house style" in, 147; 1936 Building Boom, 143; public architecture in, 142–47, 157; *Three-Dimensional View of Flat Blocks*, 158; wealth in, 180–81

Journalism as poetry, 10–12

Judeo-Christianity, 4, 23, 38, 42; Nietzsche's critique of, xxii–xxiv. *See also* Religion

Judiciary, xxvii

Justice, xxii–xxiii, 20; poststructuralist approach to, 183; theories of, 20–21; transitional justice, 21–22, 43–44

Kahn, Louis, 137

Kanin, Garson: and Ruth Gordon, 57. *See also Adam's Rib*

Kant, Immanuel, 38

Kantorowitch, Roy, 160

Knowledge, 181–82

Kojeve, Alexandre, 197

Kraal (Zulu), 136, 162, 164

Kristeva, J., 196

Krog, Antjie: on abuses of apartheid, 6, 7, 10–13; *Country of My Skull*, 6; on the three versions of the killing of Mothasi, 32–36; on the Truth and Reconciliation Commission, 24–25, 26

KwaZulu-Natal province: violence in, xii, xiii, 45; Zulu identity in, 125

Laager form of architecture, 150–51

Land Act of 1913, 3

Landscape, the African, 85–86

Langa, Pius, Judge, 28

Language: cultural politics and, 80–82, 84, 91–92, 102–3; English as preferred, 69–71, 76, 79–80, 88–89, 106; of instruction, 106; of Mbeki (neoliberalism), 71–72, 91–94, 102; Xhosa, 69, 106; Zulu, 69, 106

Language games, 182, 183

Lapsley, Michael, Father, 23–24, 45

Laub, Dori, 10–11

Legitimation capital, 91, 182, 192, 213n.19

Le Pen, Jean-Marie, 21, 30, 31

Liberal democracy: applicability to the Middle East, 199–200, 208; aspects of globalization contradicting, 208–10; as capitalism humanized through conflict, 209–10; as containing no contradictions (Fukuyama), 202, 203, 205, 207–8; economic development not necessarily related to, 208–9; as the "end of history" (Fukuyama), 196–200, 207; free-market system linked to, 197, 198; as satisfying human aspirations, 197, 199, 203–5; South Africa's emergence as, 175

Liberalism: neoliberal language, 71–72, 91–94; nonracialist liberalism needed, 102

Libya, 210

Linguistic code switching, 126

Luthuli, Chief, 76–77

Lyotard, Jean-François, 11, 21, 181–83, 186

Macpherson, C. B., 198

Mahmoud, Ismail, Judge, 78

Maki: testimony of relatives, 14–15

Makins, Andrew, 171

Malthusianism, 99

Mamasela, Joe, 33–35

Mamdani, Mahmoud, 25, 28, 156, 214–15n.17

Mandela, Nelson, President, 189; biography or character of, xi, 69, 82; on HIV/AIDS treatment, 98; iconic international stature of, xiii, 55, 91; pan-Africanism in, 82, 83

Mandela, Winnie, 25

Maré, Gerry, 104–5

"Margins" of modernism, 129–30, 136, 138–41, 165

Market fetishism, 182

Market Theater, 157–58

Martienssen, Rex, 145–46, 160; House Stern, 145

Marx, Karl: on capitalism, 209; Marxism as a grand narrative, 183

Master-slave relation: and reversal, 52–54, 56, 165; sexual variation of (*see Adam's Rib*)

DANIEL HERWITZ is director of the Institute of Humanities and Mary Fair Croushore Professor of Humanities at the University of Michigan, Ann Arbor. At the time he was writing this book, he was chair and program director of philosophy and director of the Centre for Knowledge and Innovation at the University of Natal in South Africa. He has published widely on aesthetics, the avant-gardes, and postmodern culture, and his books include *Making Theory/Constructing Art: On the Authority of the Avant-Garde* and *Husain: Drawing, Painting, Water Colour, Graphic, Sculpture, Architecture, Photography, Tapestry,* which received a National Book Award of India in 1988.